Managing records
a handbook of
principles and practice

Managing records

a handbook of
principles and practice

Elizabeth Shepherd

and

Geoffrey Yeo

© Elizabeth Shepherd and Geoffrey Yeo 2003

Published by
Facet Publishing
7 Ridgmount Street
London WC1E 7AE

Facet Publishing is wholly owned by CILIP: the Chartered Institute of Library and Information Professionals.

First published 2003
Reprinted 2003, 2004, 2005, 2006

British Library Cataloguing in Publication Data
A catalogue record for this book is available from the British Library.

ISBN-13: 978-1-85604-370-0
ISBN-10: 1-85604-370-3

Typeset in 9.5/13pt New Baskerville and Franklin Gothic Condensed by Facet Publishing.
Printed and made in Great Britain by MPG Books Ltd, Bodmin, Cornwall.

Contents

Preface

This book describes and discusses the principles of records management and its practical implementation in contemporary organizations. It provides more extensive coverage than most other recent publications on records management. The book does not assume that readers will have any prior knowledge of the subject, but is intended to be of value to experienced practitioners as well as newcomers to the field.

The discipline of records management has grown so much in the last ten or twenty years that it now seems scarcely possible for a single book to cover the whole range of relevant issues. Although space has not permitted full discussion of every topic, we have nevertheless tried to make this book as comprehensive as possible. While addressing a largely English-speaking readership we have sought to maintain an international perspective. As a result, we have given relatively little emphasis to legal or other topics that are specific to a single country, and have concentrated on areas of professional principles and practice that are applicable worldwide.

We are indebted to numerous individuals who have contributed directly or indirectly to the genesis of this book: records management students from many countries across the world who have shared their experiences with us; archivists and records managers with whom we have worked in the UK, continental Europe and Africa; and many others, particularly in North America and Australasia, whose writings have informed our understanding of the subject. We are also grateful to our present and former colleagues at University College London, especially Anne Thurston, Clare Rider, Vanda Broughton, Chris Turner and Anna Sexton.

Elizabeth Shepherd
Geoffrey Yeo

Editorial note

The following abbreviations are used:

AS: Australian Standard
ASCII: American Standard Code for Information Interchange
BS: British Standard
EDI: Electronic Data Interchange
EDM: Electronic Document Management (software applications)
ERM: Electronic Records Management (software applications)
FOI: Freedom of Information
ISO: International Standards Organization
OCR: Optical Character Recognition
XML: Extensible Markup Language

Web addresses given in this book were correct in August 2002, but may be subject to change.

Figure 1.5 was supplied by Frank Upward of Monash University, Australia, and is reproduced with his permission.

Introduction

Why keep records?

Every organization needs records.

Organizations use records in the conduct of current business, to enable decisions to be made and actions taken. Records may be required for business purposes whenever there is a need to recall or prove what was done or decided in the past. Records provide access to precedents or previous work and thus save time and money by eliminating the need to create resources afresh. Records are also kept to guard against fraud and to enable organizations to protect their rights and assets at law.

Organizations also use records to support accountability, when they need to prove that they have met their obligations or complied with best practice. Organizations are accountable in many ways: they must meet legal, regulatory and fiscal requirements, and undergo audits and inspections of various kinds; and they must be able to provide explanations for decisions made or actions taken. The use of records is the primary means by which organizations can defend their actions if they are called to account for their conduct.

Such external accountability is particularly important to public sector bodies, which are responsible for their actions both to governments and to the wider public. Companies are responsible to their shareholders, besides having a level of responsibility to the wider community. Every organization is liable to be called to account by legislators, regulators or auditors. Organizations use their records to respond to challenges made against them, whether in a court of law or elsewhere, and to justify their actions and decisions in response to enquiries or in the public arena.

Within the organization, records support internal accountability. Those working at lower levels are responsible to their seniors for the work they perform, and records are used to prove or assess performance.

While records are created in the first instance for the conduct of business and to support accountability, organizations may also use them for cultural purposes, both for research and to promote awareness and understanding of corporate history.

Figure 0.1 illustrates these three broad reasons for keeping records.

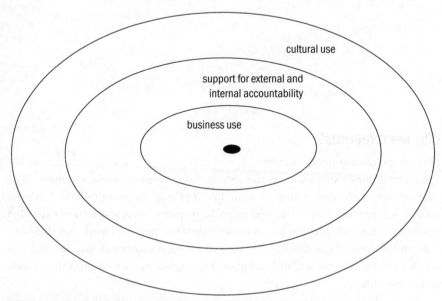

Fig. 0.1 *Why keep records?*

Outside the organization, the wider community also has expectations that records should be kept. When records are used for purposes of accountability they are not merely supporting organizational needs for compliance or self-defence; they also meet the requirements of society for transparency and the protection of rights. Other organizations and individuals may use records for historical, demographic, sociological, medical or scientific research. Records kept for cultural purposes also serve the values of society and its need for collective memory.

Why is good records management important?

Many organizations do not yet have a formal programme of records management, but all organizations need to manage the information and evidence that their records provide.

In organizations where records are not properly managed:

- records will often be inadequate for the purposes for which they are needed
- records will often be lost
- some records will probably be destroyed prematurely and others retained unnecessarily.

Excessive retention of records will give rise to retrieval difficulties as well as wasted resources; but a failure to create adequate records or to maintain them appropriately will probably have more serious consequences:

- The organization may be unable to prove that it did what was required of it, or that policies and procedures were correctly followed.
- It may be unable to defend itself if liability claims are made against its products or services or the actions of its employees.
- It may be unable to prove its rights or protect its assets.
- Business operations may be compromised if critical information is unavailable when required.
- The rights of customers, citizens and the wider community may also be impaired.

Increasingly, organizations are recognizing the benefits of well-managed records and are implementing programmes to ensure that the right records are created and retained. An effective records management programme will also ensure that records are available for use when needed, that privacy and confidentiality are maintained and that redundant records are destroyed.

How can this book help?

This book provides a detailed introduction to the concepts and practice of records management, for organizational staff who have responsibility for establishing, maintaining or restructuring a records management programme.

Throughout the book, approaches to managing records in both electronic and traditional media are considered. Chapter 1 provides an overview of the principles of records management and an introduction to records management programmes and systems. Chapter 2 describes some techniques that records managers can use to gain an understanding of the context for their work. Chapters 3 to 7 discuss the components of records management systems and their application in the context of an established programme. The final chapter gives advice on developing the necessary infrastructure and provides a discussion of practical business issues surrounding the implementation of records management in a contemporary organization. For further reading, an extensive bibliography is provided.

The focus of the book is on managing records to support the conduct of business and accountability. The management of records for cultural purposes is treated more summarily, but references to further information on this topic are included in the bibliography.

1
Understanding records management

This chapter introduces the core concepts and terms used in the book. It describes the broad professional context of records management and outlines the intellectual frameworks that underpin it.

Defining the key terms in records management

What is records management?

Records management is the 'field of management responsible for the efficient and systematic control of the creation, receipt, maintenance, use and disposition of records . . .' (ISO 15489-1:2001, clause 3.16). As a discipline, it developed from 20th-century office efficiency programmes and from the older profession of archives management. Archives were originally records kept to support the rights and obligations of organizations and individuals, but the archives profession came to be seen as concerned only with older records, kept to support historical research. By the mid 20th century, records managers were employed by archival institutions in the public sector, with the aim of controlling the inflow of 'modern records' into historical archives. While this is still one of the functions of records management, it is no longer the only role, nor even the predominant role, of the records manager. Records management now covers the management of records, regardless of age, to meet the needs of private and public sector organizations and the wider society as well as the research community. It earns its place in the life of an organization through its contribution to business aims and organizational goals.

Records management is a necessary part of the work of almost all employees within an organization (and also of individuals in their personal lives). This book focuses on the organizational context, where records managers are the specialists in records management but rely on the co-operation and participation of all employees.

To understand records management more fully it is necessary to look at the meaning of the word *record*. In the past, records management was equated with the management of papers located in organizational filing systems. The growth of new technology and information management has led records managers to seek a more rigorous definition of records, in order to explain what distinguishes them from other organizational resources, and to show how managing records differs from managing documents, data or information.

What is a record?

Originally *record* was a legal term: records were writings preserved in courts of law and accepted by them as authentic testimony of a completed action. Now it has wider connotations, and in this book the word *record* is used to mean any *recorded evidence of an activity*.

A record is not defined by its physical format or storage medium, its age, or the fact that it has been set aside for preservation. Nor is it simply a form of recorded information. The essential characteristic of a record is that it provides evidence of some specific activity.

Other definitions are sometimes found in the literature on records management, but the concept of records and archives as evidence of activity goes back to the earliest days of archival theory and can be found in the works of Dutch, British, Italian and American authors (Muller, Feith and Fruin, 1898; Jenkinson, 1922; Casanova, 1928; Schellenberg, 1956).

The word *evidence* is not used here in a legal sense. Records provide evidence that can be used in any situation where proof of a particular activity is required. In this book the phrase *legal evidence* is used where a specific legal connotation is intended.

What is an activity?

An *activity* may be defined as *an action or set of actions undertaken by an individual, a group of individuals or a corporate body, or by employees or agents acting on its behalf, and resulting in a definable outcome*. An activity has identifiable start and end points, although the end point may not always be known when the activity is begun.

Some activities, such as drafting or note taking, may involve only one person, but in an organizational context most activities involve two or more parties, with some form of transaction or communication taking place between them. One or more of the parties may be external to the organization (typically a customer or supplier). Other transactions may be purely internal (perhaps between a manager and a staff member, or between one department and another). The word *transaction* is occasionally used to denote an activity in which only one party participates, but it normally refers to a bilateral activity (Saunders, 1990, 322). In this book it denotes an activity involving two parties or more.

Most organizational activities involve the participation of one or more members of the organization's staff, but some may be largely or wholly automated. For instance, in a banking transaction conducted at an automated teller machine or over the internet the customer communicates only with the bank's computer. Some activities, such as automated stock ordering, may be performed without any direct human agency.

What is the connection between an activity and the creation of a record?

Records are a product of organizational activity, created or received during or after completion of the activity itself. Where more than one party is involved in an activity, each party may create its own record; alternatively the second party may receive and retain the record transmitted by the creator, while the creator retains a copy of it.

Records may be created either in the course of an activity, or afterwards in a conscious act of record keeping. In the case of a letter, invoice or purchase order, the transaction is effected in whole or part by the creation or transmission of the record. Some records of this kind are created within the organization, while others are received from outside. The way in which business is done leads naturally to the creation of records, and the parties concerned are likely to be more conscious of the activity being performed than of the fact that they are incidentally creating a record of it. In other cases (for example, staff training records, equipment maintenance records or minutes of meetings) the purpose of creating records is to provide evidence of activities that are already complete. Records of this kind are consciously created within the organization to meet specific needs for record keeping, and are not usually sent to or received from outside parties. In many jurisdictions the distinction between these two types of records has been recognized at law: for example in the UK in *H v Schering Chemicals*, 1983, Lord Justice Bingham offered a definition that records 'either give effect to a transaction itself or . . . contain a contemporaneous register of information supplied by those with direct knowledge of the facts' (Saunders, 1990, 30–1).

How are records created?

Traditionally, organizational staff created records manually, using pen and ink or a typewriter. In the modern world most records are created using digital technology, by interaction with a computer program. Records can also originate when communications are received from outside the organization, by letter, fax, e-mail or other messaging system. In this book *creation* is often used as a shorthand term for *creation or receipt* of records.

What media are used to create and maintain records?

Until very recently almost all records were on paper, but modern organizations are increasingly using digital media. Records maintained digitally are known to records managers as *electronic records* (or *digital records*). Both terms refer specifically to records created or received electronically, which are then *maintained* in electronic form, as opposed to records which are created using word-processing or other software and then printed onto paper.

Records are usually textual but can also contain, or be associated with, non-textual material such as sound, images or three-dimensional objects. Parker (1999, 5) gives examples of clothing, drugs and even a piece of railway sleeper, which have been attached to records of legal investigations or court proceedings. Spoken messages (such as voicemail) and visual items (including drawings, photographs and moving images) can also be records in their own right.

What is meant by 'capturing' a record?

The term *capture* refers to the actions that are taken to secure a record into an effective records management system, where the record can be maintained and made accessible for as long as it is needed.

Some records are captured as soon as they are created, others after an interval; ephemeral records can be destroyed before capture. Writers on records management sometimes reserve the term 'records' for those that have been formally captured, but records exist before they are captured, and even the most ephemeral record is evidence of activity within the organization. However, systematic capture is essential if records are to be retained and managed effectively over time. Strategies for records capture are discussed in Chapter 4.

What are archives?

The word *archives* is popularly used to refer to older papers or computer files that have been consigned to secondary storage. Sometimes *archives* and *records* have been used as synonyms. Archives are also perceived as records kept for research purposes. However, in records management terms, archives may be defined as *any records that are recognized as having long-term value*.

These are likely to be only a small proportion of the total number of records captured in a records management system. Most records have a limited lifespan and will eventually be destroyed. *Archives* may include records that have continuing significance in the conduct of business, for example as evidence of the organization's constitution or its ongoing rights and obligations. They may also include records that are no longer expected to be required for operational use or to support accountability, but are kept indefinitely as part of the corporate memory of the organization or for research or other cultural purposes. The word *archives* is also used to mean an institution or business unit responsible for managing records of long-term value.

The life of the record

The lifecycle concept

The *records lifecycle* is a concept in common use. It indicates that records are not static, but have a life similar to that of biological organisms: they are born, live through youth and old age and then die. The idea was developed in North America by Schellenberg (1956, 37), who wrote about the 'life span' of records, which included their current use and final destiny. Similar concepts are employed in other disciplines, notably the 'information lifecycle' models used in information management and technology.

Since the 1950s many variants on the records lifecycle concept have been modelled. Most models aim to show a progression of actions taken at different times in the life of a record: typically, its creation, capture, storage, use and disposal. Some writers show this as a linear progression, while others describe a loop or circle (see Figure 1.1).

A different model (see Figure 1.2) suggests that records pass through three 'ages', or stages: a *current* stage, when they are used for business; a *semi-current* stage, when their business value is reduced; and a *non-current* stage, when they have little or no business value but may be used for other purposes.

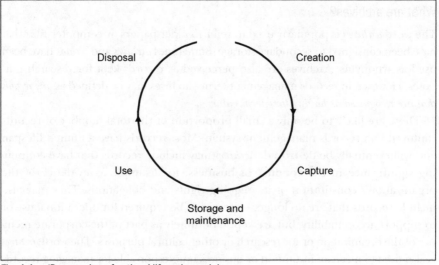

Fig. 1.1 *'Progression of actions' lifecycle model*

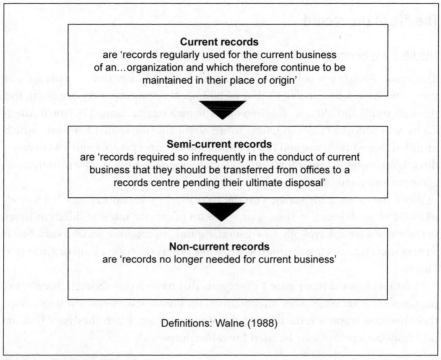

Fig. 1.2 *'Three ages' lifecycle model*

This model assumes that records are kept initially for organizational purposes, and implies that they may be transferred into archival custody when the passage of time has reduced their business value to the organization. Writers who use this model (such as Couture and Rousseau, 1987, 37) have generally emphasized the physical movement of paper records to alternative storage at each phase of their life, together with the destruction of unwanted records at each stage. Some records managers have argued that the semi-current stage is redundant, and that a record is either current or non-current.

Some writers refer to the stages of the lifecycle as 'active', 'semi-active' and 'inactive'. In this book, however, the word *active* is used to describe records that are in use at a given moment, as opposed to those which lie inactive in storage. In this sense, records are most active in the early part of their life, but there is often a resurgence of active use for secondary reasons later in life (see Figure 1.3).

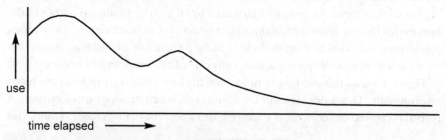

Fig. 1.3 *Typical usage levels during the life of a record*

In recent years the lifecycle concept has been subject to much adverse criticism. First, critics have noted that some records do not 'die', but are retained indefinitely because of their continuing value. Secondly, the division between stages of the lifecycle in the 'three ages' model is seen as artificial: for example, records thought to be non-current may have a renewed period of currency if the activity that gave birth to them is revived. The lifecycle models do not allow for the repetition of stages, or for stages to be omitted, although in practice this frequently happens. It has also been argued (McKemmish, 1997) that the lifecycle concept perpetuates an artificial distinction between records kept for business purposes and records kept for cultural reasons, and thus between the professional perspectives of archivists and records managers.

Critics of the lifecycle concept also suggest that it is too focused on records as physical entities and on operational tasks, especially those associated with the custody of paper records. Electronic records rely on logical rather than physical structure, and the tasks associated with the physical storage of paper are largely irrelevant to their management.

A record 'entity life history'

It is possible to refashion the lifecycle concept to meet contemporary needs, using the *entity life history* method developed by Jackson (1983). This is a method employed by systems analysts to represent different events that affect materials or other entities used in the conduct of business.

Following this method, an entity (such as a record) is seen as having a life history constructed of sequences, iterations and selections of objects and actions. This is represented diagrammatically using boxes in a kind of 'family tree', where each 'parent' box can have one or more 'children'. A sequence is shown by a horizontal row of unmarked boxes: the actions in a sequence can occur only in the order shown, reading from left to right. An iteration, indicated by an asterisk in the top corner of the box, means that each instance of this object or action can occur zero or more times. A selection, indicated by a small circle in the top corner of a child box, means that for each instance of the parent action, only one of the child actions occurs.

Figure 1.4 uses this method to model the life history of records in a structured environment. This model is valid for all records, whether paper or electronic. A record is created or received, is captured into a records management system, and

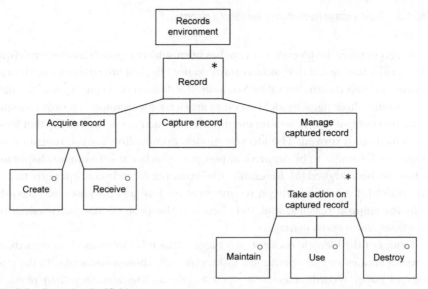

Fig. 1.4 *Record entity life history*

is then subject to actions (maintenance and use), which may be repeated as necessary until the record is destroyed. For records of continuing value, destruction need never occur, but when it does occur it is the final event in the life of the record.

The continuum concept

The *records continuum* concept (see Figure 1.5) was developed in the 1980s and 1990s in response to criticisms of the lifecycle models. In a continuum there are no separate steps: managing records is seen as a continuous process where one element of the continuum passes seamlessly into another.

The dimensions in the continuum are not time-based, but represent different perspectives on the management of records. The circles move out from the creation of records of business activities, to ensuring that records are captured as evidence and to their inclusion in formal systems for records management within the organization, while the fourth dimension looks out towards the needs of society for collective memory. In contrast with the older view that records are kept for organizational purposes during the early stages of their lives, and only later come to meet the needs of a wider society as archives, the continuum model 'embraces

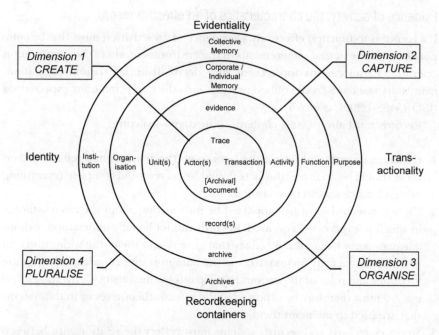

Fig. 1.5 *Records continuum* (© Frank Upward; all rights reserved)

the view that records function simultaneously as organizational and collective memory from the time of their creation' (McKemmish, 1997).

The continuum is a flexible and inclusive concept that reflects a range of issues surrounding the role of records in contemporary organizations and society. It emphasizes that the same principles apply to the management of all records, whether newly created or inherited from the past. Many archivists and records managers, especially in Australia, have rejected the lifecycle models altogether and promote the continuum as offering a more holistic view of record keeping. However, the two are not incompatible. The true objection to the older models is not to the lifecycle concept itself, but to those manifestations of it that reflect an underdeveloped view of records management or try to introduce excessive practical detail. Specific practices will vary from one working context to another, but models based on the lifecycle concept or the entity life history can help to identify stages and actions within a records management programme, and thus provide a useful framework for planning and implementation.

Records as evidence and as sources of information

Evidence of activity: the characteristics of an effective record

If a record is to function effectively as evidence of an activity, it must first be compliant with any external requirements in the environment where the organization operates. Requirements for records may derive from legislation, regulation, mandatory standards, codes of best practice and ethics, or community expectations (ISO 15489-1:2001, clause 5).

Records must also possess content, context and structure:

1 *Content*: a record must reflect the facts about the activity. For a reliable record these should be accurate (the facts should be correct) and complete (everything of significance should be recorded).
2 *Context*: a record must be supported by information about the circumstances in which it was created and used. Records cannot be fully understood without adequate knowledge of the activity that gave rise to them, the wider function of which that activity forms part, and the administrative context, including the identities and roles of the various participants in the activity. Contextual information must therefore be captured in the records themselves or in the systems that are used to maintain them.
3 *Structure*: records and records systems must reflect the relationships between

their constituent parts. In a business letter, for example, there is a formal structural relationship between the details of the addressee, the date, the body of the text divided into paragraphs and the signature at the end. There are also structural relationships between the individual letters in a file or folder, and between records in a series.

The structure of a record forms a link between content and context. Structure organizes the content in such a way as to denote context, and thus contributes to users' understanding of the record.

Archival theory emphasizes the need to preserve *provenance* and *original order*:

1 Traditionally understood as referring to the administrative origin of records, the term *provenance* is now often reinterpreted to include an understanding of the functions and activities that underlie records creation and maintenance.
2 Other aspects of the context of a paper record can be ascertained from its physical juxtaposition to other records, typically in a file or cabinet. The principle of retaining the *original order* relates to records in the paper world: it preserves context by protecting their physical structure. To extend this concept into the digital world, where storage is random and the physical juxtaposition of records has no significance, it is necessary to reinterpret it in terms of the intellectual relationship between one record and another.

These longstanding principles are still valid: records managers need to ensure that information about the provenance and interrelationship of records is not lost.

According to the international records management standard (ISO 15489-1:2001, clause 7.2), records should have qualities of authenticity, integrity, usability and reliability. The authenticity and integrity of records need to be guaranteed over time, so that users can be confident that records are genuine and trustworthy and that no illicit alterations have been made to them. Records need to be usable: they must be accessible to authorized users and provide sufficient evidence of the context of their creation to support users' understanding of their significance. Records created within an organization should also be reliable and accurate in their content.

For this to be achieved, records must be created and maintained systematically. Sufficient measures are needed to allow proof 'that records are what they purport to be and that their purported creators have indeed created them' (AS 4390.3-1996, clause 5.3). Weaknesses in these areas will diminish the weight of a record as evidence of an activity. Records may be destroyed when no longer required, but for as long as they are kept they should remain unaltered. Moreover their usability must be protected so that they can be retrieved, consulted and interpreted when they are needed. Systems to manage the content, structure and context of records, and to ensure their integrity and usability over time, are discussed in later chapters of this book.

Records provide information as well as evidence

Records can be used as sources of information as well as evidence. The information in a textual record may be in the form of raw data (name, address, etc.) or may be derived from narrative. Records typically contain information relating to the parties involved in an activity and to the contents or subject matter of the activity itself, but may also contain information relating to other matters such as the political, organizational or social environment within which the activity occurred. Users may refer to a record to obtain information of this kind, quite independently of any need to use the record as evidence. Users are also likely to employ other methods of obtaining information, and may not consciously distinguish between records and other information sources.

In the past, information professionals often made a distinction between published sources (which were the responsibility of the librarian) and unique or unpublished materials (which were seen as the province of the records manager). However, this distinction is no longer as valid as it once was: with the growth of computer technology and the proliferation of copying devices in the modern office, a record is no longer necessarily seen as a unique object. Even the distinction between an original and a copy of a record has become increasingly blurred in the digital era. Moreover the establishment of a corporate website or intranet means that materials can be 'published' without creating multiple physical copies, while the intranet may also be used to provide access to repositories of organizational records. In a world where electronic objects can be viewed remotely on demand, the traditional division between published and unpublished materials is hard to maintain.

However, there remains a critical distinction between records, which provide evidence of activities as well as information, and materials produced for informational purposes alone. Information products are consciously designed to disseminate information or ideas on a defined subject, and the importance that an organization attaches to them will relate directly to the comprehensiveness, accuracy and currency of the information they contain. An online reference source or a CD-ROM containing inaccurate or obsolete information is of little value, and a librarian is unlikely to recommend it. Records generated outside the organization are assessed differently: an incoming business letter containing false information has little value as an information source, but as a record it may still be valuable as evidence of the writer's ignorance or intention to mislead. Most records can be expected to contain information that is accurate at the time of their creation, but if they are to function as evidence they cannot be updated after their capture in a records management system. The use of records as information sources often involves using them for a purpose that their creator did not intend.

While library materials and other information products are usually managed as discrete objects, a record normally forms part of an accumulation of related records. Library systems are focused on information, but records management systems have to meet both informational and evidential needs. A records management system should provide search tools that allow records to be used for reference purposes, but must also ensure that users can interpret records in their context. These issues are explored further in Chapters 3 and 7.

Records, documents and data

What is a document?

The term *document* is used in many ways, both in popular speech and in technical areas such as law and computing. Some records managers have used *document* and *record* as if they were synonyms; others have defined a document as 'work in progress, not yet captured as a record'. Neither usage is followed in this book.

A more helpful definition is given by Robek, Brown and Stephens (1995, 4) who state that a 'document' usually 'means "the smallest unit of filing", generally a single letter, form, report, or other item housed in a filing system'. Roberts (1994, 19) identifies two further characteristics: a document is 'discrete and identifiable from other documents', and there are logical relationships between each of the textual (and sometimes visual) elements of which it is composed. These definitions can be applied to both paper and electronic documents.

Not all documents are records

Completed application forms, letters, invoices, register books and hard-copy ledgers are all documents. They are also records, since each of them provides evidence of activity.

Blank forms, picture postcards, advertising posters and reference books are also documents, but they are not records (see Figure 1.6). The form can become a record

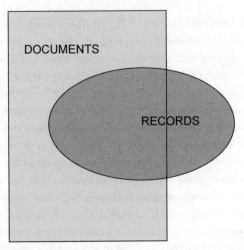

Fig. 1.6 *Relationship between records and documents*

if it is completed and transmitted to initiate some action; the postcard can become a record if it is used to send a message. Until then they are documents but not records, because they have not participated in a business activity.

What are data?

Data are 'raw' facts or figures, usually represented in a formalized manner. Typical data are names, titles, locations, dates, quantities, costs, and so on. Data *elements* are commonly organized using pairs, with each pair consisting of an *element name* (for example, 'location' or 'price') and a *value* (for example, 'London' or '$100').

In the pre-computer era, the maintenance of data was largely confined to documentary formats: data were typically kept on index cards, and processed manually using tabulated analysis on paper. Computer systems allow data to be maintained independently of documentary formats.

Data used in current information systems are not records

Organizations need data about their operations, finances, stock levels, customers or suppliers, and about the wider business environment, in order to provide information to managers or other staff. The usual requirement is for such data to be as up to date as possible, and to be capable of reuse in different parts of the organization. Data of this kind are processed, manipulated, analysed or interpreted to support decision making, business control or operational tasks.

Computers allow data to be updated, to flow wherever they are needed and to be processed electronically in current information systems. Systems of this kind include many corporate and departmental databases, single 'line of business' applications and integrated business support applications such as enterprise resource planning (ERP) systems. Data in these systems are clearly distinguishable from documents:

1 Data in current information systems are processed chiefly at the output stage. Their internal structure need not be visible in output.
2 Documents are processed at the point of creation; when viewed subsequently they are intelligible without further processing, and their internal structure is always reflected in output.

Data are frequently extracted from documentary records, and sometimes from other documents, for processing and analysis in a current information system. Data extracted from records are ultimately derived from business activities, but data used in this way are not themselves evidential records. Electronic data in current information systems are dynamic, in the sense that they are manipulable and subject to update, whereas records are stable and fixed in time.

Data in electronic transaction systems are records

Before the advent of technology, records of transactions were also inextricably tied to the documentary format; a business activity could not be recorded without using a document. However, in an electronic environment records need not be in the form of documents. Computer technology allows a transaction to be recorded using data alone.

In many areas of work, data entry has replaced the creation of documents as the preferred method of creating records of completed activities. For example, staff operating a telephone helpline may enter data such as name, date and subject of enquiry into a database and these data may constitute the sole evidence of the handling of each enquiry. These data are not dynamic, since they are not subject to update after they have been entered in the database. Some computer systems include both dynamic data and evidential data.

Besides their use in recording an activity that is already complete, data-centric systems can also be used to perform the activity itself. Systems of this kind are increasingly employed in automated transactions for ordering goods or transferring money. Examples include electronic data interchange (EDI) and internet commerce, as well as electronic funds transfer (EFT) and bank cashpoints (automatic teller machines or ATMs). In these technologies a standard set of data is transmitted from customer to supplier in order to effect a transaction, and the data that comprise the record of the transaction exist independently of document constraints. As electronic commerce develops, there will be more records of this kind.

Evidential requirements apply equally to records such as these. To function effectively as a record, the data that form the evidence of the transaction must have context and structure as well as content. Although there is no documentary structure, it is nevertheless essential to have a structure that identifies and binds together the set of data representing each transaction. The record must also be compliant with legislation and regulations; and measures will be needed to ensure its authenticity and integrity. While current informational data are intended to be updatable, evidentiary data need to be fixed in time. The issues are the same for all records, whether they take the form of documents or data.

The complexity of digital records

At present, most records in most organizations are paper or electronic text documents, produced using word-processing or similar software. Data are usually seen as the domain of separate applications built around database technology.

In one sense, however, documentary records themselves contain data. The data are the words, numbers or images used by the creator of the document. Data of this kind may not be composed of named 'elements'. Instead, in a record such as a letter, the creator conveys meaning by imposing a sequential structure on the words that are used.

The association between document and data can be seen most clearly in the use of forms. A completed form is a documentary record, but its content is less closely tied to the documentary structure than is the content of a letter. While the documentary structure is essential to an understanding of the meaning of a letter, the text on a form is composed mainly or wholly of discrete elements of data. Element names are provided by headings or prompts on the form, and if the ordering of the elements were to be changed their meaning would not be lost. The user's understanding of the data on a paper form is determined largely by the element names, not by the order in which the elements are presented.

Particularly in electronic systems, forms can be seen as documents that are designed to facilitate the capture of data. An electronic form may be posted as a document on a website, but it is the set of data that a customer enters that will be used to process a transaction and will constitute the record.

Conversely, some digital records are created and captured as data, but may acquire something resembling a documentary format when they are output to a printer or converted to another medium for long-term storage. Voicemail and other spoken messages acquire documentary characteristics when they are transcribed or when voice recognition technology is applied.

In the future many records are likely to be seen as 'digital objects' composed of both document and data characteristics. Particularly in the areas of enterprise resource planning and customer relationship management, automated systems are being developed where data forming evidence of routine transactions can be associated with non-standard documentary materials such as correspondence. At the time of writing, extensible markup language (XML) is seen by many as the key to managing composite records of this kind, because of its utility in combining data and document functionality in a single environment. XML is likely to be the language of choice for web-based transactions both on the internet and on corporate intranets and extranets, and research is in progress into its use in areas such as medical records and in supply chain management, where it is seen as a catalyst to enhance the value of EDI.

Even within the world of documentary records, the growth of technology has led to the creation of more complex records than was possible when paper was the only medium. 'Compound' records are those where the electronic document is composed of several parts, each created in a different computer application. Text documents that include spreadsheets or graphics are now common. More complex multimedia records, in which the document includes video or sound files, are also possible (though still relatively rare in the transactional environment). With the growth of remote conferencing and web technologies, multimedia records may become commonplace.

Records management and related disciplines

How does records management differ from document management?

While the future may bring many new types of record, at present most records are in documentary format and most records management activities involve dealing with documents. At a physical level it is the document that is filed, consulted, moved, retained or destroyed. The term *document management* is usually associated with computer packages sold as 'electronic document management systems', and these sometimes provide much (though rarely all) of the functionality that is required for managing electronic records.

Much of this book is devoted to the management of documentary records in paper and electronic media. However, records management has to deal with records in all formats and not just those that are documents. Records management also emphasizes the need to maintain the authenticity and context of records, with which document management is rarely concerned. 'A document management system which is used to ... provide access to documents which have no or insufficient evidential characteristics is an information system not a recordkeeping system' (O'Shea, 1996).

How does records management differ from information management and knowledge management?

Like records management, *information management* is concerned with materials in any format. However, information management focuses on information products used to support business activities, rather than the evidence of the activities themselves. These products include in-house publications, reference books, journals, technical manuals, CD-ROM publications, data mining and decision support systems, and websites and informational databases whether maintained by the organization itself or externally. Some may be the province of the librarian, while others may be managed by computing specialists. All these products have content and structure, and their reliability and accuracy are seen as important, but where their context is recognized as an issue it is likely to be perceived as a matter of authorship or publication rather than business activity.

The term *knowledge management* has been used to mean many things, but generally signifies an integrated approach to the management of various types of information resource, often in association with attempts to capture 'tacit' knowledge, particularly the expertise of members of staff and the knowledge that they as individuals bring to their jobs.

Information management and knowledge management are also concerned with the information that is contained in records. Most definitions of knowledge management explicitly mention information to support corporate memory (for which records are a prime source) as well as dynamic information typically associated with database applications. Records management on the other hand is concerned with managing records for their value as evidence of activities, as well as for the information they contain.

Managing records and other information sources

In practice the distinction between records management and information management is often blurred, especially in smaller organizations where records management may be undertaken by an information manager. In organizations that support a dedicated records management service, records managers are often expected to maintain information sources that are not records. Information management is sometimes perceived as concerned only with current information, and older or historic information may then be seen as the province of the records manager. Records managers are rarely asked to manage externally generated information products (whether published texts or external data) but may have custody of, or some responsibility for, information products generated internally in paper or electronic form.

Records managers may be interested in information products for a number of reasons. First, internally generated information products are created within a business context. The data in a typical corporate database are collected in the course of business, to provide an information tool. The existence of internal publications or a corporate website indicates that organizational activity occurred when they were created.

Secondly, information products are used in the course of business activities. Just as the actions involved in creating and editing the product are business activities, so are the actions involved in using it. Although consultation of a database or a procedural manual usually leaves no trace, sometimes it may be necessary for a record of each consultation to be maintained. In some cases a record may not be complete, or fully understandable, unless the information sources used in its preparation are identified. Sometimes an information product such as a database is compiled for the purpose of a single activity; in such cases it can be appropriate to retain the product in close association with the record of the activity concerned.

Thirdly, the use of information products may involve transmitting or publishing them. A common business activity is the sending of information products from one person or organization to another: for example, brochures are sent to clients, or news cuttings attached to a memo to the boss. When an information product is included in a transaction of this kind, it is normally appropriate either for the product to be incorporated into the record of the transaction, or for its identity to be documented so that it can be traced when the record is used on a later occasion.

Finally, the use of websites is of interest to records managers. Websites may be consulted as information sources but are also used for carrying out business. Web transactions are effected by transmission of data from one party to another, but the static content of a website can also form part of the evidence surrounding the transaction. Organizations may wish to consider the longer-term retention of their web pages, not only for informational reasons, but also as part of a programme for the management of evidence.

Scope of this book

The focus of this book is on the management of records. Since records managers may also wish to preserve other sources such as informational databases, websites or internal publications, methods that may be used to capture products of this kind are discussed in Chapter 4. However, the book gives priority to records created as evidence of organizational activity. As Kennedy and Schauder (1998, 7) state, 'records managers must give priority to [records] which have evidential value, as the risk of not managing these is higher than for other informational documents'.

The book also gives priority to records in documentary format. Paper records are always in the form of documents, and at present most digital records also have documentary characteristics. The world of records management is still largely document-centred, and much of this book has a similar emphasis.

Managing paper and electronic records: the hybrid environment

Paper has a long history as a record storage medium. Paper-based records can be read without the need for a computer as intermediary; they are familiar and reassuring, and despite the inferior quality of much modern paper they offer an apparent prospect of longevity.

Electronic records present the records manager with new challenges, not least in their dependence on computer software, hardware and operating systems, and in the measures that are needed to ensure their continuing accessibility in a world of rapid technological change. On the other hand electronic systems for records management offer not only substantial space savings, but also the possibility of a speed of retrieval and range of functionality unmatched in the paper world.

With electronic records, filing is no longer a time-intensive manual activity. Multiple options for retrieval can be provided without using elaborate cross-references or making duplicates for filing under different headings. While a paper file can only be consulted in one place at any one time, electronic systems allow simultaneous access by multiple users, and physical proximity to storage areas is no longer a prerequisite for speedy access: records can be delivered almost instantly to distant as well as local users. Finally, the risk of loss can be substantially reduced. Unlike their paper counterparts, online electronic records are not liable to damage by being handled, nor can they be accidentally misplaced. If security copies of electronic records are required they can be created with a minimum of effort.

The introduction of electronic systems into an organization can be seen as falling into two phases. In the first phase computer technology is used for informational databases, and as a mechanism for creating paper documents, which are then forwarded or retained using traditional means. In the second phase electronic systems are used to effect transactions (such as the transmission of a document to its recipient) and automate work processes, and for the retention of records. Almost all organizations are now entering the second of these phases, but as yet few organizations have a paperless office. For the foreseeable future, most will have a hybrid environment, where some records are created or received on paper while others, perhaps relating to the same activity, are created or received in digital form.

Broadly speaking, if records are created or received in both media, the options for retention are:

- printing electronic records to paper
- making digital copies of paper records
- maintaining a hybrid system, with some records in paper form and others maintained electronically.

Where records are printed to paper (or to another analogue format such as microform), electronic systems may be used for drafting or messaging, but are not used for the retention of records. This is a simple approach, but at best it is an interim solution. The 'print to paper' option preserves static content but the ability to search, disseminate and retrieve records electronically is lost. If sets of electronic data are to be kept as records, only data dumps or report outputs can be retained on paper. Records that contain dynamic links or multimedia elements lose their functionality when printed out; with spreadsheets the underlying formulae are almost always lost. Printouts of electronic mail messages may fail to identify senders and recipients, or may refer to them only by an alias that is meaningless outside the e-mail system. In the longer term, printing is not a cheap solution, because of the storage and retrieval costs associated with paper.

If a wholly digital approach is used, records are created, transmitted and received electronically where possible, and all records are retained in electronic form. Paper is not used as a storage medium, and paper records are copied to digital format using imaging technology.

Both of these approaches may raise issues of authenticity. The paper printout is not the original record of an electronic transaction; and although many jurisdictions have moved towards legal recognition of electronic evidence, the digitized image is a copy and not the original record of a paper-based activity.

In practice it is often necessary to maintain a hybrid system, where some records are retained on paper, others electronically. The issue then is how to manage records that are closely related in terms of context and content, but physically divided between paper and digital media.

This book is based on the premise that the task facing most records managers at the beginning of the 21st century is to manage records in a hybrid situation. It endeavours to show that the principles underlying the management of electronic records are the same as those that support the more familiar paper systems. The practical application of those principles may differ according to the needs of one medium or the other, but where records in both media are to be managed in tandem there is a need for as much commonality as can be achieved. This book aims to assist records managers in designing programmes and systems to manage records effectively in a hybrid environment.

Records management programmes, systems and standards

What is a records management programme?

In any organization, managing records should be a strategic function, with a continuing programme that is effective across the organization as a whole. Records management programmes vary from one organization to another, but typically comprise a number of elements. These include:

- setting and monitoring policies and standards for records management throughout the organization
- designing and implementing records management systems
- informing and educating staff about records management.

In a small organization the operation of the programme is likely to be the responsibility of a records manager working alone. A larger organization is likely to require a records management unit with a number of staff, in order to operate the programme effectively. Depending on local needs and circumstances, the records management unit may also be responsible for:

- day-to-day management of the storage, retention and disposal of records
- provision of access to stored records or to the information they contain

- advice and assistance to business units in managing their own records
- performance measurement of local or centralized records management systems.

The organization should have a formal records management policy stating its agreed position with regard to its records, and responsibilities and accountabilities within the programme should be clearly specified.

What is a records management system?

A system is 'a set of components that interact to accomplish some purpose' (Senn, 1989, 16). An organization can itself be viewed as a system, and will have numerous subsystems, of which the records management programme is one example. Within the programme, systems are needed to ensure that records remain trustworthy as evidence of the activities that gave rise to them, that they are protected against loss or damage, and that the records and the information they contain are accessible and usable over time. In this book the term *records management system* is used to refer not to the records management programme as a whole, but to a unified set of resources, responsibilities, procedures and equipment designed to maintain and provide access to records within the programme.

Records that are to be successfully managed need to be captured within a formal records management system. In the paper world it could be said that a record is 'captured' on paper as soon as it is created, but for effective control of records it is the capture of the paper document into a records management system that is the critical action. In this sense the term 'capture' applies equally to records created within the organization and to those received from outside. Records created electronically exist only in the computer's temporary memory until they are 'saved' to a digital storage medium or printed to paper; again, further action is likely to be required to ensure their capture into a records management system.

A records management system needs a physical infrastructure: paper-based systems use a range of stationery and storage equipment (including files, boxes, cabinets and shelves); electronic records require hardware (computers and storage media) as well as software. Paper files and computer hardware both need accommodation that provides adequate security. However, physical storage is only part of the picture. People have an essential role in any records management system: those who design, implement and support the system and those who are its customers. Records must be accessible to those who are authorized to use them, and information about the context of the records must also be provided. Subsystems are needed to manage the capture, classification, maintenance and disposal of records, to provide access to them and to ensure that they remain accessible in future. These issues are discussed further in Chapters 3 to 7.

Records management systems also need an intellectual basis. This can be provided in part by an organizational records management policy, but policies are unlikely to be effective unless they are backed up by measures to ensure their implementation. In paper-based systems, a set of operational procedures is required, together with staff training in their use, directives that enforce them, and monitoring of their application. Similar measures are also likely to be needed in systems that are partly or wholly automated, but computerization can allow some parts of a system to operate invisibly, without direct intervention on the part of users. The ideal system is one that is minimally intrusive to staff undertaking a business activity.

In small organizations, a single organization-wide records management system may be a practical possibility, but in an organization of any size it is likely that there will be a need for separate systems in different functional areas. Each system will support particular types of activity, and the operational needs of those activities should determine the structure of the system (see Figure 1.7).

Sometimes the procedures used in individual records management systems can be common to all areas of the organization, even though each system is distinct and operates at local level. Alternatively there may be a need for different procedures for records capture and maintenance in different areas. However, it is desirable that all records should be classified to a common model, that disposal practices across the organization should be harmonized, and that there should be a single point of access for information about all the records of the organization.

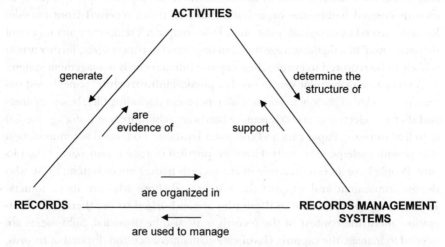

Fig. 1.7 *Relationship between activities, records and records management systems*

When is it appropriate to design a records management system? Who should be responsible for its development?

There may sometimes be the opportunity to design a records management system when an organization or business function is newly established. More commonly, the requirement is for an existing system to be redesigned, perhaps following a restructuring or re-engineering exercise, or (very often) simply because existing practices have proved inadequate.

The development of a comprehensive records management system is a complex operation with many facets, and is likely to be a multidisciplinary exercise. It involves planning, designing and implementing subsystems for the capture and physical storage of records, for their classification, maintenance and disposal, and for the provision and regulation of access. It requires input not only from the records management unit, but also from managers and staff of business units, from legal advisers and auditors, and from information managers and computing specialists, including network administrators and application developers. If the organization employs compliance or quality assurance managers, they should also be members of the project team. External consultants might be hired if skills are needed that are not available within the organization. Directors or senior managers will not be expected to participate in the design activity, but the system must take account of their requirements. Systems design is discussed in more detail in Chapter 8.

Who should be responsible for operating the system?

In the paper world the operation of the system is tied to the physical custody of the records, which may be the responsibility of the records management unit, of individual business units, or a mixture of both. Some aspects of the service, particularly the custody of older or less frequently used records, might also be outsourced to an external contractor.

If paper records are in the physical custody of the records management unit, it is usual for the staff of the unit to manage all aspects of the system. End-users are seen as clients of the records management unit, and have to approach records management staff when requiring access. If physical custody of some or all records is devolved to business units, local staff will be responsible for the daily management of the system, with the records management unit providing advice and monitoring quality control.

In the electronic world, while physical custody normally rests with information technology staff, access to digital records can be provided at the desktop and no intermediary is required. In this situation technical support is provided by computing specialists; the role of the records management unit is to provide advice, non-technical support and quality control. However, older digital records may be retired to offline discs or tapes; if these are stored by the records management unit, it may still have a custodial role. In a hybrid environment records managers may have a mixture of custodial, support and monitoring roles.

The use of software in a records management system

The earliest records management software applications were designed for managing files in a paper environment. They provided features to control the registration, storage and retrieval of paper files, to record the use and movement of files within the organization and to manage their retention and disposal. Commercial packages of this kind are still available, often with an additional facility to provide pointers to the location of records in microform or digital format; but software suppliers have increasingly sought to develop products that offer a closer interface with document imaging, electronic document management or workflow software.

Electronic records management applications currently on the market are designed to support electronic records in documentary format, and can broadly be seen as enhancements of electronic document management packages, developed to meet the needs of the records management community. A reputable product will support the authenticity and evidential characteristics of records, and will provide for their integrity over time as well as managing the information they contain. It will also support the management of contextual information about the records and the control of their retention and disposal, although no software package will obviate the need for intellectual analysis of functional classification and retention needs. The best applications are able to manage digitized images of paper records as well as records 'born digitally', and can also handle information about records that are to be maintained in paper form, thus providing a high level of integrated control in a hybrid environment. Of course, they will only be fully effective when employed as part of a planned and structured records management system, under the control of trained and competent staff.

Standards for records management

There are numerous published standards of interest to those responsible for developing and operating records management programmes and systems. In particular, the international standard ISO 15489-1:2001 *Information and documentation – records management*, published by the International Standards Organization, and the Australian national standard AS 4390-1996 *Records management* provide benchmarks against which records management programmes and systems can be measured.

There are also many standards that may be relevant to particular parts of a records management system. These include standards that relate to:

- legal admissibility and compliance
- security
- preservation
- media conversion
- information retrieval
- quality assurance.

In the world of electronic and hybrid systems it is particularly important for records managers to be aware of technical standards that can be used to manage the dependency of records on computer hardware and software, in order to maintain digital records for long-term access.

Besides standards published by national or international standards organizations, there are others promoted by commercial or professional bodies. For example, the UK Public Record Office has published *Standards for the management of government records* (1998 et seq.), which offer guidance on many aspects of records management, with special emphasis on the needs of public sector organizations.

A select list of standards relevant to records management is given in Appendix B.

Managing the life of the record

Traditionally, records managers were empowered only to deal with records no longer required for the current business of the organization. Storage and preservation systems were seen as their main concerns, together with the provision of access to older records and the disposal of those that were redundant. In many organizations this may still be the case: the management of current records may be left to operational managers and their staff, and the remit given to a records manager may be limited to retention scheduling, the transfer of older records to off-floor or offline storage and the management of the storage areas and their contents.

In a paper-based organization, it is possible to run a records management unit that deals only with semi-current and non-current records. However, a service that focuses on the records that are least active (see Figure 1.3, page 7) will only be able to make a limited contribution to the effectiveness of the organization. It will be impossible for the records manager to ensure that records are reliable and complete, and that all the records of the organization are accessible and usable. At best, the records management unit will try to achieve these aims but will lack the authority to co-ordinate records creation practices effectively; it will be obliged to do the best it can with the records it receives from the creators, in whatever state these records arrive. At worst, it will come to be perceived as a dumping ground for unwanted files, irrelevant to the 'real' business of the organization.

In the world of electronic records and hybrid systems this is not a viable option. When the technical aspects of electronic storage are necessarily managed by computing specialists, a 'back room' approach to electronic records management offers little or no role for the skills of the records manager. More importantly, this approach is unlikely to lead to the maintenance of adequate records of the organization's functions and activities. Many staff who create records will neglect to capture them in a system that supports preservation and access, or will fail to plan for their disposal in a systematic fashion. The creation and preservation of the records that the organization needs cannot be guaranteed unless records management issues are addressed when records creation systems are designed and implemented. Just as an effective records management programme should cover records in all media, electronic as well as paper, so it should accept responsibility for all records of the organization regardless of their age.

References

Casanova, E. (1928) *Archivistica*, Lazzeri.

Couture, C. and Rousseau, J.-Y. (1987) *The life of a document: a global approach to archives and records management*, Véhicule Press.

Jackson, M. (1983) *System development*, Prentice Hall.

Jenkinson, H. (1922) *A manual of archive administration*, Clarendon Press.

Kennedy, J. and Schauder, C. (1998) *Records management: a guide to corporate record keeping*, 2nd edn, Addison Wesley Longman Australia.

McKemmish, S. (1997) Yesterday, today and tomorrow: a continuum of responsibility. In *Proceedings of the Records Management Association of Australia 14th National Convention, 15–17 September 1997*, Records Management Association of Australia. Also available at http://rcrg.dstc.edu.au/publications/recordscontinuum/smckp2.html.

Muller, S., Feith, J. A. and Fruin, R. (1898) *Handleinding voor het ordenen en beschrijven van archiven*, Groningen; English translation by Leavitt, A. H. (1940) *Manual for the arrangement and description of archives*, H. W. Wilson.

O'Shea, G. (1996) Keeping electronic records: issues and strategies, *Provenance: the Electronic Magazine*, **1** (2). Available at www.provenance.ca/1995-2000backissues/vol1/no2/features/erecs1a.htm.

Parker, E. (1999) *Managing your organization's records*, Library Association Publishing.

Public Record Office (1998 et seq.) *Standards for the management of government records*, [UK] Public Record Office. Also available at www.pro.gov.uk/recordsmanagement/standards/.

Robek, M. F., Brown, G. F. and Stephens, D. O. (1995) *Information and records management: document-based information systems*, 4th edn, Glencoe/McGraw-Hill.

Roberts, D. (1994) Defining electronic records, documents and data, *Archives and Manuscripts*, **22** (1), 14–26. Also available at www.records.nsw.gov.au/publicsector/erk/dtf/define-1.htm.

Saunders, J. B. (ed.) (1990) *Words and phrases legally defined*, Vol 4, Butterworths.

Schellenberg, T. R. (1956) *Modern archives: principles and techniques*, F. W. Cheshire.

Senn, J. A. (1989) *Analysis and design of information systems*, 2nd edn, McGraw-Hill.

Walne, P. (ed.) (1988) *Dictionary of archival terminology*, ICA Handbooks Series, Vol 7, 2nd edn, K. G. Saur.

AS 4390-1996 *Records management*, Standards Australia.

ISO 15489-1:2001 *Information and documentation – records management – part 1: general*, International Standards Organization.

2
Analysing the context for records management

Records managers need to understand the context of their work at a number of different levels. They need knowledge of the records that are produced, the organizational activities that generate records and the systems used to control them. In addition, they should have a thorough understanding of the organization itself and how records management contributes to its objectives.

To gain this understanding, records managers must analyse the role and responsibilities of the organization, study its structures and working methods and discover how these have changed during its life. They also need to identify the broader issues that influence the way the organization operates, including its corporate culture and the interests and expectations of stakeholders within the organization and externally. Knowledge of the organization's operating environment is a key element in designing an effective records management programme.

When the records manager has investigated these broader aspects of the organization, the next task is to acquire a deeper understanding of its functions and the activities that are performed to support them. The knowledge gained from these investigations can then be used to assess how each of these factors affects the organization's needs for evidence and information, and the degree to which its needs are met by the existing records and records systems. Putting all these pieces together, the records manager can design and implement a programme that fits the organization's requirements.

This chapter examines analytical techniques that records managers can use to develop a wide view of an organization and their role within it. These techniques may be used when establishing a new records management programme and also in responding to changing circumstances when a programme is in operation.

Using analytical techniques

What techniques are available?

Records managers need to undertake a range of analyses, using techniques appropriate to each task (see Figure 2.1). One of these techniques, the records survey, has been developed by records managers themselves, but others were invented outside the records management field. Techniques for investigating the environment, culture and structure of organizations have been developed by management analysts, while functional and process analysis techniques are borrowed from information technology and systems analysts.

Analysis is an iterative process, since issues raised when one technique is used will often need further investigation using a related technique. The choice of an initial technique depends on the purpose of the analysis and the object to be analysed. Traditionally, records managers have begun at the bottom, with detailed surveys of records. This book suggests that the initial focus should be at macro levels (the organization and its environment), followed by micro-level analysis (of records systems and existing records) to complete the detailed picture.

Planning and managing an analysis project

In any analysis there are likely to be four phases: definition of the object and purpose

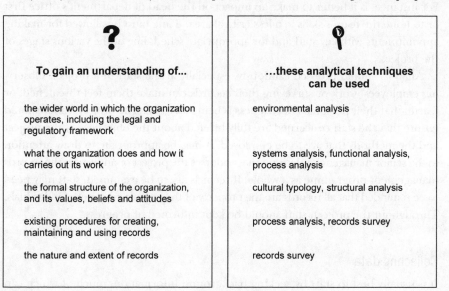

To gain an understanding of...	...these analytical techniques can be used
the wider world in which the organization operates, including the legal and regulatory framework	environmental analysis
what the organization does and how it carries out its work	systems analysis, functional analysis, process analysis
the formal structure of the organization, and its values, beliefs and attitudes	cultural typology, structural analysis
existing procedures for creating, maintaining and using records	process analysis, records survey
the nature and extent of records	records survey

Fig. 2.1 *Analytical techniques to gain an understanding of an organization*

of the analysis, data collection, examination and interpretation of the data, and a final phase which may include constructing a model based on the results of the analysis, or drawing up conclusions or recommendations for further action. Most analyses are carried out using project management techniques and standard approaches to data collection.

Senior management support is vital. For larger projects it may be appropriate to set up a steering committee, with senior management representation, to approve the resources and oversee the direction of the project. The scope of the project must be agreed in advance: for example, which parts of the organization will be investigated? A pilot exercise may be used to establish the project parameters.

Projects need to be broken down into the component actions or tasks required to accomplish the objectives. Decisions are needed on who will carry out the work: records management staff, staff from other parts of the organization, contractors or consultants? The availability of appropriate skills will affect the design of the project and, if more than one person is involved, the roles assigned to each participant. Where records managers work in a multidisciplinary team with other professionals, resource demands can be shared and a wider range of skills deployed. A project leader will be needed, to keep the project on schedule and deal with any problems that arise.

Projects should be planned carefully, taking into account their objectives and scope. The project leader needs to define the sequence in which tasks will be undertaken. For instance, is it better to make an impact on the head of department's office first or to hone the team's skills in a less critical area? Time must be allowed for making appointments with key staff and for appropriate scheduling of the various stages of the project.

Analysts should proceed cautiously, especially at the start of a project. Observing employees' work or surveying their records can make them feel threatened, or fearful that their personal effectiveness is being assessed. The project leader should ensure that the staff concerned are fully briefed about the objectives of the project and the methods that are to be employed. It may be appropriate to draw attention to the senior management decision that endorses the project or authorizes the records management programme as a whole. If records are to be examined, staff may need to be reminded that all records are the property of the organization, not of individuals. Throughout the project, staff should be kept informed of progress.

Collecting data

It is usually best to start by seeking background information, much of which can be obtained from internal and external publications such as those listed in Figure 2.2. Many of these should be accessible through a library or information centre, or by using the internet or an organizational intranet. Some may have to be sought from human resources departments or elsewhere in the organization. Recent projects in other areas of management may have involved the collection of similar data; if existing work can be reused the need for research can be reduced. However, internal documentation must often be treated with caution: it may be out of date, incomplete or representative of an official viewpoint that has little relation to actual practice. Information obtained from desk research generally needs to be supplemented by contacting individuals or groups of stakeholders, using questionnaires or interviews.

External sources for preliminary research include:

- 'trade press', directories and other publications specific to the employment sector
- government and other legal and regulatory publications
- standards and codes of practice.

Internal sources include:

- annual or other reports
- business plans and other strategic planning documents
- standing orders and operational directives
- policies and procedural manuals
- organization charts and job descriptions
- internal directories or staff lists
- documentation of existing records systems
- site and floor plans
- organizational histories
- previous systems analysis reports, consultancy reports or records management surveys.

Fig. 2.2   *Sources for preliminary research*

Questionnaires provide a simple means of gathering data from a large number of respondents. They can be used within an organization or to collect information from external stakeholders.

Questionnaires can be distributed on paper or electronically. They should be carefully designed to meet their specific purpose and to support the proposed method of data analysis. A good questionnaire:

- covers all relevant topics
- takes account of the respondent's expected level of knowledge
- is clearly laid out, with questions in a logical order
- uses concise and plain language, not jargon
- avoids ambiguity and vagueness

- uses 'open' questions to seek opinions and 'closed' questions to discover facts
- includes a section to identify the respondent, where appropriate.

Recipients must be told what the questionnaire is for and what they have to do with it; this information can be given on the form itself or in separate guidelines. Before distribution, questionnaires should be tested by asking a third party to review them, particularly to identify any parts that are unclear or difficult to understand.

While questionnaires may be easy to administer, they usually achieve low rates of return. Personal contact is lacking, and the usefulness of the answers depends on respondents understanding the questions and being willing to reply thoroughly and accurately. Follow-up enquiries are often needed to clarify or complete responses.

An alternative is to use more direct methods of data gathering, such as interviews. Although they can be time-consuming, especially in geographically dispersed organizations, interviews have the benefit of providing personal contact with individuals and give an opportunity to 'sell' the records management programme. It is often possible to collect more detailed information from interviews than from questionnaires. Informal or anecdotal information can also be gathered, such as opinions on existing systems or suggestions for their improvement. Interviews allow supplementary questions to be asked on the spot and thus offer greater flexibility in following up initial answers.

The selection of staff to be interviewed should be determined by their knowledge, not by seniority. Interviews may be one-to-one, or a number of interviewees may be brought together in a focus group. Face-to-face interviews are usual, but telephone interviews may be employed if interviewees are distant.

Interviewing is a skilled task and expert advice in the design and execution of interviews may be helpful. Preparation for an interview includes defining its purpose, designing a suitable structure and setting questions. Interviewers should prepare well, listing the topics that need to be covered, doing background research and obtaining security clearances and appointments in advance. Decisions are also needed on how to record the interview (using a laptop computer, tape recorder or paper notes) and an appropriate venue. The ideal setting is a private area that is familiar to the interviewee but free from interruptions.

An interview generally has three phases:

1 Introduction: the interviewer explains the background and purpose of the interview and its benefits to the interviewee, and gives reassurance that information will be treated in confidence.

2 The main part of the interview: each topic is taken in turn, with initial questions followed by further probing to explore and clarify responses.

3 Conclusion: the interviewer summarizes to ensure that key points have been understood, and any follow-up actions are noted.

Interviewers need tact, diplomacy, perseverance and patience to ensure that information is gathered in a professional manner. The results should be written up as soon as possible after the interview, while the information is fresh.

When questionnaires and interviews are used, opinions may be easier to gather than facts, since respondents may not have full or accurate knowledge of the issues concerned. Their answers may need to be corroborated from other sources, and discrepancies explored.

Questionnaires and interviews can be supplemented by direct observation and measuring of systems and work practices. Observation may include walkthroughs of working or storage areas, investigating current systems in practice and studying workflows and patterns of communication. Measuring provides specific data such as the time required to perform an activity or the number of records stored or retrieved in a particular period.

Using these methods takes time. Normally only a snapshot can be observed, and employees may behave differently if they know that they are being watched. Nevertheless, observation is a useful means of confirming whether official procedures or work descriptions are reflected in reality. Observation or measuring may be essential if other information sources are unreliable or unavailable.

A useful guide to data collection for records managers has been produced by the National Archives of Australia (2001).

The organization and its environment

What is environmental analysis and why is it useful in records management?

Records managers need to learn about the environment in which the records management programme operates. This includes developing an understanding of the internal and external pressures on the organization as a whole, as well as those aspects of the environment, such as legal and regulatory requirements, that have a direct impact on records management.

The term 'environment' needs some explanation here. In this context it is used to mean everything outside the particular universe that is the subject of study. As Dawson (1996, 78) says, the environment 'is inevitably an arbitrary concept in that it embraces everything outside any particular organization'. The designation of the organization and its environment and the drawing of a boundary between them is always subjective to some degree.

Actors in the environment include regulatory agencies, potential and actual customers, suppliers and competitors, as well as the wider community. Organizations draw resources (materials, labour and technology) from their environment, besides supplying products or services to it. The environment is the source of external demands made on an organization, and also of opportunities for the organization to develop and grow.

Environmental analysis and strategic management

Environmental analysis techniques have been developed to help with strategic management in organizations. Johnson and Scholes (2002, 16) suggest that strategic management has three elements: gaining an understanding of an organization's strategic position, choice of strategy and implementation. Since strategic decisions taken at senior levels affect the long-term direction of the organization, the analysis that precedes them needs to look at the match between organizational activities and the operating environment, as well as matching activities to the organization's resource capability.

Various strategic analysis techniques are available to study the environment in which an organization operates, its objectives and its resources. These range from the simple SWOT analysis (identifying *strengths*, *weaknesses*, *opportunities* and *threats*), discussed in Chapter 8, to sophisticated software-based tools that can be used to analyse financial markets and identify investment opportunities or competitive advantage. While records managers are unlikely to use the more advanced strategic analysis tools, they can benefit from an understanding of the strategic approaches being proposed for the organization as a whole in order to evaluate the impact on records creation and retention.

At a lower level, strategic management is also critical to the success of individual programmes within the organization, including the records management programme. Strategic management is a responsibility, not just of corporate managers at the top of the organization, but also of managers at business unit and operational levels. They too have to plan for the effective functioning of their own work areas, within the overall policy framework determined at higher levels. Thus records managers can make use of strategic analysis both in assessing organizational needs for records and in directing the staff and resources of the records management unit.

Records managers may find that analyses of environmental influences have already been made elsewhere in the organization. However, time spent undertaking an analysis of their own will help them to gain a deeper understanding of the context of their work. Besides surveying the top level of the organization and the environment in which it operates, they should consider which influences are currently most significant for the management of the organization's records and which issues are likely to be important in the future.

The political, economic, social and technological environment

One way of auditing the environment is to undertake a PEST analysis, which seeks to identify the different influences that currently affect the organization in the present. The acronym PEST refers to the *political, economic, social* and *technological* environment within which the organization functions.

A simple way of undertaking a PEST analysis is to consider each of the four headings and review the issues in the environment that might affect the organization and the management of its records. The first part of the analysis can be done by an individual or a small team, for instance in a brainstorming session, to identify key issues. Additional research then follows, looking at market reports, government papers or press coverage, to confirm whether the initial findings are complete and to develop them in more detail. Figure 2.3 gives examples of issues that might emerge in an analysis of this kind.

	Political	new or proposed legislation effects of government policy on the organization change of government following an election
	Economic	economic upturn or downturn globalization, opening of new markets taxation changes privatization changes in prices or sources of supply
	Social	lifelong learning consumer movements interest in ecological and green issues flexible employment practices, part-time working cultural policies how is the organization perceived by society?
	Technological	new types of hardware and software new communications technologies new production techniques research and development technology obsolescence

Fig. 2.3   *PEST analysis*

The legal and regulatory environment

As well as identifying the broader political, economic, social and technological issues, records managers must make a more detailed assessment of the legal and regulatory environment in which their organization operates. Legislation may take the form of statutes, legal instruments or byelaws. There may also be precedents derived from decisions in the courts (case law) and rules imposed by regulatory agencies at local, national or supranational level. The details will vary from one country to another and organizations operating internationally will need to take account of the law in each country concerned. This book cannot give advice on legal and regulatory requirements in every country, but the following paragraphs outline the kinds of issues that need to be addressed, based on the common law traditions of English-speaking countries.

Records managers need to be aware of legislation imposing *explicit requirements* for the creation or management of records. Such legislation may specify:

- types of records to be created in particular operational contexts
- the form in which such records should be maintained
- the period for which records should be retained
- the circumstances in which older records are to be transferred to an archival institution
- the rights of individuals, corporate bodies or governments to have access to records
- limitations on access in the interests of privacy or confidentiality
- protection of copyright or other intellectual property rights.

These requirements will not be found in a single piece of legislation. Statutes such as the UK Public Records Act 1958, the Australian Archives Act 1983 or the National Archives of South Africa Act 1996 relate to the keeping of records of central government bodies; local governments and private bodies may be subject to separate but often less stringent records legislation. Records requirements will also be found in enactments whose title does not mention records or archives. For example, obligations to create or retain records may be imposed by laws or regulations that are specific to a particular employment sector (such as commerce, education or healthcare) or a particular activity (such as the handling of drugs or chemicals), and also by general legislation affecting all employers (on matters such as health and safety, taxation, financial probity and racial or sexual discrimination).

Most countries have specific laws on copyright, and access and privacy rights are also frequently the subject of specific legislation. The latter may be limited in scope: some privacy laws, and most laws on freedom of information, apply only to records of public authorities. Some legislation may apply only to records in particular media: for example, data protection laws in European countries cover both private and public bodies, but have only recently been extended to records held outside computerized systems.

The records manager also needs to be aware of *implied requirements*, where laws and regulations do not mention records but still have an impact on records management. For example, many laws require organizations to disclose information to higher authorities, or to provide evidence of compliance with legislation, and thus imply a need to maintain records. Similarly, records are not usually mentioned in laws that impose time limits for bringing legal action in a dispute, but such laws do indicate the period of time for which evidence may be needed.

Records as legal evidence

In countries whose legal systems derive from the English common law, organizational records were traditionally considered inadmissible as legal evidence. The courts rejected them as second-hand or 'hearsay' evidence, which cannot be verified, as opposed to 'real' evidence given by a witness in person. This rule has been substantially eroded in most countries, both by legislation (such as the UK Civil Evidence Act 1995 and the Australian Commonwealth Evidence Act 1995) and by precedent of decisions made in the courts. The current position is summarized by Smith (1996, 71–2): 'The modern trend of the courts is to treat most evidence as admissible and to allow the judge to decide what weight to attach to the various items of evidence . . . . It is only a slight exaggeration to say that the question of admissibility . . . is trivial.'

A further issue may arise if a copy of a record, rather than an 'original', is to be produced in court. Under common law, the so-called 'best evidence' rule traditionally required the production of 'original' records, or permitted the use of duplicates as legal evidence only in closely defined circumstances (for example, if the original was in the possession of a third party who could not be made to release it). Again, in recent times the 'best evidence' rule has been reviewed in many common law countries, to take account of the widespread use of copying and information technologies. In many jurisdictions the use of reproductions is acceptable, whether or not the original is still in existence, if the copy is suitably authenticated and the absence of the original can be satisfactorily explained.

Until recently lawmakers were able to assume that all records would be maintained on paper or copied to another 'analogue' medium such as microform. The growth of digital technology and electronic commerce has invalidated this view. Digital imaging systems have invaded the traditional role of microform, while increasing numbers of records are both created and maintained on computer systems. At the time of writing the law regarding records of electronic communications and transactions is rapidly changing. Generally, the trend is away from insistence on paper as the only legally acceptable medium, and towards acceptance of new technology; but the pace of acceptance differs from country to country.

In most common law countries the 'hearsay' rule is now largely irrelevant to the records manager, and the 'best evidence' rule is also of declining significance. Today the greater risk is not that a record will be ruled inadmissible, but rather that the court may judge it to carry insufficient weight as evidence, or that its accuracy or reliability may be impugned by the other party in the case. In this context the real issue for records managers and lawyers is how to ensure that records will carry sufficient weight and not be open to challenge. It is wise to ensure that best practice is followed in record creation and capture, and in any conversion of records from one medium to another: issues that are considered at greater length in Chapters 4 and 6.

Identifying legal and regulatory requirements

Wherever possible, records managers should consult legal advisers or auditors for advice. Often, however, research has to be undertaken by records managers themselves in order to obtain a full picture of the current legal or regulatory position.

Research can begin with records management textbooks, which often give an account of laws and regulations in the country where they were published. However, much of the legal information in these books quickly becomes out of date, and most textbooks provide little or no international coverage. In North America there are various CD-ROM publications on records retention legislation (see www.arma.org/Bookstore/), and these offer quarterly or annual updates. Some have limited international coverage but their main focus is on US and Canadian law. Outside North America it is usually better to rely on sources compiled for the legal profession, which tend to be updated more frequently than records management publications. The online information service *LexisNexis* is useful, but available only to subscribers (see www.lexisnexis.com/). The *SOSIG Law Gateway*, www.sosig.ac.uk/law/, and the Law Library of Congress *Guide to Law Online*, www.loc.gov/law/guide/, are free services that provide links to legal resource websites worldwide. Websites that can be used to trace legislation in specific regions include:

- *AustLII*, the Australasian Legal Information Institute, www.austlii.edu.au/
- Australian Attorney General's Department legal information site, http://scaleplus.law.gov.au/
- *BAILII*, the British and Irish Legal Information Institute, www.bailii.org/
- Her Majesty's Stationery Office (UK legislation), www.legislation.hmso.gov.uk/
- *LII*, the US Legal Information Institute, www.law.cornell.edu/.

Identifying other requirements for records

Other factors in the wider environment also have an impact on the organization's need to create and maintain records. There are likely to be codes of conduct for corporate governance and other voluntary standards that the organization has adopted for reasons of good practice, competitiveness or public image. These may include technical or industry standards as well as more general standards such as the ISO 9000 series on quality management. The records manager should identify the standards to which the organization subscribes and the records that need to be created or kept as proof of compliance.

Other external influences on the organization's requirements for records are the prevalence of litigation in the community that it serves, the extent to which it is liable to audit or inspection by regulators and the expectations of members of the public and society as a whole for access to its records.

Understanding organizational cultures and structures

Types of organizational culture

An organization's culture is the set of shared values and assumptions held by those who belong to it. The members of an organization are rarely conscious of its culture: attitudes and beliefs are usually taken for granted. A simple typology of organizational cultures (see Figure 2.4) is suggested by Handy (1993, 181–91), who notes that the nature of the organization's environment can be a crucial determinant in its culture.

The *power* culture has a strong source of power at its centre, like a spider in a web, with lines of influence radiating outwards. Usually there is a central entrepreneur who controls everything by personal influence. Resources are centralized. Divisions or departments are represented by the lines going out from the centre. Organizations like this have few rules, procedures or bureaucracy: instead, 'in a power culture certain persons are dominant and others subservient' (Pheysey, 1993, 17). Examples

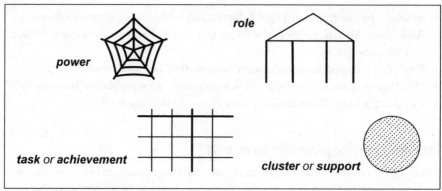

Fig. 2.4   *Handy's organizational cultures*

include many trade unions and small specialist enterprises managed by one family or individual. Power cultures often find it difficult to grow: the methods of control break down when the organization becomes too large.

The *role* culture is typically built on bureaucracy. Handy (1993, 185) depicts it in the shape of a Greek temple. Power lies with senior management in the triangular pediment at the top and the pillars of the temple represent departments, which carry out the functions. There is little room for individuality but much reliance on formal procedures and checking mechanisms. 'The word "role" . . . refers to the way in which the occupant of each position in the firm is expected to act . . . . A role culture is one which emphasizes conformity to expectations' (Pheysey, 1993, 16). Such organizations are reliable, but may not always be responsive in times of change. There may also be communication problems between departments, since the structure encourages vertical communication but provides few opportunities for cross-departmental liaison. Role cultures are often associated with government agencies and large companies in stable industries.

The *task* or *achievement* culture focuses on projects or outcomes, rather than roles or processes. Handy (1993, 187) sees this culture as a net, whose threads represent the specialist skills of the workforce, which meet at nodes where actions are taken and decisions made. 'In an achievement culture people are interested in the work itself and have a personal stake in seeing that it is done' (Pheysey, 1993, 17). Power and influence are dispersed through the organization. Such organizations have swift communications structures and the capability to bring together groups of experts to carry out specific projects. Vertical hierarchies may exist but can be bypassed in the interest of achieving spontaneous solutions or innovative results. However, centralized control is difficult, so accountability is problematic. Typically, organizations have achievement cultures to develop new products or take creative risks, but not where strong management or budgetary control is needed.

The *cluster* or *support* culture is the least common and the least structured. In this culture, members of the organization derive satisfaction from mutual relationships or shared commitment, which drives their contribution to the common goal. Individuals retain control of their work and may have more allegiance to their professional group than to the organization. Decisions are shared, and management hierarchies and control mechanisms difficult to establish. Barristers' chambers, architects' practices and small consultancies of self-employed people are examples.

Identifying organizational cultures

Analysis of an organization's culture helps the records manager to understand why the organization operates as it does and to assess its records management needs and evaluate suitable records systems. The checklist in Figure 2.5 indicates some key characteristics of the four simple cultural types and can be used to identify the predominant culture in the organization.

Organizational cultures vary over time, as organizations grow and environmental influences change. For example, a small team of people may work together in a support culture, but as their numbers grow the founder members start to dictate to the others and a power culture develops as a top management group becomes divorced from the workforce. Local branches may begin to seek more autonomy by fostering an achievement culture; then in an attempt to control local autonomies a role culture may be introduced, with formal procedures imposed throughout the organization.

In practice, these four types of culture are not exclusive. Different cultures may exist simultaneously within the same organization. For example, health visitors or academics typically pursue much of their work in a support culture, but their support mechanisms coexist with the wider role culture of health service or university management. Most organizations display complex combinations of cultural attitudes, and writers such as Brown (1998) and Robbins (2001) have suggested further indicators of cultural orientation, such as the extent to which organizations are focused on competitiveness, co-operation, loyalty, trust or employee welfare.

❑ Does the organization have these characteristics?

- It is strongly hierarchical, with numerous committees and departments.
- Its functions and structures have remained fairly stable for a long period.
- It puts emphasis on job descriptions and the formal status of staff members.
- It is averse to taking risks and innovation is discouraged.
- It relies heavily on forms and procedure manuals, especially for repetitive tasks.
- Resource allocation requires several levels of approval.
- It uses official memoranda as the chief method of conveying information from management to staff.
- Employees are offered security and long-term rewards.

*If so, it is predominantly a **role culture**.*

❑ Does the organization have these characteristics?

- It has a flexible structure which encourages people to work in project teams or groups.
- It is focused on results.
- It responds quickly to change or external pressures.
- It encourages communication, both formal and informal, between its project teams.
- Teams work autonomously, and decisions are taken locally not centrally.
- Individuals are employed because of their specialist skills.
- Few procedure manuals or forms are used.
- The organization cannot easily handle routine repetitive tasks or large-scale production.

*If so, it is predominantly an **achievement culture**.*

❑ Does the organization have these characteristics?

- It has one or two dominant individuals who make all the decisions.
- It has few formal methods of internal communication.
- It has little bureaucracy and few committees.
- It operates informally and does not document decisions routinely.
- It wants to be judged by results not means.
- It can react to change quickly when driven by the controlling personality.
- It might be vulnerable if the central figure were to leave or die.

*If so, it is predominantly a **power culture**.*

❑ Does the organization have these characteristics?

- It is loosely structured.
- It has no formal bureaucracy or rules.
- It exists for the benefit of its individual members.
- It depends on those individuals for its existence.
- Important decisions are made communally.
- Roles are shared according to expertise.

*If so, it is predominantly a **support culture**.*

Fig. 2.5 *Organizational cultures: checklist*

Organizational culture and records management

Organizational culture has implications for records managers because different types of organization require different approaches to records management. No single approach is right for all organizations; the records manager should adopt a strategy that will work within the prevailing culture.

Each culture tends to favour its own internal control mechanisms. Role and power cultures control by *regulation*; achievement and support cultures by *appreciation* (Pheysey, 1993, 22–7). In achievement and support cultures a records management programme based on a regulatory approach is unlikely to succeed. Power cultures rely on day-to-day supervision of lower levels by the powerful and may not have a systematic approach to regulation. Instead of following procedures, subordinates are expected to appeal to a superior for a decision before initiating action. Only in role cultures are there likely to be formal control systems and regulatory procedures. Records management programmes that depend heavily on regulation are best suited to organizations with a role culture.

Different cultures also have different attitudes to accountability. Role culture organizations may accept the need to account for their actions, although they may also try to limit liability by using 'small print' or by seeking to prove that responsibility for errors lies elsewhere. The power culture on the other hand 'tries to regulate its environment by conquest and confrontation' (Pheysey, 1993, 26), buying out the opposition or taking it to law. Thus records management based on the need for external accountability may be more marketable in a role culture than in a power culture. Internal accountability is an important issue in both role and power cultures, where staff must show that they have acted as the organization or its leader requires. In achievement cultures risk-taking and getting results are seen as more important than accountability. However, accountability can be surprisingly important in a support culture since there is a strong concept of mutual accountability for the work that is done.

In role cultures, records management units have a formal position in the organizational hierarchy. Strong vertical reporting structures mean that records managers can seek to use high-level authorization to ensure compliance, but it can be difficult for them to work effectively across departmental boundaries. If their status is low, there may be little incentive for other departments and senior officers to take their advice. On the other hand, bureaucratic organizations can work to the records manager's advantage. A records committee can be set up, or policy papers written for senior management, and these are good ways of gaining support. Procedure manuals can be used to establish rules for records management. Most actions and decisions will be well documented and in general the culture will support the creation and systematic maintenance of records.

In organizations with an achievement culture, many records will reflect the work of project teams. Records managers need to be aware of how projects are approved and established, so that project leaders can be approached and records management requirements built into project planning. If this is not done, it may be difficult to identify the provenance or ownership of project records or to impose records systems retrospectively when project teams have been disbanded.

Managing records in support or power cultures is rarely easy. Such organizations work informally and frequently do not document their decisions, so few records are created. Structures and activities are fluid, so records managers have few fixed points to rely on. Individuals, especially powerful ones, are likely to perceive records as a personal rather than an organizational resource, and may oppose the establishment of centralized control systems. Records management will only work if it has the explicit backing of the central power or the mutual agreement of the collective.

The structure of the organization

All organizations, even the most informal, have a structure of some kind. In many organizations the structural hierarchy is formally defined and staff are very conscious of its importance. Elsewhere structures may be more flexible and less prominent, but they still exist. These two types are often distinguished as 'mechanistic' and 'organic' structures (Robey and Sales, 1994, 86–92). Mechanistic structures are typically found in large organizations and role cultures. Organic structures are those where responsibilities are less rigidly defined, allowing individuals to perform a variety of tasks according to need. They are more characteristic of small organizations and of power, support or achievement cultures.

In organizations with a mechanistic structure, the workforce may be grouped in a number of different ways. Business units may be organized on the basis of:

- activities (bringing together individuals who share similar skills or work processes)
- output (e.g. workers on product A in one unit, workers on product B in another)
- market segment (e.g. domestic and commercial customers served by separate units)
- geography (e.g. local or regional offices).

In practice, mixed structures are common: for example, manufacturing units within an organization may be grouped by product line, sales units by geography. There may also be different forms of grouping at different levels: for example, each geographically based sales unit could be subdivided by market segment.

Structures are rarely static for long. Organizations make changes by:

- moving to a more organic or more mechanistic structure
- altering the basis of the structure (e.g. by moving from a geographical structure to one based on output)
- redistributing activities, outputs, market segments or regions between business units, perhaps by increasing or reducing the responsibilities assigned to particular units
- reallocating the responsibilities of individuals or workgroups within a business unit
- changing the number of employees reporting to a single manager (by introducing or removing 'flatter' structures, as in Figure 2.6).

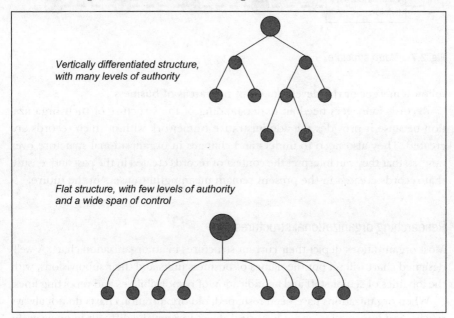

Fig. 2.6 *Organizational structures*

Larger organizations may set up or abolish subsidiary organizations. They may also introduce or revise so-called 'matrix' structures, which attempt to combine different structural bases using a more complex model (see Figure 2.7).

In a typical organization many such changes will be made over time, as managers seek to improve internal communications or controls, maximize the use of resources or respond to changes in the wider environment. Restructuring may also

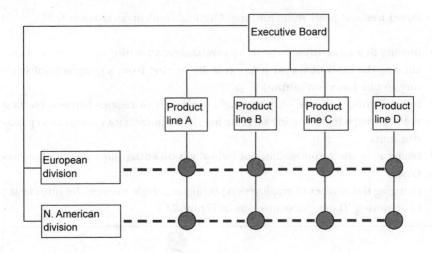

Fig. 2.7 *Matrix structure*

follow a merger or the development of new areas of business.

Records managers need an understanding of the structure of their organization because it provides the administrative framework within which records are created. They also need to understand changes in organizational structure over time, so that they can interpret the context of records created in the past and ensure that records created in the present remain meaningful to users in the future.

Researching organizational structures

Most organizations depict their current structures in an organization chart. A well-designed chart will set out the names of business units and their subdivisions, with the job titles of senior staff and an indication of responsibilities and reporting lines.

When organizations have been reshaped, old organization charts do not always survive and information about historical structures may be difficult to uncover. In any case, organization charts do not always tell the full story: sometimes they are ideal representations and do not reflect reality. Interviews with staff can help to build up a picture of the true structure, both present and historical, and the records manager may be able to fill other gaps in the historical picture by studying the records themselves.

Understanding organizational systems, functions and activities

The purpose of the organization

Whatever the culture and structure of an organization, the nature of its records will be determined by its overall purpose and by the actions that are taken to fulfil it.

An organization's purpose is often defined in documentation associated with its foundation. Purposes are also frequently expressed in mission statements; these may be aspirational rather than realistic, but they are a guide to how organizations want to be seen. They are often supported by further statements of organizational and divisional aims and objectives, set out in strategic business plans. Previous versions may be compared with the current version to give an insight into the organization's changing perceptions of itself over time.

Systems theory and organizations

To carry out their purposes, organizations undertake a number of actions. Schellenberg (1956, 53–5) analysed these in terms of functions, activities and transactions. He defined functions as 'the responsibilities assigned to an agency to accomplish the broad purposes for which it was established'. He suggested that each function can be broken down into a number of activities, which he defined as 'actions that are taken in accomplishing a specific function', and that each activity also comprises a number of parts, which he referred to as 'transactions'. His analysis has been very influential in the records management field, and many other writers on records management have followed Schellenberg's terminology while developing his ideas.

These concepts are not unique to records management. They derive from systems theory, which was developed in the 20th century as an analytical approach to viewing objects as part of a whole and looking at the relationships between them. As noted in Chapter 1, a system is a set of interacting components. It may exist on any scale, from the solar system to a single cell. At its boundary it has an interface with the external environment. Internally it comprises subsystems, which together serve a common goal. The system is governed by rules that determine the relationships between the subsystems. It can be viewed at many levels, and each subsystem can also be seen as a discrete system in itself. As Maddison and Darnton (1996, 13) suggest, 'what is perceived as a component at one level may be perceived as a system at another level'.

An organization can be seen as a business system, made up of interacting processes, which work towards a common purpose. Business systems can be broken down (or 'decomposed') into a hierarchy of component parts, which different writers describe as functions, processes, activities or transactions.

In writing of activities, Schellenberg (1956, 54) distinguished two types: substantive and facilitative. Substantive activities 'are those relating to the technical and professional work of the agency, work that distinguishes it from all other agencies', while facilitative activities are 'those relating to the internal management of the agency, such as housekeeping activities, that are common to all agencies'. He further differentiated between policy and operational transactions, stating that policy transactions determine the policy to be followed, while operational transactions are those carried out in line with policy decisions.

Similar distinctions have been made by writers outside the records management field. For instance, Earl (1996, 61–7) identifies four types of process: core, support, business network and management. Core processes are those that are central to the functioning of the organization and relate directly to external customers; support or 'back office' processes are those that have only internal customers; business network processes relate to suppliers and business contacts; while management processes are 'those by which firms plan, organize and control resources'.

Earl also discusses these actions in terms of their 'structuredness' and their strategic value to the organization. In Earl's view, core and support processes are both usually highly structured, but core processes have a high perceived business value, while support processes are seen as strategically less important. He suggests that business network processes are typically less structured than either core or support processes, while management processes are knowledge-based rather than task-based, and therefore their 'structuredness' is likely to be low.

Discussion of these issues is complicated by the different terminology used by different writers. Earl's 'core processes' and Schellenberg's 'substantive activities' are very much the same, yet for Earl a 'process' may apparently exist at any level of the systems hierarchy, while Schellenberg locates his 'activities' specifically at the middle level. Similarly, some systems writers use the word 'function' to indicate a high-level system or subsystem, while others (particularly those writing in the context of North American corporate business) use it as a synonym for 'division' or 'department'. Many of the terms used by systems theorists and writers on records management, including words such as 'function' and 'process', can have a variety of meanings in British and North American usage. It is necessary to consider these terms further to clarify their use in this book.

Organizational functions

The overall purpose of an organization can be broken down into a number of high-level *functions*. Some of these are substantive functions that relate directly to the organization's purpose; in a commercial organization, these typically include manufacturing, marketing and sales functions. Others, such as administering the organization's finances or property, are facilitative functions, providing the infrastructure that enables the substantive functions to proceed. While they are unlikely to be mentioned in a mission statement, facilitative functions are effectively subsystems of the organizational purpose since the organization's aims and objectives are unlikely to be achievable without the support they provide. Finally, there is the general management function, which determines the direction both of the organization as a whole and of its constituent parts.

Functions are the major responsibilities undertaken by the organization in fulfilling its purpose. They are distinct from the organization's formal structure, described earlier in this chapter. The functions of an organization are logical entities and are described using transitive verbs (making, selling or doing something); the structure provides the operational framework within which the functions are performed.

In practice, functions and structural divisions sometimes coincide. Personnel management, financial administration and other facilitative functions are often assigned to business units that focus exclusively on undertaking the function concerned. Business units may also be organized around substantive functions, but when they are organized on the basis of outputs, market segments or regions, the structure no longer follows the functions of the organization. Functions cross departmental boundaries, and each division is multifunctional.

When organizational aims and objectives change, new functions may arise, or existing functions may be discontinued, but these are usually fairly rare occurrences. Most high-level functions can be expected to continue for the life of the organization. The location of a function may move within the organizational structure, but at the time of its inception a function is normally envisaged as continuing into the future without a known time limit.

Functions may have sub-functions, which can also be expected to continue without limit of time. For example, the function of managing property could have two sub-functions: maintaining the fabric and administering occupation of property. These too could be subdivided.

Activities and steps

For a function to be carried out, *activities* must take place. In Chapter 1 an activity was defined as 'an action or set of actions undertaken by an individual, a group of individuals or a corporate body, or by employees or agents acting on its behalf, and resulting in a definable outcome'. If two or more parties are involved in an activity, it can be referred to as a transaction. Unlike a function, an activity is time-limited: it has a definable beginning and end.

While functions are generic (for example, providing insurance), an activity is specific (for example, selling a policy, or handling a claim from a particular customer). Every activity forms a part of its parent function, and its completion contributes to the carrying out of the function as a whole.

A completed activity should have a result, known as an 'output'. Systems theory sees the activity as taking one or more resources, known as 'inputs', and transforming them into an output. In a manufacturing system a piece of metal may be transformed into a machine tool; in an insurance claims system an application may be transformed into the acceptance and payment of a claim.

Most activities are composed of a number of *steps*, each of which may be undertaken by the same person, by different people or in different parts of the organization. Thus an insurance claim may be received in one place and assessed in another, while payment is issued in a third. Each of these steps is likely to generate records. The records of the various steps may then be aggregated to form a record of the activity as a whole (see Figure 2.8).

Just as activities may be composed of steps, so each step may have further components, which might be called sub-steps. An outline of the full system model is shown in Figure 2.9.

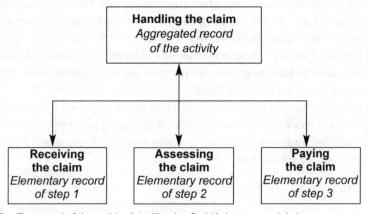

Fig. 2.8 *The record of the activity 'handling Joe Smith's insurance claim'*

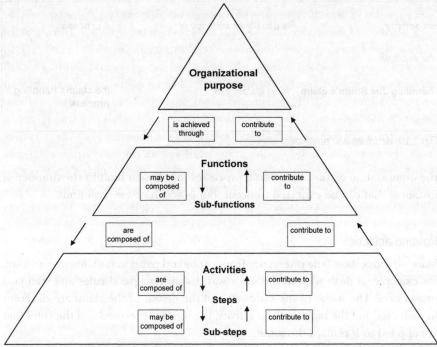

Fig. 2.9   *Outline of the system model*

Steps, like functions, may have further subordinate levels (sub-sub-steps). Logically, there is no limit to the number of possible subsystems. In practice, a point is always reached where further decomposition is either impossible or futile. In systems language a 'primitive' or 'elementary' subsystem is one where there is no value in decomposing it any further. In records management terms the elementary level is that at which the simplest record is created, and for practical purposes this is the lowest order of steps.

Activities and processes

Most organizational activities are of a broadly repetitive nature: they are instances of a *process* that will recur many times (see Figure 2.10).

The creation of a business plan, the recruitment of an employee and the sale of a particular product are all activities that recur. While each individual activity is time-limited, with a definable beginning and end, the process itself is ongoing. Insurance claims continue to be received, or products sold, throughout the life of

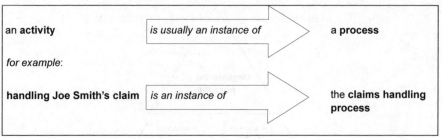

Fig. 2.10 *Activities and processes*

the organization or function. Some processes may have a limit to the number of instances that can be expected to occur, but others have no such limit.

Routine activities

Many activities show little divergence from a standard pattern. Each insurance claim, for example, is dealt with in the same way, following agreed rules and standard procedures. The name of the claimant and the details of the claim are different in each case, but the nature of the activity, the way it is executed and the rules that are applied to it remain the same.

In this book, activities that are determined in accordance with standard procedures are called *routine* activities. They are often undertaken by junior staff and they create homogeneous records, each of which is similar to the records of other instances of the same process. These are often called *case records* or *particular instance records*.

The rules that are applied to a routine activity will determine the steps required to complete it. Just as each activity is an instance of a process, so each step is an instance of a sub-process. The relationship between routine activities, processes and their subsystems is illustrated in Figure 2.11.

Creative activities

In contrast to these routine tasks, most professional and managerial activities are more varied and do not conform to a regular pattern. Some have elements of structure but others are partly or wholly unstructured. Some are simple but others are highly complex, involving the participation of numerous individuals to make up a project team. All may be called *creative* activities.

A creative activity may be large or small (building a hospital or writing an academic paper). It may be concerned with policy making or it may be purely

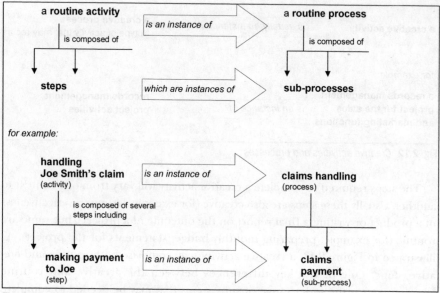

Fig. 2.11 *Routine activities, processes and their subsystems*

operational. A formal project may be planned meticulously while informal activities may not be subject to detailed planning; but all are defined activities with an identifiable beginning and end. The key distinction between routine and creative activities is not one of scale, policy, planning or timing; rather it is that each creative activity is different and the steps required to complete it are distinctive from the steps taken in other activities.

A further characteristic of creative activities is the unpredictability of the triggers that set them in motion. Whereas routine activities are launched by predictable and repetitive events, such as the submission of a purchase order or completion of a reporting period, creative activities are usually initiated individually. They may be self-assigned, or undertaken in response to instructions from regulatory bodies or higher management levels. At the top of an organization, the trigger might be a need to respond to political or economic pressures. At a lower level, it is likely to be a request for information or action from senior managers within the organization.

Despite the relative unpredictability of creative activities, most are nevertheless instances of types of activity that can be expected to recur. Activities such as target setting, policy development, report writing or project management all recur many times in the life of an organization. Thus they may be called instances of a *creative process* (see Figure 2.12).

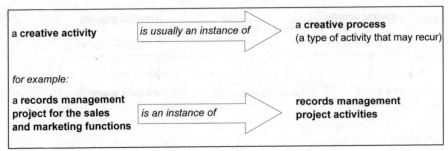

Fig. 2.12 *Creative activities and processes*

The steps required to complete a creative activity will vary from one context to another. Usually these steps are also creative (for example, testing the effectiveness of a product or writing a final report on the outcome of a project), but some are routine (for example, preparing monthly budget statements for the project). As illustrated in Figure 2.13, a creative activity may comprise both routine and creative steps. One of the key differences between the creative and routine environments is the wider range of subsystems that may be needed to complete a creative activity or step (see Figure 2.14).

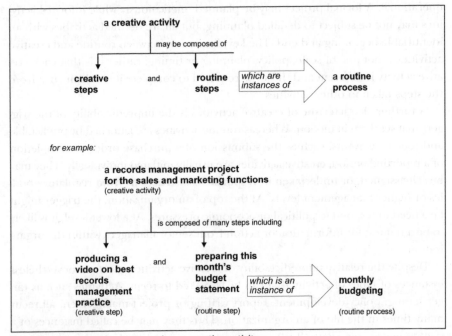

Fig. 2.13 *Steps required to complete a creative activity*

Nature of activity or step	Component subsystems
▪ Routine	Routine components only
▪ Creative	Creative and/or routine components

Fig. 2.14 *Subsystems*

In practice a greyscale is often found. Some creative processes may be subject to general guidelines; some routine processes may allow deviations from the standard pattern. Nevertheless the distinction between creative and routine processes is an important factor in the design of systems for records management. This issue is explored further in later chapters.

Analysing and modelling systems

Systems analysis in the organizational context

Many analytical techniques have been derived from systems theory. Much of the impetus has come from the worlds of information technology and corporate management. Particularly in the 1980s and early 1990s, systems analysis was widely used to match the development of computer systems to the design of organizational processes. Writers on systems analysis use different terms and their methodologies differ in detail, but the general principles are well established.

Systems analysis can be used to identify and define the functions and activities that are undertaken to deliver the objectives of an organization. It can provide information about the relationships between activities, people and organizational structures. It may also be used to redesign activities in order to improve performance, or on a larger scale to support business process re-engineering, which fundamentally rethinks and restructures organizations.

Using systems analysis in records management

Systems analysis techniques are used by records managers to show the relationships between records and the organizational systems that create and use them. They help to ensure that records management systems are designed to support the functions and activities, and thus ultimately the objectives, of the organization. They can be applied equally to records in paper, electronic and hybrid environments, and can be used in establishing new records management systems or in refining those that already exist.

The following sections of this chapter discuss two approaches that can be of particular value in records management: functional analysis and process analysis. Functional analysis techniques build a broad picture of organizational systems and construct a hierarchical model of functions and activities, while process analysis gives insights into the creation and use of records within a particular process. Functional analysis provides a logical basis for records classification and appraisal and is thus a key tool in planning and implementing a records management programme.

Functional analysis

Functional analysis maps organizational functions and activities using a top-down approach: that is, the analysis starts at the highest level needed and breaks down the system concerned into its component parts. The highest level is that which provides the widest or most general view of the system. The components at the next level are those subsystems that together achieve the objectives of the higher-level system. These are then broken down in their turn, and the analysis continues until the required level of decomposition has been achieved.

It is not essential to start at the level of the organizational purpose: a single function or sub-function may be selected for analysis. Equally it is not always necessary to continue the breakdown to the 'primitive' or 'elementary' level of subsystems. When the reason for conducting the analysis has been achieved, there is no need to extend it further.

Typically, the information needed for functional analysis is gathered through a combination of desk research, interviews and observation. Much relevant information can be gained from annual reports, planning documents or staff manuals, although information derived from them should be confirmed by discussion with relevant stakeholders. At lower levels, functional analysis is concerned with processes rather than individual activities, but to obtain a full picture it is often necessary to examine and analyse particular tasks undertaken by workgroups or individual employees.

Interpretation of the initial findings may not be easy. Especially at higher levels, there is often more than one way of viewing the components of a function. Different stakeholders, or members of a team of analysts, may vary in their definition of each part of the system or their understanding of the relationships between subsystems. To resolve such difficulties it may be helpful to consider the outputs from the system. A function usually has a generalized output such as 'profit' or 'customer satisfaction', while lower-level subsystems have much more specific outputs. Outputs can also be a key indicator of the relationship between subsystems and higher-level systems. If the output from one part of the system aggregates with other outputs to contribute to a higher-level objective, a subsystem relationship is indicated.

The result of the analysis is a logical model of the structured hierarchy of systems and subsystems. This can be represented visually using charts or diagrams (see Figures 2.15 to 2.17). Rough diagrams can be created to assist in working through the analysis. The finished model can be represented on a decomposition chart showing the system levels and the decomposition of the system into its component parts. If the model is complex, several interlinked charts may be needed.

An example of functional analysis

Figure 2.15 represents an early stage in an analysis of the human resources function within an organization. The analyst has identified some of the components of the function.

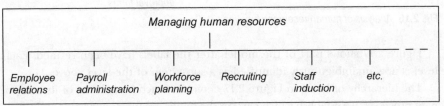

Fig. 2.15 *Analysis of human resources function (1)*

On further analysis, it is recognized that *Payroll* is not a subsystem of *Managing human resources*, but forms part of a financial function; *Payroll* is therefore removed from the model. In addition, *Staff induction* is identified as a subsystem of *Employee relations*, and it is decided that an intermediate level is needed to embrace *Workforce planning* and *Recruiting*.

Figure 2.16 shows the model at a later stage, when these changes have been made and one part of the function has been decomposed to a lower level.

When the decomposition is complete, the analyst checks the labelling of the subsystems. In this context *Advertising* is a subsystem of *Recruiting*, but the analyst recognizes that elsewhere it could be a subsystem of (for example) *Marketing*. At a lower level, *Signing approval forms* is equally ambiguous: these are unlikely to be the only approval forms used in the organizational system. To avoid possible confusion, the analyst needs to replace these with terms that are more specific.

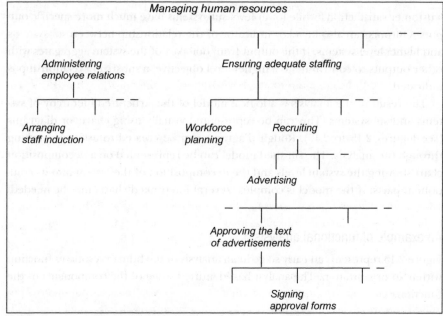

Fig. 2.16 *Analysis of human resources function (2)*

Figure 2.17 shows part of the model after the labels have been refined. Each level is now unambiguously identified as a subsystem of the level above.

The hierarchy of levels in Figure 2.17 depicts a function and one of its component processes. To establish which parts of the model are functional levels and which are process levels, the analyst seeks to identify the levels that can be realized as particular instances.

Managing human resources to meet organizational objectives and *Ensuring optimum staff numbers and skills* cannot be realized as particular instances. From this the analyst infers that these are functional levels: one is a sub-function of the other.

Recruiting staff for vacant posts can be expected to have numerous instances of particular posts that need filling. Recruiting for each vacancy will follow broadly the same pattern and work to the same rules. Therefore it is a routine process, and the subsystems below it in the model are its sub-processes.

Decomposition has been taken to the point where a specific record (a signed approval form) is created. It would be possible to decompose the process further – for example, to the level of *Finding a pen to sign the forms* – but there is no practical value in doing so. The analysis has reached the elementary level of decomposition.

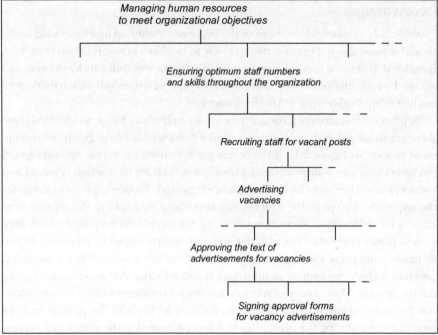

Fig. 2.17 *Analysis of human resources function (3)*

Functions and responsibilities

The final stage in a functional analysis is to define the relationships between functions and processes and the business units of the organization. The recruitment process in Figure 2.17 may be undertaken within a centralized human resources unit, or part or all of the process may be performed locally by operational units. Where organizational structures are not based on functions, related tasks are necessarily carried out in different parts of the organization. Records managers need to identify and document the processes for which each business unit is responsible; they also need to maintain information about changes to the allocation of responsibilities over time (see Figure 2.18).

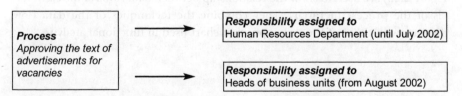

Fig. 2.18 *Changes in functional responsibilities*

Process analysis

Process analysis takes one or more of the processes identified in a functional analysis and investigates the process more closely to establish how it is carried out. Like functional analysis it focuses not on individual instances, but on the process as a whole. Process analysis is not valid for every type of organizational activity: generally it is applicable only to routine processes.

In practice, instances of a routine process are unlikely to follow an identical path: there are usually alternative options within a predetermined range. In the recruitment process in Figure 2.17, if the text is not approved the forms are not signed, but something else is done instead. Possibly a redrafting instruction is issued and some of the earlier steps in the process are repeated. Process analysis investigates the sequence of steps in the process, the conditions that lead to the repetition of steps or the selection of alternative steps, and the inputs and outputs for each step.

A step may have other controls that support, inform, direct or constrain its performance, and these too may be investigated. Controls may be of many kinds but generally include the sources of information and evidence that are used in carrying out the process. Most processes rely to some degree on access to information, which may be derived from documents or data forming an input to the process or from records created during the process itself. A record created in the course of a process may be used to provide evidence or information for another process, for another instance of the same process or for a later step in the same instance.

Systems analysts have developed a variety of types of charts and diagrams to represent different aspects of a process. Many of these are variations on the 'flowchart' (see Figure 2.19), which represents the process pictorially, using symbols to depict objects, actions, procedures and decisions.

One of the types of chart most commonly used is the data flow diagram, derived from the work of DeMarco (1978) and others. Data flow diagrams indicate the sources and destinations of data used in a system and provide a view of the way that data move between processes or between parts of a single process. They can also show procedural details of the process and the relationships between each part of the process and the external controls. 'Levelled' or 'multilevel' diagrams (see Figure 2.20) are used to show the relationship between data flows at different levels of the process hierarchy. They combine the techniques of the data flow diagram with those of the decomposition chart used in functional analysis.

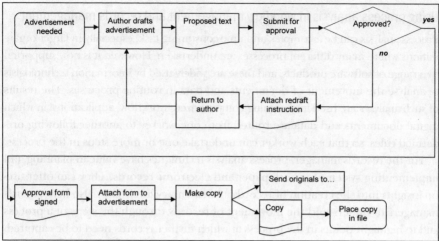

Fig. 2.19 *Standard flowchart*

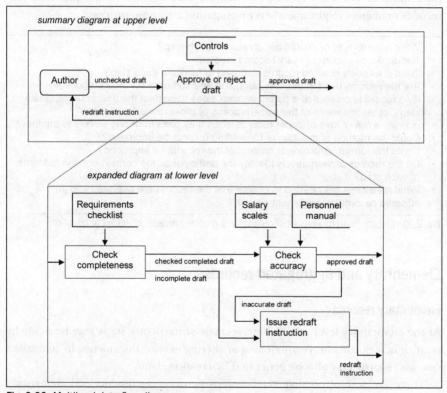

Fig. 2.20 *Multilevel data flow diagram*

Using process analysis in workflow management and records management

Process analysis can be a complex and time-consuming task, especially in larger organizations where many different processes are undertaken. However, it is now supported by a range of software products, and these are widely used by information technologists to analyse the movement of documents and data in routine processes. The results of such analyses are used in designing computerized 'workflow' applications, in which digital documents and data are routed from one worker to another following pre-defined rules, so that each worker can undertake one or more steps in the process.

For the records manager, process analysis techniques have value in planning and implementing systems for both paper and electronic records. They can offer useful insights into the creation of records at elementary level. They also help records managers to understand the movement of records through the steps of a process and to highlight points in the process at which further records need to be captured. In automated environments they can be used in assessing the records management capabilities of workflow applications. Figure 2.21 suggests some questions that records managers might ask when investigating a routine process.

- What records are, or should be, created at each step?
- Are duplicate or unnecessary records created?
- What previously created records are used to facilitate each step?
- Are the records used in this way adequate and sufficient for their purpose?
- If no record is created at a particular step, does this affect the performance of later steps, other instances of the same process or other related processes?
- Is there a risk of loss of paper records when they pass from one worker to another?
- Could the method of creating or forwarding records be improved?
- Could the format, structure or content of the records be improved?
- Do the records authoritatively identify the participants, the context and the outcome of each step?
- What measures are needed to ensure that the records are captured into an effective records management system?

Fig. 2.21 *Creation and movement of records in a routine process: checklist of questions*

Elementary and aggregated records

Elementary records

At the elementary level of activities, records of particular steps may be made by creating new documents or annotating or altering existing documents. In automated systems records may also be generated by creating data.

There are several possible relationships between documents and elementary records:

1 The record of a single step may be represented by a single document.
2 A single step may be represented by more than one document (e.g. a letter and an attachment).
3 Particularly in paper-based systems, several steps in an activity, or several instances of a process, may be represented by entries on or changes to a single document such as a register or ledger.

Aggregation of records

The record of a single step (or sub-step) may be of little significance in its own right. It acquires meaning when combined with the record of other steps, to form a record of the activity as a whole.

In principle there is no limit to the number of levels of aggregation. Records are created at the elementary level of the system, and these elementary records are the building blocks from which the records of higher levels are constructed. At the upper levels of the system, activity and process records aggregate to form records of sub-functions and functions, and at the topmost level these in turn aggregate to form the record of the business of the entire organization.

The aggregation of records parallels the logical model of functions, processes and activities. However, the logical model is usually constructed from the top downwards, while records may be seen as aggregating upwards from the elementary level.

The concept of the record series

An understanding of the aggregation of records is the foundation of much of a records manager's work. Records managers often use the word *series* when referring to record aggregations, although the meaning attached to this word is frequently imprecise. According to the International Council on Archives (2000, 11), a series may be composed of records that were accumulated or filed in the same way or result from the same activity, or records that 'have a particular form, or . . . some other relationship arising out of their creation, receipt or use'. Sometimes the word 'series' has been used loosely to mean an assemblage of records of a convenient size, or records that have little in common apart from being stored in the same place by their creators.

In this book, a record series is defined in systems terms: a series comprises the records of all the activities that are instances of a single process. A series may be large or small: it is distinguished, not by its size, but by the fact that it provides evidence of a particular process. If an activity takes place that is unique, rather than an instance of a process, its records form a series in their own right.

Surveying records and records management systems

What is a records survey?

Records management programmes cannot be established, maintained or improved without an understanding of the organization's existing records and the systems used to control them. Indeed, at the start of a programme, it is possible that more time will be occupied in dealing with so-called legacy records inherited from the past than in designing new systems for the future. To acquire the necessary knowledge records managers generally undertake a survey of records and records management systems, investigating what already exists and analysing what is needed, as a basis for making decisions about what ought to exist in future. Records managers also undertake surveys when preparing to modify existing programmes in response to changing circumstances.

Traditionally, surveys were carried out to establish where records were held and the nature and extent of each record series. Such surveys were typically undertaken as a prelude to drawing up or revising retention guidelines and arranging for older records to be moved away from business offices and operational areas. The focus was on listing and counting records, and in the older records management literature surveys are often called censuses or inventories, terms which reflect this limited perspective.

In recent times, records surveys have acquired a wider scope. Besides discovering what records exist, a full survey seeks to:

- identify the interrelationships between records, and their relationship to organizational functions and activities
- investigate the existence and effectiveness of intellectual control systems for records management
- assess the physical state of the records, including their location, media and quantity
- ascertain who is responsible for maintaining them
- review the needs of different users and the extent to which they are satisfied by the existing records and systems.

Figure 2.22 sets out the steps in a records survey.

⇨ Establish objectives and scope of the survey
  ⇨ Obtain resources and approvals
    ⇨ Undertake background research
      ⇨ Prepare survey forms or database
        ⇨ Assemble and train survey team
          ⇨ Hold initial meeting with operational managers and staff
            ⇨ Identify location of records
              ⇨ Observe and measure records and systems
                ⇨ Document findings
                  ⇨ Analyse findings and make recommendations

Fig. 2.22 *The steps in a records survey*

Planning and conducting a survey

It is likely to be difficult to examine records and systems throughout the organization in a single survey. Hence surveys usually focus on particular business units or functional areas. Surveys may be carried out by staff from the records management unit, or some or all of the work may be undertaken by staff from the functional areas being surveyed. Locally based staff should have good knowledge of the records and the systems in use, but will need training in survey techniques. Another approach is to bring in specialist contractors. Ideally, a survey team is led by a records manager and includes representatives of records creators and users, and relevant specialists such as information technology staff.

Surveys generally aim to collect information at the level of the record series. An inventory of series is compiled, electronically or on paper, as the survey progresses. Information about existing systems and procedures for managing the records may be common to a number of series. Figure 2.23 summarizes the elements of data that may be collected. In practice, some may not be needed: the purpose of the survey will determine the precise information that is required.

Observation and measuring are usually the primary methods employed, but are unlikely to be effective in isolation. Surveys need to build on prior knowledge of the functions and structures of the organization, and of changes to functions and structures over time, and it is essential to find out as much as possible before the work begins. Managers and key staff members should be interviewed before any records are inspected, to determine the nature of their work and the types of records they create or use, and to gain access to documentation or tacit knowledge of existing records systems. Stakeholders can also be interviewed at later stages in order to fill any gaps in the information available to the surveyors, but a survey is unlikely to succeed if undertaken with no prior knowledge at all.

Data elements for record series:

- title
- alternative or informal titles
- date range
- media and format (e.g. optical discs, paper files, volumes, microfilm)
- extent (e.g. megabytes, cubic or linear metres, number of boxes or cabinets)
- provenance (i.e. the process that created the series, and the business unit/s responsible for the process)
- scope and content, including the subject matter of the records, the completeness of the series and reasons for any gaps
- quantity and frequency of accruals (e.g. new records added to the series per week, month or year)
- location of series or parts of series, and custodial responsibilities for the records
- storage equipment used
- existence and location of back-ups or duplicates
- relationship to other series
- actual and potential uses of the records
- frequency and urgency of use
- conditions governing access, including legal and security restrictions
- technical requirements, such as software or hardware needed to gain access to the records
- retention period, and reason/s why records are kept for a given length of time.

Note existing systems and procedures for:

- creation and capture of records
- classification and arrangement
- identification, description, indexing and retrieval
- access control
- protection and preservation
- transfer of older records to a different site or custodian, or conversion to more compact or long-term storage media
- disposal of records at the end of their retention period.

In each case it is appropriate to discover how the system is structured, managed and documented, and to assess its effectiveness and any constraints that apply (such as time, money or expertise).

Fig. 2.23 *Data elements for a records survey*

Surveys can often be combined with process analysis, to examine the ways in which records are created or used in a particular business process and to investigate the flow of records through the process. If processes are partly but not wholly automated, process analysis can help to show how records are divided between paper and electronic media.

Surveyors may also find that a series is split between different locations or different software applications. Several software applications may be used in creating records of a single process, while older paper records may have been moved to off-site storage. It is usually beneficial to identify all the records created by a specific process and to collect data for the series as a whole, rather than separately by medium, application or storage location.

Surveys, processes and computer systems

In practice, it can sometimes be difficult to isolate the records of a single process. If past record-keeping practices have been unsystematic, the records of several different processes are likely to be intermixed. Nevertheless, the surveyor should try to identify the various processes and the records created by each of them. The aim should be to obtain separate data for each underlying record series, rather than simply documenting the existing accumulation of records as a single unit.

With paper records, this can usually be achieved by persisting with the survey until the underlying picture becomes clear. In computerized environments, however, it can be very difficult, especially where employees keep word-processed documents or e-mail messages in personalized storage. If records of a variety of processes have been stored at random on individual hard drives or diskettes, surveys based on observation and measuring will be almost impossible and the use of interviews may be the only practicable fact-finding option.

Records of data-oriented processes are often easier to investigate than records of processes that rely on unmanaged electronic documents. The reason is that word-processing and electronic mail applications are widely used across the boundaries of organizational processes and activities, while data-centric 'line of business' computer systems, and those that support facilitative functions, such as purchasing and financial management, generally correspond to one or more defined processes. When looking at electronic systems of this kind it may be feasible to identify the records of each process separately, but it is often easier to consider the system as a whole, with a view to assessing its data output in records management terms.

Besides using data-centric systems for transacting business, most organizations also use them for informational purposes. Computing specialists often do not see a distinction between data that supply up-to-date information and data needed to provide evidence of business transacted, and many computer systems used in conducting transactions are designed primarily to satisfy current information needs rather than records management requirements. For this reason, records managers may wish to survey all the data-centric systems within the organization, to determine which of them are used in conducting transactions and to investigate what records management functionality they have. A survey of this kind need not attempt to examine individual records, but should focus on testing the ability of the computer application to capture a full history of past transactions.

Using the survey results

When the results of the survey have been collected, they must be analysed and interpreted. Database or spreadsheet software may be used, but mental creativity as well as quantitative analysis is generally needed if worthwhile conclusions are to be drawn. It should not be assumed that every piece of information collected during the survey is equally important; the analysis should concentrate on the issues that form the main focus of the survey.

If a survey is carried out after benchmarks of good practice have been established, the records manager can match the findings on the ground against the standard that the organization requires. If existing systems are found to be satisfactory, no further action is required. Usually, however, a need for improvement is identified. A comprehensive survey normally leads not only to the production of an inventory of existing records, but also to drawing up recommendations or proposals for new or improved records management systems. Some of the findings of the survey may be primarily for use by the records manager, but usually a report is written for the business units whose records have been surveyed or for the senior management team.

Proposals might include new retrieval systems, procedures to ensure that older records move out of current storage or the provision of better or more capacious storage equipment. If the survey was targeted on current records, there might also be proposals for improved records capture systems or for eliminating unnecessary duplication between paper and electronic records. At later stages of the records lifecycle, recommendations might focus on media conversion, off-site accommodation or appropriate handling of archival materials. These and other components of an effective records management system are discussed more fully in later chapters.

From analysis to implementation

Using the analytical techniques outlined in this chapter, the records manager can gain an understanding of the organization and its needs for records management, and can assess the extent to which existing records and records systems meet the requirements of the organization and the wider community. Using this knowledge as a basis, the records manager can then propose and oversee implementation of new records management strategies, either locally or across the organization as a whole.

The analysis can (and should) be repeated as necessary, since the working context for records management is subject to constant change and records managers must ensure that their awareness remains current.

References

Brown, A. D. (1998) *Organisational culture*, 2nd edn, Financial Times/Prentice Hall.

Dawson, S. (1996) *Analysing organisations*, 3rd edn, Palgrave.

DeMarco, T. (1978) *Structured analysis and system specification*, Yourdon Press.

Earl, M. J. (1996) Business process re-engineering: a phenomenon of organization. In Earl, M. J. (ed.) *Information management: the organizational dimension*, Oxford University Press.

Handy, C. B. (1993) *Understanding organizations*, 4th edn, Penguin.

International Council on Archives (2000) *ISAD(G): general international standard archival description*, 2nd edn, International Council on Archives. Also available at www.ica.org/biblio/com/cds/isad_g_2e.pdf.

Johnson, G. and Scholes, K. (2002) *Exploring corporate strategy: text and cases*, 6th edn, Financial Times/Prentice Hall.

Maddison, R. and Darnton, G. (1996) *Information systems in organizations: improving business processes*, Chapman and Hall.

National Archives of Australia (2001) *DIRKS: a strategic approach to managing business information*, Part 3. Available at www.naa.gov.au/recordkeeping/dirks/dirksman/dirks.html.

Pheysey, D. C. (1993) *Organizational cultures: types and transformations*, Routledge.

Robbins, S. P. (2001) *Organizational behaviour*, 9th edn, Prentice Hall.

Robey, D. and Sales, C. A. (1994) *Designing organizations*, 4th edn, Irwin.

Schellenberg, T. R. (1956) *Modern archives: principles and techniques*, F. W. Cheshire.

Smith, G. J. H. (1996) PD 0008: a lawyer's view of the legal admissibility of document images, *Records Management Journal*, **6** (2), 71–4.

ISO 9000 series: ISO 9000:2000 *Quality management systems – fundamentals and vocabulary*, ISO 9001:2000 *Quality management systems – requirements* and ISO 9004:2000 *Quality management systems – guidelines for performance improvements*, International Standards Organization.

3
Classifying records and documenting their context

Records are kept to be used over time. The creator of a record may return to it to seek information or evidence of past activity. It is also likely to be used by others but, unlike the creator, later users may have little or no personal knowledge of the events surrounding its creation.

Completeness and reliability of the *content* of records are often the aspects of most concern to their creators. The *context* that gave rise to the record is usually self-evident to the creator, but may be less obvious to others who use the record in the future. To meet the needs of these later users, a record must carry sufficient evidence of its meaning and context to enable them to identify and interpret it correctly.

Building on the concepts discussed in Chapter 2, this chapter considers how records are classified and organized to ensure that contextual information is available and users' needs are met.

Understanding the context of records

Context and classification

Users of paper records can usually gain some understanding of their meaning from their physical appearance and internal structure, and from data contained within the text. A user can distinguish a business letter from a private communication by its structure and format, and can identify the sender and recipient from the contents of the letter. Sometimes, however, essential data may be lacking; for example, the name or job title of the sender may have been omitted from the file copy of an outgoing letter.

If the letter has been filed with other related items, its context is also illuminated by its relationship to the other items in the file. Again, critical items are sometimes missing from files, so that the full context of those that remain is not apparent. However, paper records that have been filed systematically provide users with the structural and contextual information that is needed to reveal their meaning.

A key element that underlies the interpretation of records is the *classification scheme*, which in a paper-based system determines the identity of the file in which each item is housed and the place of each file within the records management system as a whole. Classification schemes play an equally important role in electronic records systems, where paper files do not exist, and in hybrid systems, where paper and electronic records exist side by side.

Classification schemes are based on an analysis of functions, processes and activities. They document the structure of a records management system and the relationships between records and the activities that generate them. They provide an essential basis for the intellectual control of records and facilitate their management and use over time.

The Australian records management standard defines classification as 'the process of devising and applying schemes based on the business activities which generate records, whereby they are categorized in systematic and consistent ways to facilitate their capture, retrieval, maintenance and disposal' (AS 4390.1-1996, clause 4.8).

The primary uses of a classification scheme are in:

- providing links between records that originate from the same activity or from related activities
- determining where a record should be placed in a larger aggregation of records
- assisting users in retrieving records
- assisting users in interpreting records.

Classification schemes can also be used to provide a framework for determining, assigning and documenting:

- custodial responsibilities
- access rights
- security precautions
- retention periods.

Why classify records by function?

Records are created in the course of business activities. Each record provides evidence of the activity that generated it, the process of which the activity is an instance and the wider function of which the activity forms part. Classification schemes based on functions, processes and activities firmly connect records to the context of their creation.

In the past, records have often been viewed as products of particular departments or business units. However, the activities carried out in each business unit contribute to the purpose and functions of the organization as a whole, and the systems used to manage the records of those activities should reflect an organization-wide perspective. Classification schemes based on functions are also more flexible than those based on administrative structures. When temporary project teams with cross-departmental membership are formed, records are created outside the formal structure of the organization. Moreover, organizational structures are increasingly subject to change and classification schemes must be able to reflect this fluidity.

In a typical restructuring of an organization, functional responsibilities are redistributed and the records of processes previously undertaken in one business unit need to be acquired for use by another. If records are on paper, they probably have to be physically moved from one location to another. If the classification scheme identifies the records of each process separately, it should be relatively simple to identify those that need to be moved. However, if classification has been based on organizational structure it is often difficult to divide the records appropriately, with the result that two business units may require access to, and claim 'ownership' of, the same set of records. In this situation, continuity between the records generated before the restructuring and those generated afterwards is often impossible to maintain, even though the nature of the activities that they support is effectively the same.

'Business classification schemes are not based on the organizational structure of an organization. Functions and activities are more stable than organization structures' (AS 4390.4-1996, clause 7.2). The business units and workgroups responsible for records creation should be identified in the documentation of the records management system, but should not be used as the basis for classifying records.

Designing a classification scheme

The need for systematic classification

In many organizations, inherited records systems are poorly structured. They may be based on administrative arrangements (past or present), on subject content or on some combination of the two. It is often difficult or impossible to gain contextual information from file lists or other documentation. Each business unit may have its own system, with no consistency across the organization. Older systems may be restricted to paper records, leaving electronic records to be organized at the discretion of individual members of staff.

The provision of systematic and consistent classification schemes across the organization is an important part of a records manager's work. Ideally, a single classification scheme should be designed to encompass all the records of the organization. Every record should have a known place in the scheme, and its relationship to records in other parts of the scheme should be fully documented. However, in a complex organization this is a demanding task requiring considerable time and expertise. In well-resourced organizations it is a realistic objective in the short or medium term. Elsewhere resource limitations may mean that it could only be achieved after many years of work.

Records managers have used many approaches to classification. One approach to the design of a classification scheme is as follows.

Step 1: identify functions

The starting point is to draw up a logical model that identifies and defines the functions of the organization and maps out the relationships between each function and its major sub-functions. If a comprehensive exercise in functional analysis has already been undertaken, the functional decomposition chart will provide the model that is needed. Where no prior analysis has been undertaken, or where only parts of the organization have been analysed, records managers must make their own definition of the organization's functions. The techniques required have been discussed in Chapter 2. At this stage only the upper levels of the functional hierarchy need be analysed and the scope and boundaries of each function recorded.

Some functions, such as the management of property or finance, exist in almost every organization, while specialist functions may be unique to a particular organization. When considering functions that are common to all organizations, or to those in a particular business sector, it may be possible to use an existing model. The *Administrative functions disposal authority* issued by the National Archives of Australia (2000) provides an analytical listing of administrative functions common to Australian government agencies, but much of its content can be applied more widely. Functions in UK universities are modelled in Parker (1999). If a generic model is to be used, records managers must confirm how far the model is applicable to their own organization. For functions that are unique to the organization or for which no generic model is available, analysis undertaken locally is the only option.

Step 2: prioritize classification work and extend the logical model

The next step is to prioritize functional areas for undertaking more detailed classification work and to extend the model in the priority areas identified. Priorities will depend on many factors including resources, management support and the adequacy of existing systems. For an initial exercise it is usually best to select a function or sub-function that is carried out within a single business unit. Functions split between several units are more difficult to model and should not be chosen as pilot projects.

The components of the function or sub-function then need to be identified, and the relationships between them mapped, following the advice given in Chapter 2. The model should be developed to process level (the level of decomposition where activities occur, each with a beginning and end, in contrast to functions and sub-functions that continue without limit of time). The objective in this step is to identify the processes that make up each function or sub-function. Individual activities are not considered, but the overall scope of each process needs to be defined.

If a generic model is available it may also prove helpful with this step. However, generic models differ in their terminology and the rigorousness of their construction, and may not always match the records manager's requirements. They may also differ in the number of levels of decomposition that they provide. Commonly two or three levels will be sufficient but occasionally more will be needed.

It is essential to focus the analysis on functions and processes, not on subject terms. For example, 'conferences' is a subject term that might be found in a library classification scheme; but in a functional classification scheme 'attending conferences' and 'arranging conferences' are different processes and must be classified separately.

It is also important to differentiate the management of a process from its operation. Management functions include the supervision and monitoring of operational tasks as well as policy making, and these should be classified separately from the implementation of policies at operational level.

Sometimes, especially in smaller organizations, a function will be found to comprise only a single process. For example, in a small business with a single product line, the manufacturing function may be represented by one process rather than many. Usually, however, a number of different processes will be identified.

When the model has been extended to cover all the known processes within the system, this step is complete. The modelling exercise has reached a level that corresponds to the record series as defined in Chapter 2.

In any organization some activities take place that are not instances of a recognized process. These activities cannot be predicted until they occur and do not feature in the logical model at this stage. Instead they have to be classified, and new record series created, as and when they arise. In most organizational systems, however, such activities are the exception rather than the rule.

Step 3: assess the need for further decomposition

The next step is to consider the value and the feasibility of extending the model further. In theory, any process can be decomposed to elementary level. In practice, records managers must decide whether the work done so far will provide adequate control of records classification, or whether a greater degree of detail is required. Their decision may be influenced by the volume of records generated by each process: in general, the larger the number of records in a series, the greater the need for detailed classification. In addition, as Kennedy and Schauder (1998, 67) suggest, the degree of detail may be determined 'by how critical the particular function is to achieving the goals of the organization, and how important the recordkeeping is to protecting the organization in the case of legal and other challenges'.

Another factor is the extent to which modelling can be reused. Since routine processes are undertaken to defined rules, every step can be mapped in detail: the records created at each step will be consistent over time and the model will remain valid for as long as the process is carried out in the same way. Some creative processes can also be mapped in some detail, if they broadly follow an established pattern.

Where formal project management techniques are applied and project tasks planned in advance, the project plan can form the basis of a logical model of a creative activity. Each part of the project forms a step or sub-step within the activity as a whole. Project records are less uniform than routine process records, but if they are mapped using a detailed project plan their structure will provide an accurate reflection of the project. This approach can be applied to any managed project but is most useful where existing plans are reused for later projects, as the model then remains valid over time.

In less structured environments, where creative activities are largely unplanned, it is impossible to foresee what steps will occur or what records will be created. If records need to be classified in detail this can only be done at or after their creation. Detailed modelling is unlikely to be worthwhile, since the model cannot be reused.

In Figure 3.1, the routine steps undertaken in recruiting staff are modelled in detail down to elementary level, because the same model can be used for every recruitment episode. In the more creative area of public relations, the steps that

77

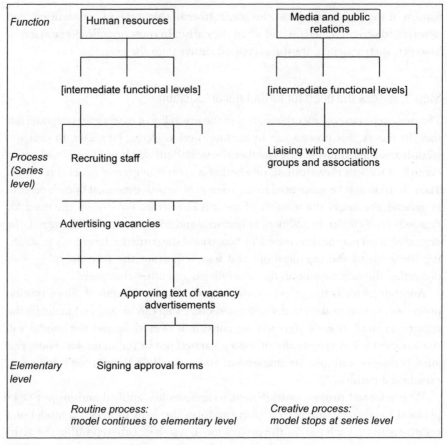

Function | Human resources | Media and public relations

[intermediate functional levels]   [intermediate functional levels]

Liaising with community groups and associations

Process (Series level) | Recruiting staff

Advertising vacancies

Approving text of vacancy advertisements

Elementary level | Signing approval forms

Routine process:
model continues to elementary level

Creative process:
model stops at series level

Fig. 3.1 *Comparison of process models*

occur when the organization makes contact with community groups are different on each occasion and there is little value in extending the model below series level.

Figure 3.2 shows an intermediate model. Information technology staff undertake many software acquisition and development projects. Differing customer requirements mean that the detailed steps at lower levels are unlikely to be the same, but many of the higher level steps are common to every project. In modelling this process, the records manager will again be influenced by the extent to which the model will be suitable for reuse. In Figure 3.2 the model extends below series level, but not to the level of the elementary record.

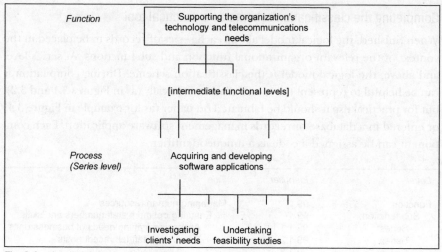

Fig. 3.2 *Intermediate process model*

Step 4: review the model and label the components

The model should now be reviewed for consistency, and clear and unambiguous names agreed for the components at each level. As noted in Chapter 2, functions and their components are described using transitive verbs. In practice it is often possible to invert the wording and replace the verb with an equivalent noun form (see Figure 3.3).

Level	Name: verb + predicate	Inverted name: noun form
Function	Managing human resources	Human resources management
Process / Series	Recruiting staff	Staff recruitment

Fig. 3.3 *Inverted names*

At function level, the verb or verbal noun can sometimes be omitted altogether. 'Human resources', for example, may be an acceptable label at this level.

At lower levels, the verb or verbal noun should always be present. 'Recruiting staff' and 'Remunerating staff' are acceptable, as are 'Paying invoices' and 'Issuing invoices'. However, 'Staff' and 'Invoices' are not acceptable labels by themselves because they do not adequately describe the process.

Completing the classification scheme as a practical tool

When finished, the logical model allows each series of records to be placed in the context of the relevant organizational function and sub-functions. At series level and above, the logical model *is* the classification scheme. During compilation it can be helpful to represent the model diagrammatically (as in Figures 3.1 and 3.2), but for practical use it should be tabulated on paper (as for example in Figure 3.4) or entered in a database or records management software application. Each component can be assigned a code as a unique identifier.

Level	Identifier	Title
Function:	99	Managing human resources
Sub-function:	99.1	Ensuring optimum staff numbers and skills
Series:	99.1.1	Assessing staffing needs of business units
Series:	99.1.2	Recruiting staff for vacant posts
Series:	99.1.3	...
Sub-function:	99.2	Administering employee relations
Series:	99.2.1	...
Series:	99.2.2	...

Fig. 3.4 *Outline functional classification scheme at series level and above*

The logical model also provides a framework for capturing the context of records below series level. However, further work is likely to be needed before a classification scheme can be extended to lower levels. Below series level, the logical model is not the only factor that has to be taken into account: the scheme may also need to document the arrangement of the records and their grouping into paper files or electronic folders. Particularly in paper-based systems, classification and physical arrangement are closely linked. Although the logical structure of a process is independent of the medium or format of the records that it generates, in practice the options for arranging the records within a series depend on whether they are kept on paper or electronically or whether a hybrid system is in place; the needs of users may also require an arrangement that diverges from the logical model of the steps of the process. These issues can have a significant impact on the way in which a classification scheme is finalized, and their implications are discussed in the following sections of this chapter.

Organizing and classifying records in paper-based systems

Arranging records within the series

If the logical model of the process has been extended below series level, it may be used as a basis for arranging paper records within the series. For example, the recruitment process is divisible into at least three sub-processes: advertising, short-listing and interviewing. Each of these generates its own records. For storage and retrieval purposes, the records of each sub-process can be housed together (see Figure 3.5).

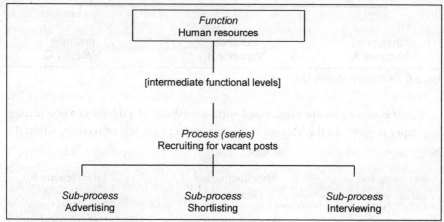

Fig. 3.5 *Arranging records (1)*

If the logical model has not been extended below series level, other methods of arrangement must be sought. For example, in the process 'Liaising with community groups and associations' (see Figure 3.1), no logical model below series level is available and records must be grouped in some other way. Such groupings are often based on 'particular instances' of the process that gives rise to the series as a whole. In this case, each grouping might bring together the records that arise from a particular episode of contact with a single community association.

Such groupings are not limited to situations where extension of the logical model below series level is impractical. Even where a logical model is available below series level, the records manager may choose not to use it for the physical arrangement of the papers. In organizing recruitment records, for example, it may be prefer-able to arrange the records by 'instance', keeping together all the records of a particular recruitment episode (see Figure 3.6).

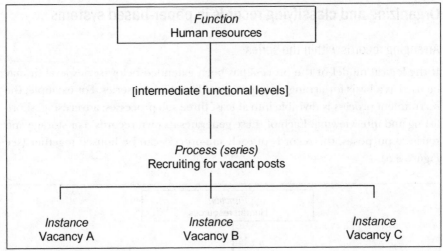

Fig. 3.6 *Arranging records (2)*

Records managers are often faced with something of a dilemma when arranging paper records. In this example there are in fact nine sets of records within the series:

Advertising for vacancy A	Shortlisting for vacancy A	Interviewing for vacancy A
Advertising for vacancy B	Shortlisting for vacancy B	Interviewing for vacancy B
Advertising for vacancy C	Shortlisting for vacancy C	Interviewing for vacancy C

The physical arrangement of these records should reflect users' requirements for retrieval. However, users may want to see any one of the nine, or may want 'all the advertising records' or 'all the records of vacancy A'. How can the records be organized to meet all these potential user needs? In practice, storage methods for paper mean that some degree of compromise is required.

Housing each record separately may be an option if the quantity of records is small, but usually paper records must be grouped in some way if they are to be managed effectively. Most solutions rely on the nesting of one type of physical arrangement inside another. In Figure 3.7, the logical model is followed to group records at sub-process level; a secondary grouping is then introduced, which matches particular instances. In Figure 3.8, this approach is reversed: an instance grouping is introduced immediately below series level, and the scheme then returns to the logical model.

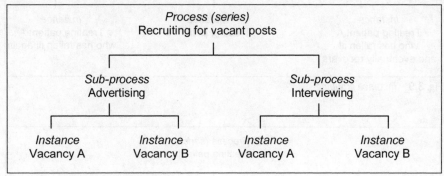

Fig. 3.7 *Arranging records (3)*

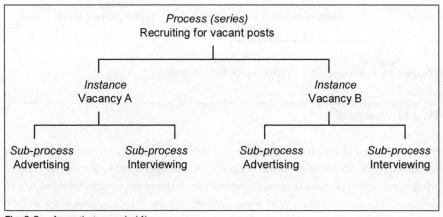

Fig. 3.8 *Arranging records (4)*

Groupings can also be based on the participants or commodities involved in business transactions. In routine processing environments it is common practice to group together the records of transactions with a particular client or supplier. Thus when two separate transactions are conducted with the same client, the records of the second transaction are grouped with the records of the first. Figures 3.9 and 3.10 illustrate the distinction between instance groupings and client groupings, in the context of patients attending a medical facility.

For convenience, groupings based on commodities, clients or other participants may be called *subject* groupings. At first sight, these may appear to equate to the

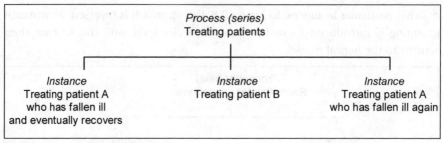

Fig. 3.9 *Instance grouping*

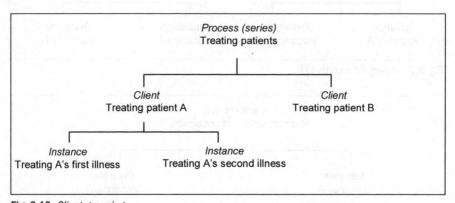

Fig. 3.10 *Client grouping*

'subject files' of library-based practice, but this is not the case: the grouping is not of 'all material about' a client or commodity, but specifically of records created while conducting particular transactions in which the client or the commodity participated. The functional context is paramount and the subject aspect is secondary.

Other possible bases for grouping include locations, agents or dates of transactions (bringing together all records of transactions performed in a particular branch or geographical area, by a particular person or on a particular date). Groupings can also be based on attributes of the participants in a transaction: for example, on the gender of clients (records of male patients in one grouping, female patients in another). However, such attributes must be stable if they are to be used as a basis for grouping records: birth dates of clients would be suitable (see Figure 3.11), but addresses or occupations are usually unsuitable as they are liable to change over time.

Groupings based on instances, subjects or attributes may be introduced at any level between the series and the elementary record. When used in paper-based records systems, they represent a conscious departure from the logical model of

84

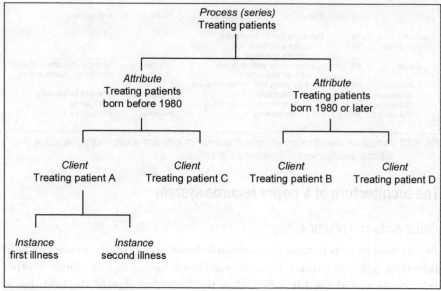

Fig. 3.11 *Attribute grouping*

a process, in order to support convenience of retrieval. They may also be used in some electronic systems, particularly those that mimic the paper environment.

When planning the grouping of records below series level, system designers have a wide range of choices. The main limitation in paper systems is that only one arrangement is possible at any one time. If an alternative arrangement is required, the records must be physically reorganized or duplicate copies made.

Decisions about grouping should be determined by the needs of those who use the records for the business of the organization. Records may be required to facilitate later steps of the activity in which they were created, or to support other activities or other processes. If processes have been analysed in detail, the sources of evidence and information that each process requires should already have been identified, and the grouping of records below series level should be planned to reflect these needs. Decisions should be made jointly by the records manager and the business units concerned, and should then be documented in the classification scheme (see Figure 3.12).

Level	Identifier	Title	Scope	Arrangement
Function:	99	Managing human resources		
Sub-function:	99.1	Ensuring optimum staff numbers and skills		
Series:	99.1.1	Assessing staffing needs of business units	Includes...	Arranged by names of units (one file per business unit) ...
Series:	99.1.2	Recruiting staff for vacant posts		
Sub-series:	99.1.2.1	Advertising	Includes ...	Arranged by vacancy ...
Sub-series:	99.1.2.2	Shortlisting	Includes ...	Arranged by ...
Sub-series:	99.1.2.3	Interviewing	Includes ...	Arranged by ...

Fig. 3.12 *Functional classification scheme at sub-series level and above, indicating scope and internal arrangement of series and sub-series*

The architecture of a paper records system

Constraints and practicalities

Paper-based records systems are necessarily based largely on the management of records as collective entities. Typically, each *item* is housed in a *file* alongside other related items, and the file rather than the individual item is the unit that is retrieved, used and returned to storage. Items are created or received individually, but for most practical purposes they lose their separate identity when they are placed within the file. Arrangements of this kind are a practical necessity: paper records have to be managed collectively because the resources needed to manage them individually cannot normally be justified.

The arrangement of items within a file is mirrored by the arrangement of files within a hierarchical filing system. Each file is placed in a drawer within a filing cabinet within a sequence of cabinets, or on a shelf forming part of a bay of shelving within a sequence of bays. The file serves the purpose of keeping related items together, and thus ensures that users of the records get a coherent picture of past actions; the cabinets or shelving bays keep related files together.

It would be simple if it were possible to invent a rule that each activity, or each step in a process, should always correspond to a single file for physical storage. In practice the mapping depends on the working context. For example, a process where every instance is a complex transaction with a client may generate many thousands of paper documents each year. Large numbers of file covers are required to hold them, and at least one file is needed for every transaction. In another process where there are many small transactions with each client, a file for every transaction may be unnecessary, and a file for each client may be more appropriate. In both cases, the record series may occupy many metres of shelving or fill numerous cabinets. However, in the former case each file corresponds to one transaction, while in the latter case one file contains the records of several transactions.

In a process where each transaction generates only one document, and only five or six transactions take place annually, the records do not require extensive storage facilities. In fact, a single file cover can house them all, and the file corresponds to the process rather than the transaction or the client.

Thus a series of paper records may occupy a shelf, a roomful of shelves, or several rooms, or it may consist of a handful of files or even a single file, sharing space in a filing cabinet with other series. If a process is carried out at more than one location (at a number of regional offices, for example) the series is necessarily divided between the localities concerned. All these configurations are acceptable for paper records. The variables arise because the functional model is purely logical while the practical arrangements have to reflect the physical constraints of records storage.

File architecture

All but the very smallest record series will need to be physically subdivided into a number of separate files. The file is the unit that is consulted by the user while a business task is carried out. Ideally it would contain only the items that the user might require to carry out the task, but different users have different needs and records managers normally have to seek a compromise that meets the needs of most users for most of the time.

In defining the scope of a physical file unit, the issues to be considered are:

- the need to keep related items together
- the logical level at which users wish to retrieve records
- the options for the grouping of records
- the limitations of file size.

The logical level of retrieval will vary from one business context to another. In a policy-making environment, the requirement may be for a file containing the total record of each activity. Where operational records of a complex project are concerned, users may prefer a file that contains only the record of one aspect of the project.

The business requirements of the organization also determine the use of groupings. Sales records, for example, could be grouped by client name, by product range or by client name within each range of products. If there is a conflict between the requirements of different users, it is necessary to decide where the business need is greatest.

The architecture of paper files is also influenced by stationery costs, efficient use of storage space and physical convenience of filing and retrieval. If a series is very small, it may not be an economic use of stationery and space to open a file for each transaction. On the other hand, if numerous documents are created, the bulk of each file unit must be kept within reasonable bounds. When a file reaches a certain size it has to be closed and a continuation file opened.

In practice this gives a number of options: the record of a particular activity, or a particular subject or attribute grouping, may equate to a file, a part of a file or several files. Business needs must be balanced against physical constraints to determine the choice.

Intermediate levels

Sometimes there is a need for physical representation of further levels, above or below the level of the file unit. This may not be easy to achieve: design options are limited when paper files must be arranged on a shelf or in a cabinet, and documents in a file cover. Nevertheless intermediate levels can be represented by establishing subsequences of files within the series, or by making internal subdivisions within the file.

However, only a limited number of subdivisions can be made. Where large numbers of intermediate levels are required it may be difficult to represent them all in the physical world. Logical relationships should be documented in the classification scheme, even if they cannot be replicated physically.

Elementary records

In paper systems it is rare for the physical arrangement of records to be based on the elementary steps in a process: users generally prefer groupings based on activities, subjects or attributes at a higher level. For example, users are likely to prefer an arrangement where completed application forms are housed with the records of their scrutiny and approval, in groupings based on the identity of the applicant, rather than having them grouped with other application forms. For this reason, fully extended process models are rarely essential when planning the arrangement of paper records.

Sometimes, however, users' preferences for activity, subject or attribute groupings are inhibited by an external requirement that steps from different activities must be recorded on a single document. For example, there might be a legal or auditing requirement to keep a register book, where each instance of a critical step in a process is recorded; another step in the same process might be to refer an authorization request to a committee, whose decisions are recorded in a minute book. Because the books are indivisible, the records of these two steps must be physically separate from the records of other steps that could be brought together within file covers.

In practice, it is unlikely that records managers will be able to justify the time required for modelling every process to elementary level. In the 1990s a study by Darnton found that a typical financial institution had more than 15,000 elementary procedures (Maddison and Darnton, 1996, 141–2). Undertaking a full analysis of each would be beyond the resources of most records management services, and only critical processes are likely to be chosen for detailed analysis. Nevertheless, if resources allow process models to be extended to elementary level, it is possible to identify all the types of elementary record that are likely to be created in routine processes and to define precise rules for their management (see Figure 3.13).

Elementary record type	Series for filing	Verification required	Filing instructions
Signed approval forms	File in series X, which is arranged by name of applicant.	Before filing, check that form has been signed by two managers at grade 3 or above. Refer unsigned forms to ...	Place form at the front of the applicant's file.

Fig. 3.13 Filing rules for elementary records

Metadata for paper records

Records managers need to maintain information about the organization's records, including information about their nature, extent and location, the context of their creation or receipt, the means of access to them, and decisions concerning their future management. The term used to describe such information is *metadata*.

Literally meaning 'data about data', the term *metadata* can be used for any data that provide information about a resource, from machine-readable tags to formally published catalogues of libraries and archives. In records management the term is often used to mean data about electronic records, but it is equally applicable to records on paper or any other medium.

The logical model of functions and processes supplies metadata about the context of records. These metadata are set out in the classification scheme, from the highest level down to the point where instance, subject or attribute groupings are required. As shown in Figure 3.12, the scheme may also indicate the nature of these groupings and their arrangement in physical files.

The classification scheme need not provide a complete list of file titles. In a traditional paper system, individual file titles are held in a separate file list or index (see Figure 3.14). Classification schemes only need updating when a new process starts, but file lists have to be updated whenever a new file is opened.

Paper documentation is sometimes still used for paper records systems, but it is now common practice for classification schemes and file level metadata to be maintained in electronic form and delivered to users through corporate networks or intranets. If a database or records management software application is used, file lists and indexes can be combined with the classification scheme in a single application and different views of the database taken as necessary.

FUNCTION: HUMAN RESOURCES

SERIES A98   RECRUITING FOR VACANT POSTS

LIST OF FILES

1. Personnel Department: personnel officer .... Oct 2001

2. Records Management Department: administrative assistant .... Dec 2001

3. Finance Department: administrative assistant.................................... Feb 2002

4. Finance Department: accountant.. May 2002

5. Records Management Department: records clerk .... Sep 2002

6. Personnel Department: secretary.. Oct 2002

7. Records Management Department: records clerk .... Jan 2003

Index to departments
  Finance Department: A98/3, 4
  Personnel Department: A98/1, 6
  Records Management Department: A98/2, 5, 7

Index to posts
  Accountant, Finance Department: A98/4
  Administrative assistant, Finance Department: A98/3
  Administrative assistant, Records Management Department: A98/2
  Personnel officer, Personnel Department: A98/1
  Records clerk, Records Management Department: A98/5, 7
  Secretary, Personnel Department: A98/6

Fig. 3.14 *Paper file list*

Whether held on paper or in an automated system, metadata are also required to document the business units responsible for each function or process, and changes to their responsibilities over time (see Figure 2.18, page 61). Metadata relating to the management, accessibility and use of records over time also need to be maintained. These are discussed further in Chapters 5 to 7.

A database or records management application should support the maintenance of all these types of metadata. A well-designed application should also avoid the need to enter the same data more than once: metadata should be attached at the highest applicable level to avoid repetition at lower levels. An automated system should also facilitate searching of metadata and provide analysis and reporting tools. Software applications for managing paper records usually offer a range of features of this kind.

Classifying electronic records

Principles and practice

Where records are maintained electronically, the principles of classification remain the same but the methods used to apply them may be very different. Electronic records are created and used in the same business context as their paper equivalents, but the physical dimension of records management ceases to be of consequence and records need not be restricted to a single order of arrangement. Records can be managed collectively if required, but it is possible (and often advantageous) to exercise more control at item level. Different retrieval requirements can easily be met, and physical formats need not dictate the way in which classification schemes are implemented.

In the electronic world other rules are changed too. Automated systems are designed to store documents in ways that maximize efficient use of disc space; they do not dictate that one must be housed in physical proximity to another. Thus the contextual information provided by the physical arrangement of paper records may be absent in the electronic environment. Moreover, fewer visual clues are provided: electronic documents such as spreadsheets often bear little indication of the circumstances in which they were produced. The status of a paper draft is usually obvious from its informal appearance or the existence of manuscript annotations, but electronic drafts often look much the same as finished versions and their draft status may not be immediately apparent.

Since the risk of loss of context is so much greater in the electronic world, a rigorous approach to classification and assignment of metadata is needed in order to capture and preserve contextual and structural information. As Bearman

(1993, 183) suggests, in well-managed electronic systems 'structural information, corresponding to that provided by the form and filing of paper records . . . comes from the documentation of the system' in which the records are maintained.

Electronic records also require metadata relating to their hardware, software and operating system dependencies to ensure that they remain accessible and readable over time. Metadata about electronic records can be managed in a number of different ways: they can be embedded in the records themselves, each record can be 'encapsulated' or wrapped with a set of metadata, or records can be linked to metadata but stored separately. Rules need to be defined for what constitutes acceptable metadata, and systems need to be in place to gather those metadata and ensure that they are bound to the record. These issues are examined further in Chapters 4 and 6.

Using directories and folders in an electronic records system

Electronic records in documentary format can often be managed as collective entities, following concepts familiar from the paper world, using electronic folders or directories in place of the paper files and cabinets. Most computer operating systems provide a framework for creating electronic folders, and electronic records management packages and some other specialist software applications offer similar features. Unlike paper files, electronic folders do not physically hold the documents they 'contain': the link between a document and a folder is logical rather than physical, but to the end-user it appears that one is located inside the other.

As Figure 3.15 shows, electronic folders are not subject to many of the practical limitations of their paper counterparts. These freedoms mean that classification of electronic records can often follow the logical model of functions, processes and activities more closely than is possible with paper records. Where appropriate, the relationships between activities and steps can easily be replicated in a structure of nested folders, and higher and intermediate levels can also be fully represented. Relevant metadata must be attached to each level of the system hierarchy (see Figure 3.16).

However, some constraints still arise. Users may be unwilling or unable to handle multiple tiers of nesting. Although electronic systems provide navigational aids to allow users to drill down into a nested hierarchy of folders, the retrieval of low-level folders or individual items from a system of more than four or five tiers can be cumbersome. Some users may find it helpful if their view can be simplified, perhaps by making the upper tiers of the hierarchy invisible to them.

Paper files	Electronic folders
• File covers can only hold limited numbers of documents: files have to be closed when there is no room for further accruals.	• A folder can contain as many items as necessary.
• Stationery costs or space limitations may create pressure to minimize the number of file covers used.	• Even activities that generate only one or two documents can have their own folder.
• Most records systems are physically limited to three tiers (item in file, file in file sequence).	• Systems can have as few or as many levels of nested folders as necessary.
• Delivery to users is normally at file level.	• Delivery can be at any level: a single item, a folder or an aggregation of folders.

Fig. 3.15 *Paper files and electronic folders*

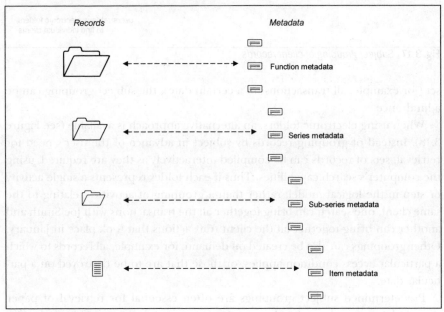

Fig. 3.16 *Metadata hierarchy*

Alternatives to subject grouping for electronic records

Just as subject groupings of paper records allow users to retrieve the records of a particular set of transactions (for example, all transactions with a named client) within a single physical file unit, so in an electronic system users locating a 'subject' folder in a directory structure may find that the set of records they need has already been brought together (see Figure 3.17). However, if they require a different

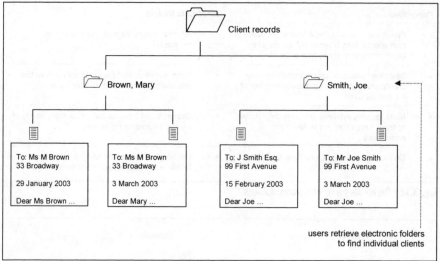

Fig. 3.17 *Subject grouping of client records*

set (for example, all transactions on a certain date), the subject grouping can be a hindrance.

When using electronic folders, an alternative approach is available (see Figure 3.18). Instead of grouping records by subject in advance of the user's need for retrieval, sets of records can be compiled interactively as they are required, using the computer's search capabilities. Thus if each folder represents a single activity or step in the logical model, rather than a grouping of activities relating to the same client, one search can bring together all the transactions with Joe Smith and another can bring together all the client transactions that took place in January. Other groupings can also be created on demand: for example, all records to which a particular access condition applies, or those that are to be destroyed on a particular date.

Predetermined subject groupings are often essential for retrieval of paper records; in electronic systems they may be unnecessary, since technology provides a degree of flexibility that the paper world cannot match. However, effective retrieval depends on the creation of appropriate metadata for each record and the establishment of controls to ensure that all metadata are accurately and precisely defined. Normally this requires the creation of one or more *authority files* or lists of approved index terms, from which appropriate metadata are selected for each record. These issues, and other aspects of retrieval from electronic systems, are discussed further in Chapter 7.

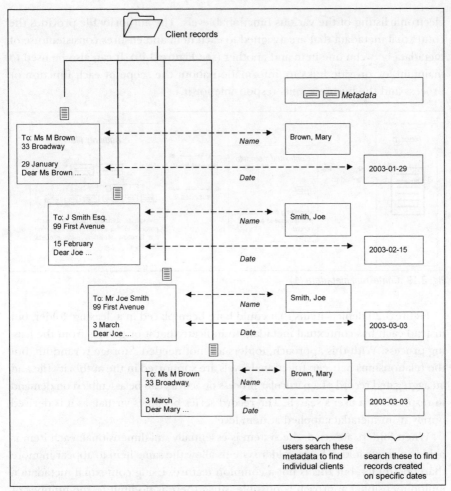

Fig. 3.18 *Metadata as an alternative to subject grouping*

Using contextual metadata to classify electronic records

The use of electronic folders produces a virtual filing cabinet, based on the concepts of the paper world. From the user's perspective the folder offers a familiar point of reference, because of its similarity to paper-based systems. However, in the electronic environment the use of folders is not essential. Instead, metadata can be used to document the context of records and allow them to be managed at item level alone.

Instead of translating the logical model of functions and processes into a hierarchy of folders and sub-folders, the model is represented in an authority file, an electronic listing of the various functional levels. The authority file provides the contextual metadata that are assigned to each item and ensures consistent use of metadata between one item and another (see Figure 3.19). It can also be used to maintain, or provide links to, information about the scope of each function or process and the business units responsible for it.

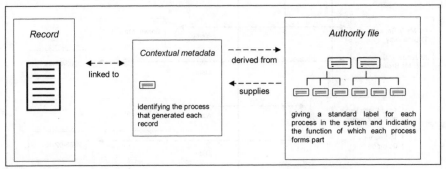

Fig. 3.19 *Contextual metadata (1)*

Figure 3.20 depicts items that could have been placed in a 'leasing' folder, but instead each has contextual metadata to indicate that it originates from the leasing process. With this approach, folders are not needed. Storage is random, but the relationships between functional levels are supported in the authority file and an aggregated record of a particular process or activity can be assembled on demand in response to a user's search. The record series becomes virtual, as it is derived purely from metadata applied at item level.

When folders are used, the system is essentially uni-dimensional: each item is held in a single folder. Some folder systems allow the same item to appear in more than one folder, but this is not a common feature. Using contextual metadata a multidimensional approach is possible, since there is no limit to the number of metadata that can be attached.

This can be illustrated by reviewing a filing problem that is familiar in paper-based records systems. If one document relates to two separate activities, should it be placed in one file and cross-referenced from the other, or should a copy be made for the second file? Some writers have suggested imposing a rule that staff should never refer to two matters in the same document, but this is impractical in real life. Multipurpose documents will continue to be created, and messages referring to a number of unrelated matters will be received. Figure 3.21 (page 98) shows a single item containing two elementary records: with multiple contextual metadata attached to it, the issue ceases to be of consequence from a records

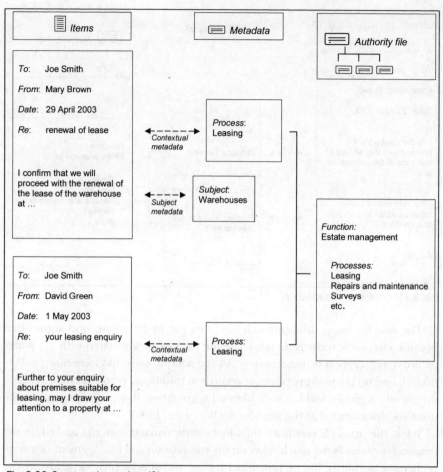

Fig. 3.20 *Contextual metadata (2)*

management viewpoint.

Contextual metadata need not be limited to identification of functions and their component processes and activities. Information about organizational rules or other mandates for records creation can be captured in metadata, as can the identities of participants in an activity and their roles (for example, as sender or recipient of a message). Metadata about individual employees can be derived from a personnel database giving their name, the business unit that employs them, their position within the unit and changes to their responsibilities over time. Such metadata attached to a record provide a full definition of the record's context for the benefit of future users.

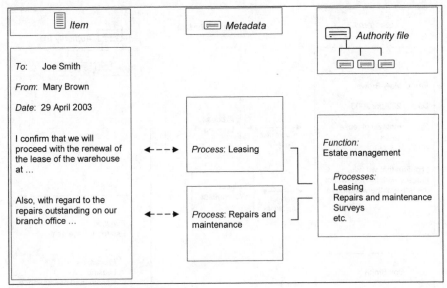

Fig. 3.21 *Contextual metadata (3)*

The case for using this approach has been put by Bearman, who argues that because electronic records do not have 'the physicality associated with . . . paper records', aggregation is unnecessary. 'All the actions we would have taken collectively, based on physical proximity of records in traditional recordkeeping systems, we can take logically, without such physical aggregation, if appropriate logical relations are documented at the item level' (Bearman, 1996).

While the principle seems irrefutable, records managers are not agreed on the practicality of this approach. It relies on the compilation and management of a comprehensive authority file of functional terms, and this in turn depends on the thoroughness with which the logical model is constructed and maintained. In comparison with the use of folders, contextual metadata are less tolerant of imprecision. If a full range of metadata is to be gathered, considerable effort will be required to analyse and identify the information that is needed and to maintain the relevant authority files. There is also concern about the need to develop appropriate retrieval techniques and presentation methods for records systems that do not use folders, and about the cultural changes that this would imply for records creators and users.

For electronic records in conventional documentary formats, there is certainly a future for systems that rely on folders and other concepts familiar from the paper world. But as new forms of record evolve such systems are likely to become less valid. The folder is an unsuitable model for databases, for websites and for data recorded in electronic transaction systems. Metadata must be used to capture contextual information about resources of this kind, and will probably be used for other types of record that emerge from future technological change. They may also be used to provide a common approach to the classification of records and electronic information products: for example, to allow the same classification scheme to be used for a published multimedia report as for the records of its drafting and issuance. The use of contextual metadata is likely to form the basis of many records management systems in the longer term.

Classifying records in hybrid systems

In most organizations records are managed in a hybrid environment, where some are retained on paper and others in electronic form. Records management systems need to be effective regardless of the media employed.

Classification schemes provide a basis for successful hybrid systems, as they allow electronic records to be co-ordinated with those on paper even though they cannot be physically stored together. The starting point is the logical model of functions and processes, since it is independent of media constraints and can be used to devise a classification scheme that is common to records in all media.

The exact approach will depend on the extent to which particular processes generate records in different media. In many organizations, routine processes are highly automated while creative processes are partly or wholly paper-based. In these circumstances it may be possible to manage the division by using a particular medium for each series, with some series being maintained wholly on paper and others entirely in electronic form.

Where a single series is split between paper and electronic media, it is usually appropriate to establish an electronic folder structure that parallels the paper filing arrangements, ensuring that consistent terminology is used in each part of the system. This will facilitate shared management and retrieval techniques and avoid the need for different systems to coexist in a single functional area.

However, the design options are likely to be more limited for a hybrid series than for a series maintained entirely in electronic form. In particular, it is wise to:

- avoid using multiple tiers of folders in the electronic part of a hybrid system, since they will be difficult or impossible to replicate on paper
- apply subject groupings (Figure 3.17) consistently across both parts of a hybrid system, even though the electronic environment could support other approaches (as in Figure 3.18).

If a paper system has several groupings in one file, or several files to represent one grouping, this is purely a matter of stationery and space usage and need not be replicated in the electronic folder structure. In this respect it is the logical and not the physical hierarchy of paper records that should be mapped to the electronic environment.

The equivalence between an electronic folder and its paper counterpart must be clearly documented, so that users know that they must look in both places. Electronic records management software packages often provide features to support this.

If some of the records in a hybrid series are held in a database or other application that does not provide a folder structure, it will be necessary to use appropriate metadata to supply pointers or cross-references from the paper or electronic folders to the database and vice versa.

Hybrid records systems are likely to remain a practical necessity for some time to come, but their limitations mean that they will probably be interim solutions. Ultimately they may be replaced by wholly electronic systems with a much wider range of functionality.

References

Bearman, D. (1993) Archival principles and the electronic office. In Menne-Haritz, A. (ed.) *Information handling in offices and archives*, K. G. Saur. Reprinted in Bearman, D. (1994) *Electronic evidence: strategies for managing records in contemporary organizations*, Archives and Museum Informatics.

Bearman, D. (1996) Item level control and electronic recordkeeping, *Archives and Museum Informatics*, **10** (3), 195–245. Also available at www.archimuse.com/papers/nhprc/item-lvl.html.

Kennedy, J. and Schauder, C. (1998) *Records management: a guide to corporate record keeping*, 2nd edn, Addison Wesley Longman Australia.

Maddison, R. and Darnton, G. (1996) *Information systems in organizations: improving business processes*, Chapman and Hall.

National Archives of Australia (2000) *Administrative functions disposal authority*, National Archives of Australia. Also available at www.naa.gov.au/recordkeeping/disposal/authorities/GDA/AFDA/summary.html.

Parker, E. (1999) *Study of the records life cycle*, TFPL. Also available at www.jisc.ac.uk/pub01/records_lifecycle/ and at www.kcl.ac.uk/projects/srch/reports/reports.htm.

AS 4390-1996 *Records management*, Standards Australia.

4
Creating and capturing records

Much organizational activity leads naturally to the creation of records, but few organizations seek to record everything that they do. Written communications generate records, but most spoken communications leave no record unless a written note is made, and manual and physical tasks can also pass unrecorded. However, new ways of working and new technologies often make it simpler to create records where none were created in the past. With the growth of e-mail, many messages that might once have been verbal are now written; digital telephony and voicemail have made it easier to capture evidence of telephone communications when records are required. The first part of this chapter examines organizational needs for the creation of records, and discusses the intellectual and practical aspects of managing records at the point of their creation or receipt.

The characteristics that records need (authenticity, integrity, usability and reliability) have been discussed in Chapter 1. Records that have these qualities provide a full and accurate representation of the processes and activities that give rise to them. They serve the purposes of business users, lawyers, auditors and regulators. They underwrite the organization's requirements for accountability and transparency as well as providing for its business needs and corporate memory. A records creation strategy helps to ensure that records meet the appropriate standards of quality, but it is also essential that they are captured into a secure and effective records management system so that these qualities will remain intact over time. The second part of this chapter considers principles and procedures for identifying what needs to be captured and for managing the systematic capture of records in paper and digital form.

Principles of records creation and capture

Identifying where records are needed

Some writers assert that a record should be created and captured for every organizational activity, or at least for every transaction involving more than one party (Bearman, 1994, 300). Others suggest that some processes or some steps within a process may not need to generate records, and that the role of records management is to identify how far each process should be recorded (Reed, 1997, 221–2). In practice this depends on the needs of the organization. Highly regulated industries and organizations whose work is publicly sensitive may need to ensure that every telephone call and every verbal transaction is documented, but in most organizations this is neither necessary nor practical.

In assessing the need for creating and capturing records, the aim should be to identify and assess:

- the requirements of the organization, or particular business units, for records that provide evidence and information for operational use
- the requirements of the organization, particular business units or external stakeholders for evidence that can support accountability
- the costs of creating, capturing and maintaining the records that are required, and the risk to the organization if it does not have those records.

Operational requirements for records may be identified through process analysis or discussion with relevant stakeholders. To identify accountability issues it is necessary to assess legal, regulatory and auditing requirements and the extent to which particular areas of business are likely to be subject to litigation. If the organization employs risk management specialists, they can help to assess the risks incurred if records are not created or captured, especially where legal or regulatory requirements are concerned.

In many organizations, decisions about whether to create and capture records are left to individuals or workgroups, but this practice is not recommended. Such decisions are a matter for policy, corporately or at the level of the business unit. Decisions about the need for records that are only expected to support the operations of a single business unit may be within the competence of the managers of the unit concerned, but records created in one area are often needed in another and it is not always appropriate for such decisions to be made at business unit level. Any decision not to create or capture records where legal or other accountability requirements exist should always be based on a risk assessment made at corporate level. Records managers must work with legal, risk and compliance specialists, as well as business managers, to identify processes and steps where records need to be created and captured.

Ensuring authenticity; managing the risk of legal challenge

If records are to serve as evidence of organizational activity, a future user must have confidence that they are authentic and intact. Particularly in the event of a legal dispute, an opposing party may attempt to repudiate or discredit a record, by claiming that it is not what it purports to be or that it has been altered in some way.

The circumstances and methods of creation of records are likely to have an impact on their openness to such challenges:

1 If there are legal or regulatory requirements for records to be created in a specific format, layout or medium, or for particular wording to be used, records may be challenged if this has not been done correctly.
2 Records made as part of a transaction are less likely to be challenged than those created retrospectively. Of the latter, those made near the time of the transaction, or by an individual with personal knowledge of it, are likely to be more trustworthy than those created long afterwards or at second-hand.
3 Records created *ad hoc* are more open to challenge than those created in the regular course of business.

Thus the organization's records management programme should support the creation of records as a normal part of business activities. In the case of records created retrospectively, it should aim to ensure that they are created as soon as possible after the activity and are created or countersigned by staff who actively participated in it. In a court of law, records may be harder to impugn if a representative of the organization can testify that they were created in the course of an identified business activity and demonstrate the records creation procedures associated with the activity concerned.

Opponents may also claim that records have been altered to suppress potentially damaging evidence. Thus the organization must be able to show that its records have been captured in systems that minimize the risk of tampering or loss and ensure that records are unaltered over time. Strategies for secure preservation of records are discussed in Chapter 6.

The existence of a records management programme will support the credibility of records as legal evidence. Systems documentation, including classification schemes and procedure manuals, can add further weight. Evidence may also be needed that procedures were actually followed. Often the existence of the records, and their classification and retention in the context of a structured records management system, will suffice; but sometimes it may be necessary to show that procedures were audited to ensure compliance.

With electronic records further challenges are possible, particularly on the grounds that a computer may not have been operating properly at the time the records were created or at some later time. To minimize this risk, records of the operation (and any malfunction) of computer hardware and software should be maintained, together with details of maintenance and recovery procedures.

In some cases, proof of execution of a record may be required in court. Under common law, records above a certain age (often 20 or 30 years) that come from 'proper custody' are presumed to have been duly executed. This presumption can sometimes extend to records of more recent date, but there may be a need for examination of handwriting, signature or attestation. The signing of records is rarely required in law, but records are often given more weight if a signature is present. Signatures can serve as proof of the identity of the person creating or approving a document, or as evidence that the signatory intended to assert the accuracy of its contents or be bound by its terms. Some jurisdictions may accept other symbols such as rubber stamps, but handwritten signatures are usually safest.

Proof of execution of electronic records is less straightforward and in many jurisdictions remains untested in the courts. Making paper copies of electronic documents needing signature is increasingly impractical, but the infrastructure to support electronic signatures is not yet universally available, particularly to individuals, who sign documents in their dealings with government or business. However, the legal acceptability of electronic signatures is currently under consideration by many governments worldwide, and confidence in new forms of signature can be expected to grow in the coming years.

The measures taken to ensure the authenticity of records will depend on the needs of the organization and the perceived level of risk attaching to each of its processes. Where issues of authenticity are critical, the use of signatures, stamps, seals or other measures will be rigorously enforced, but not all cases are equally critical. In routine processes, authentication of systems (are they designed to produce trustworthy transactions? were they functioning correctly when a particular transaction occurred?) may be at least as important as the measures used to authenticate individual records.

Creating records

'Free text' documents

In a typical organization most records are in documentary format: these include e-mail messages, letters, memos, reports, planning documents and many others. Their structure is determined partly by their creators and partly by accepted conventions such as the presence of an address, greeting and signature in a letter. The content of each document is largely 'free text' composed at the discretion of its creator. However, some organizations attempt to control aspects of content as well as structure by imposing a house style, reinforced by staff training or monitoring procedures.

While some elements of house style, such as use of approved fonts or paper sizes, are relatively unimportant from a records management viewpoint, others can support the capture of contextual data that enhance the value of the document as a record of corporate activity. For example, creators may be instructed to:

- give job titles of signatories and addressees on internal as well as external communications
- identify the originating department or officer on all copies, including file copies on plain paper
- quote reference numbers or codes used by senders and recipients
- identify drafting officers as well as signatories, where communications have to be signed by a senior manager.

Obviously such rules cannot be applied to records received from outside the organization, but for records created internally periodic monitoring can be undertaken to establish whether specific criteria have been met. An audit of a random sample of records within a series should be sufficient to highlight any defects in the series as a whole. Figure 4.1 suggests some questions that may be relevant.

If records are generated using word-processing or similar software, a range of devices can be used at the point of creation to enhance the quality of content and structure. These include spellcheckers and tools for automatic setting of heading styles and section numbers. Automatic dating tools must be treated with caution, because when a document is recalled these tools may substitute the date of viewing or printing for the date of creation.

Among the most valuable tools are those that allow templates or stylesheets to be used as patterns for creating documents, thus providing some guarantee of consistency and quality in output. Templates can define the positioning of particular

---

When records are created ...

- Are the names of creators and their job titles or professional status recorded?
- If several individuals have contributed to one record, are they all identified? Is the extent of each individual's contribution unambiguous?
- Is it clear why the record was created, in what business context and on what occasion?
- Are all records signed and dated?
- Are recipients fully identified? Are their addresses given correctly?
- Have any unexplained abbreviations been used in the record?
- Is the language clear and concise?
- Are handwritten records legible?
- If alterations have been made on a paper document, is it clear that they were legitimate? Has each alteration been signed and dated? Is the original wording still legible?
- Have security classifications, if any, been correctly assigned?

Fig. 4.1 *Checklist for auditing best practice in records creation*

elements within a document and can also be combined with standard text blocks to produce standard letters. McDonald (1995, 89) suggests that these tools may be used to good effect if records creators can be presented with icons representing business tasks or processes, rather than software applications: choosing a particular icon opens both the template and the application required to use it. This approach would help to ensure that templates are used and that records are placed in their functional context.

Forms and data

In routine processing environments records are often created using forms or other data-centric systems. These may be employed wherever creation of the record involves the capture of specific data elements, such as customer or product details, and their verification or transmission as part of a business process. In a customer service area, for example, forms may be completed by customers themselves or by staff who use them to create a record of their interaction with the client. Forms are also used in certain professional environments, where the work is skilled but its results need to be recorded in a standard format: the creation of medical records is an obvious example. A form usually serves a double purpose: it gives effect to a transaction and also collects data about the parties or commodities involved.

In most organizations paper forms are increasingly being replaced by forms that are completed and transmitted electronically. Where paper forms are still employed, they are frequently used to gather data for transfer to a database where information can be maintained and searched electronically. However, the initial creation of the record using the form remains critical, partly because the form determines the quality of the data that are transferred to the database system but also because it is the completion and transmission of the form that achieves the business transaction. Once the data have been transferred to the database the form is unlikely to be needed for informational purposes, but it still constitutes evidence of the transaction and must therefore be managed as a record.

The structure of a form is more rigidly defined than a free text document. Forms design techniques (see Figure 4.2) can help to ensure that records are accurate, consistent and complete. Good forms design also benefits organizational efficiency, since form-filling is often a large part of the work of clerical staff and well-designed forms bring productivity gains.

When forms are designed . . .

- Give each form a title that distinguishes its use and purpose, and a unique code for identification.
- With paper forms, consider whether there is a need for serial numbers for stock control, or for numbering each part of a multi-part form.
- Include the name and contact details of the organization or business unit responsible for issuing the form.
- Provide instructions for completing the form (at the top) and submitting it (at the bottom); with multi-part paper forms, state what to do with each part.
- Arrange the components of the form in the order in which users will logically complete them.
- Ensure that captions or screen prompts are unambiguous and that each is clearly related to the correct space for data entry.
- If paper forms are to be keyed into a computer or read by optical character recognition software, use 'tick marks' to indicate the number of character spaces and ensure legibility.
- Check that there is sufficient space to enter the information required.
- If the number of options is limited, preprint them on the form with a check box or use a drop-down list.
- Where handwritten signatures are required, provide spaces for signing and dating (on every page if necessary).
- Ensure that forms which capture data about living persons comply with data protection or privacy legislation.

Fig. 4.2 *Rules for forms design*

Rules for data entry can be used to govern the completion of paper forms, but quality control is often difficult. Staff manuals, training and supervisory checks can help to enforce standards when forms are used internally. When paper forms are completed by those outside the organization a lower degree of consistency is inevitable.

In many types of transaction, data are keyed directly into a computer without the use of a paper form as a preliminary. An electronic form is the equivalent of a data entry screen for a database application. Electronic forms and database systems offer scope for automatic validation of data entry and thus provide a higher level of quality control. For example, they may allow:

- fields to be designated as numeric (rejecting alphabetical characters) or accepting only certain options (such as numbers in a defined range)
- data entry in text fields to be limited to approved terms using authority files, drop-down lists or check boxes
- links to be made to other data so that, for example, entering a customer's number automatically pulls in their name and contact details; or entering a postcode or zipcode automatically identifies an address
- date and time of form-filling to be supplied automatically, and any arithmetical calculations performed by the system rather than manually by the user
- online help to replace or supplement procedure manuals
- fields to be mandatory; the computer checks that all necessary fields have been completed before users are allowed to submit the form.

Capturing records into a records management system

What should be captured?

Policy guidelines on records capture are an essential component of a records management programme. They should state the organization's policy on the capture of records to serve internal needs and to meet legal requirements or the wider expectations of society. Records capture decisions complement decisions about the length of time for which records are kept, and appraisal criteria that support these decision-making processes are discussed in Chapter 5. To avoid superfluous capture or premature destruction, guidance on the handling of ephemera, drafts and copies should also be provided. Operational controls will be needed to ensure compliance.

Ephemera

Every record created or received in an organization could be considered for capture in a records management system, insofar as its existence provides evidence of an activity. In practice, many records are likely to be destroyed before capture. For example, decisions may be made to:

- destroy or delete records immediately after creation (either as rejected drafts, or because an electronic system has been used merely as a means of preparing a paper record and the electronic version is not required when a satisfactory paper print has been obtained)
- overwrite preliminary versions while creation is in progress, by saving a new version with the same file-name
- destroy 'junk mail' and other unsolicited correspondence on receipt.

All of these are appraisal decisions. Many cases are self-evident, but guidance on what can safely be discarded will guard against premature destruction of records whose longer-term value may not be immediately recognizable.

Drafts

Some records (such as minutes and policy documents) go through multiple drafting stages. Guidelines are needed to indicate which, if any, of the drafts should be captured in a records management system.

There are several kinds of draft. Those that are merely stages in the work of an individual creator usually have no long-term value. However, drafts that are sent to others in the organization for comment or other action may then be accompanied by remarks or suggested amendments from colleagues or managers. There may be a formal workflow system or approval process through which drafts must pass before a final version is transmitted or a transaction deemed to be complete (see Figure 2.20, page 63). Sometimes only the final result is retained (as in Figure 2.19, page 63), but drafts that contain evidence of multiple authorship, or of significant stages in a workflow or approval process, may also be worthy of retention. A possible model is suggested in Figure 4.3.

- A **working draft** is for the eyes of the creator only and can (usually) be overwritten, deleted or destroyed as soon as it is superseded.
- An **approval draft** is sent for comment to others and an appraisal decision is (usually) needed on whether it should be captured in a records management system.
- A **final version** is sent to the intended recipients and should be captured in a records management system.

Fig. 4.3 *Capturing drafts*

In some cases, the concept of a 'final' version is barely applicable: building plans and technical drawings, for example, often undergo a process of almost constant revision as the building or plant is itself modified. In some areas of design-related activity, and in product or manufacturing system development, the organization may need to capture every draft to provide proof of actions taken while development was in progress.

Where intensive redrafting takes place, there is potential for an uncontrolled situation with many similar but not identical drafts and little indication of the relationships between them. In this situation procedures for *version control* are needed. Two types of version control are recognized: 'linear' versioning where only one version is current, and 'branched' or 'parallel' versioning where several drafts exist concurrently, usually as a result of collaborative authoring. In both cases, version identifiers are required to distinguish between versions. Further metadata, including dates and statements of responsibility for each change, are needed to provide a full record of the workflow or approval process in which each draft participated.

Copies

Contemporary business requires the availability of quick and easy copying facilities, and copying devices have proliferated in almost every organization. As copying becomes easier, more copies are produced. Some are made so that they can be reviewed by several individuals simultaneously, but others are made 'just in case', or sent to staff who do not need them. Unnecessary paper copies add to the organization's costs for space and stationery and eventually for waste disposal. Even electronic copies incur costs of distribution and server space. More important, however, is the cost of staff time in reading, evaluating and filing unnecessary copies. Some organizations have programmes to cut copying by reducing the size of paper circulation lists, but increasingly multiple copies of e-mail messages are circulated instead. Copying guidelines should cover electronic media as well as paper, and since it is common to find multiple copies of drafts as well as final versions they should be complemented by version control procedures.

Because a duplicate copy of a record has the same information content as the original, it may be considered redundant as soon as the immediate need for it has passed. Nevertheless in records management terms it also provides evidence of its making, sending or receipt in the course of a business activity, and a decision is needed on whether it should be captured into a records management system.

In practice, most copies are unlikely to be needed for evidential purposes. Convenience copies, made to facilitate access when records are held remotely or as templates for reuse of existing formats, do not require the formal protection that a records management system provides and should not be captured into the system, although their availability can usefully be publicized and guidance given on their eventual disposal. Controls are required to ensure that they are not retained unnecessarily.

However, some copies may need to be formally captured. These include:

- copies of paper records filed in different sequences to provide alternative retrieval mechanisms (for example, 'day files' where copies of records are filed chronologically to allow easy access to materials created on a particular date)
- duplicates retained for security purposes as part of a vital records programme
- copies required as evidence of sending or receipt, including 'file' copies of outgoing messages (the successors to the 'carbon' copies of correspondence in an earlier era).

Senders may need to capture file copies of messages even if the recipient is within the same organization. Although this means that copies of the same item may be kept in records management systems in different parts of the organization, each copy performs a different evidential function.

Choice of media for record capture

Guidance is also required on what should be captured when paper and electronic copies of the same document have been created (for example, when a letter is drafted electronically but printed to paper for transmission). Unless required for vital records security, there is no need to keep a record in both media. The rules will depend on whether a paper-based, electronic or hybrid records management system is in place.

1   If all records of the process are maintained on paper, a paper file copy should be made and the electronic copy deleted unless it is required as a template for future work.
2   If all records of the process are kept electronically, but a particular step is transacted on paper (for example, by sending a letter outside the organization), the record of that step (the file copy of the letter) should be captured electronically.
3   If the system includes both paper and electronic records relating to the same process a new record can be captured in either medium, but wherever possible all records relating to a single step in the process should be kept in one medium only. For example, either the reply to an incoming paper letter should be captured as a paper record, or the in-letter scanned so that both can be retained electronically.

External publications and reference materials

Information products acquired from external sources should be held in a library system. They need not be captured into a records management system unless they are required as evidence that they were used by, or available to, the participants in a specific activity.

If the organization or department has no library or information service, or if maps, journals, trade catalogues or other publications are required in staff offices, information files should be set up so that reference materials can be kept separate from evidential records. If a single storage unit holds information files as well as paper records, differently coloured file covers can be used to distinguish them. Where there are extensive collections of literature, the advice of a professional librarian should be sought.

Ensuring that records are captured systematically

Meeting the challenges of systematic capture

A decision about whether a record is to be captured should be made as soon as possible after its creation or receipt. It must not be postponed beyond the time when the activity generating the record is complete. If the decision is left longer than this, there is a risk that the record will be lost before capture can take place.

In the paper world, it is usually safe to assume that records will be filed when an activity is finished. Even if employees have little concern about retention and future accessibility of the record, they see 'sending it for filing' as the easiest and safest way to get finished work off their desk. Often, however, drafts, redundant copies and ephemera are filed unthinkingly. As a result, too many records are captured. Accessibility is reduced because the system is congested.

In the electronic world, saving to disc or using the delete key are often the easiest options and thus in uncontrolled environments many electronic records are either destroyed or inaccessible on personal computers. Drafts in particular are susceptible to loss, because of the ease with which they can be overwritten. Too few records are captured, and the corporate records management system does not contain all the records that are needed.

If there is a lack of confidence in the accessibility or completeness of records in corporate systems, individuals often set up private systems of their own. Private systems undermine the working of the organization because records held in them will almost certainly be irretrievable if the individual concerned is absent or leaves.

Often these problems are linked. If workers find capturing records to a corporate system difficult or inconvenient, many will capture records carelessly or seek to avoid using the system. Records will then prove difficult to locate or be missing from the system altogether. When individuals cannot be sure of finding the records that they want within the corporate system, they are likely to start private systems. A vicious circle results: as private systems are set up, the effectiveness of the corporate system diminishes further and yet more private systems appear.

The solution lies in making formal records management practices as easy as possible. Records must be accessible to those who need them, and corporate classification and retrieval systems must be known to work. Capture of appropriate records must also be made simple. The records manager's objective should be to 'decrease the time and effort that people have to invest in managing records', while reducing opportunities for human error (Hedstrom, 1997, 65). The ideal is seamless capture, where records management appears to operational staff 'not as a separate application . . . but as something that is interwoven into the normal conduct of business' (McDonald, 1995, 88).

Capture of incoming records

Traditional strategies for records capture have often been linked to procedures for handling incoming communications in paper form. These are usually sorted by mailroom staff, who may handle incoming supplies of equipment and information products such as professional journals, as well as business communications arriving by mail. Systems to separate business communications from other incoming mail should also ensure that items requiring action are routed to the appropriate officer or business unit. Most organizations have a central mailroom, which either opens the mail or distributes it unopened.

Traditionally, central mailrooms were often associated with a registry service where details of incoming letters were entered in a register or database, items requiring action attached to the appropriate file and the files sent to the relevant officers. The processes associated with mail-opening thus facilitated records capture as well as triggering an action or response. Systems of this kind are still found in some organizations. They have to be supplemented by further controls for capturing outgoing messages and records of internal activities.

Many organizations have now abandoned central mail-opening facilities, devolving the work to business units, workgroups or individuals. The growth of electronic mail and the provision of e-mail addresses for individual employees has encouraged the decentralization of mail management. Traditional strategies for records capture at a central control point can still be useful: if activities are regularly initiated by the arrival of external communications, paper messages can be scanned into an imaging system at the point of receipt, and both their routing to an officer for action and their capture into a records management system can be facilitated. In many situations, however, especially where e-mail communication is the norm, the traditional solutions have become inadequate and new strategies are required.

Capturing records of routine processes

Workflow records

In a routine environment, records capture can be incorporated into workflow management. Typically, new items arrive and are processed, and the output is passed to the next person in the chain, the customer or a defined storage location. Each instance is handled in a similar way.

Systematic capture of paper records depends on staff following established rules. Compliance may need to be monitored, but the rules can be quite simple. For example, instructions may state that when each activity is complete the resulting documentation is sent for filing; or a file may be created when an activity begins, with records added to it as a result of particular steps within the activity.

As routine processes are increasingly automated so are records capture techniques. When electronic workflow management systems are designed, decisions must be made about whether a record is to be captured only at the end of an activity or whether records of intermediate steps need capture, and the extent to which capture is to be triggered by the system or left to the discretion of the operator. Where appropriate, capture may be automatic. As discussed in Chapter 2, process analysis helps to identify points where records need to be captured; the specification of a workflow system should incorporate these requirements. To achieve this, records managers as well as computing specialists must be involved in process analysis and systems design.

Records of electronic commerce and web-based transactions

Automatic systems are particularly appropriate for records of transactions that are routinely performed by transmitting sets of data. These can include data used in EDI or internet commerce, submitted in web-based transactions with governmental or supervisory bodies, or transmitted through intranet portals acting as front ends to business support systems.

Such data must be captured to a secure repository. Capture can be fully automatic: individuals posting data need take no decision to capture a record nor even be aware that capture is taking place. For this to happen, records management functionality must be built into the electronic transaction-processing application. If goods are ordered electronically but delivered by conventional means the records management component of an e-commerce application must also have an interface with a more traditional system for recording the fulfilment of orders.

Besides data entered by the party to a transaction, the static content of a website or electronic form may comprise part of the evidence that is needed. For example, if a website presents customers with a button that merely says 'click here to buy', the evidence of what was bought and the terms of the contract are derived from the static content of the web pages as they were viewed at the time of the transaction. A records system needs to capture this information as well as any data entered by the customer, and to maintain a link between them. Many older e-commerce applications cannot easily support this requirement, but applications that offer this functionality are now becoming available.

Capturing records of creative processes

Automatic and discretionary capture

Automatic capture strategies have sometimes also been proposed for electronic records systems in creative environments. If these strategies are to be effective, systems must be designed so that capture of records is triggered by defined events. Such triggers are not easy to specify where creative work is concerned. Capturing a record every time a document is saved is rarely practical or efficient. For this reason, automatic capture strategies for creative environments usually involve capture of transactions rather than saved documents. Dollar (1992, 48) suggests that 'any transaction communicated via a network ... produces records which can be captured automatically at the point of transmission or receipt'. Bearman (1995, 235) develops this idea, suggesting that 'communicated business transactions need to cross some kind of software switch or hardware switch' in the architecture of the system, and proposing that all transactions should be captured at the point where they cross the 'switch'. In the case of internal transactions this would ensure that only a single copy of each record is captured, thus avoiding the duplication that occurs when senders and recipients keep copies of the same record.

Strategies of this kind allow evidence of transactions to be captured without any further action on the part of the originator or recipient, and thus eliminate human error from the capture process. They are sometimes used to capture e-mail messages, whose apparently transitory nature makes them prone to premature destruction if no controls are applied. Several commercial software packages are available to support automatic bulk capture of e-mail.

In its basic form this approach leads to the capture of every electronic communication, however trivial. In some organizations this may be desirable, but usually filtering is needed so that only certain types of transaction are captured. Dollar (1992, 48) suggests that 'automatic capture could occur by sending a copy of messages ... having certain characteristics' to a secure electronic store, if these characteristics can be predefined so that the system can recognize them. However, the unpredictable nature of many creative activities means that characteristics that might form the criteria for capture are hard to identify in advance.

In general, automatic capture of records of creative work is problematic. Few creative activities are carried out in a wholly automated environment, and paper records such as incoming letters are not susceptible to automatic capture. Automatic capture of electronic transactions will fail to catch non-messages, including drafts and other working papers, that might need to be formally retained. Moreover, when e-mails or other records are captured indiscriminately it is often difficult to ensure that they are adequately classified or to apply systematic retention rules or structured retrieval techniques.

Systems that do not use automatic capture require human intervention to review each item and decide whether it is to be captured into a records management system. It may be appropriate for a line manager or records manager to make the decision, but in practice such decisions are often left to the creator or recipient of the record. The records manager's role is then to provide guidance to operational staff about what needs to be captured and how and where to file it. To minimize the risk of error, records managers must also design systems that help users to make considered decisions and capture records in a sensible and structured fashion. Procedural guidelines usually need to be augmented by staff training and motivation, with technical or other controls where appropriate.

The 'domains' concept

In creative environments it is common for documents to be kept on desks or on personal computers, or circulated among colleagues, without being formally captured in a records management system. Some records managers have responded to this by developing a concept of separate 'domains' at personal, workgroup and corporate levels (see Figure 4.4).

> - Each employee has a *personal* domain: personal space which need not be controlled to corporate standards. Advice on good practice may be issued, but workers can organize their personal domain in their own way.
> - Records in the *corporate* domain are controlled, classified and organized to corporate standards.
> - The *workgroup* domain is intermediate. There may be more than one level of workgroup (team, section, department). The degree of control and standardization depends on local needs.

Fig. 4.4   *Domains*

The personal domain is used for reminders, drafts, work in progress, templates, information copies of corporate records, and personal records relating to the worker's terms of employment or social activities connected with work. Such records are not formally captured by a records management system although drafts and templates will lead to the creation of records that are then transmitted to a wider domain.

At levels above the personal domain, the concept allows different interpretations.

1   One view is that it relates to access rights and sharing of resources. If records are held in a workgroup domain, only members of the group can see and use them. If they are in the corporate domain, they are accessible throughout the organization.
2   Another view is that the workgroup domain supports collaborative drafting and editing but it is only in the corporate domain that records are formally captured in a records management system. This view is based on the understanding that all formally captured records are ultimately a corporate resource, even if some of them are restricted to authorized users.

The latter interpretation is reflected in policy-making activities in government bodies, where records typically progress through each of the three domains. According to the UK Public Record Office (1999, 24), personal workspace contains 'early work in draft', team space contains 'early formal drafts and discussion documents' and corporate space contains 'finalised documents and formal records'. In smaller organizations, only two domains (personal and corporate) may be required.

The model followed in this book is to emphasize the distinction between records that need to be subject to systematic management and must therefore be captured in a records management system, and other items, which can be modified and reused as required. The domains concept helps to formalize this distinction in a practical way.

Organizing paper in the personal domain

In organizations where there is a registry service, incoming paper communications may be captured into a records management system by registering them immediately after they are opened in the mailroom. However, in many organizations mail arrives on the worker's desktop indiscriminately. The decline of central registries places responsibility for the management of incoming mail and of records created internally on workgroups and individual employees. Initial handling takes place on the individual desktop before capture, and records are at risk of loss or confusion.

Many workers have little idea how to organize their own paperwork and organizations employ fewer secretaries and filing clerks than in the past. Records managers have an important role in advising and training staff how to handle records effectively on their desktops and in their offices. Good practice in organizing uncaptured records in the personal domain helps to ensure that those that will need to be captured are systematically retained.

Employees have broadly five choices when an incoming paper document arrives. Four of them are decisive: they can act on it, pass it to someone else, file it or destroy it. They can also postpone a decision. This range of options determines the way paper documents should be handled when they arrive on the desktop. Most office desks have one or more trays for active documents. Items to be destroyed do not require a tray, but if the desktop is to be well organized a tray is needed for incoming papers and one or more for each of the other four options. The traditional set of 'in', 'out' and 'pending' trays will rarely be enough to ensure that their contents are organized systematically. The categories usually needed are:

- in-tray for documents that have not yet been looked at
- action trays for documents that require something to be done as soon as time permits: one tray for straightforward matters requiring authorization (invoices, leave applications, etc.), one for reading (professional journals, trade catalogues) and one for items requiring a considered response or detailed investigation
- pending trays for documents where actions or decisions are needed but cannot be taken until a further event occurs (such as a meeting or the arrival of a second document)
- out-trays for items going to the external or internal mail, or passing to colleagues in a workgroup
- separate filing trays for records destined for storage in a records management system and for information products destined for a library or information system.

Out-trays and filing trays can be shared between members of a workgroup, but action and pending trays are usually personal to each employee.

If records managers understand these principles, they can not only organize their own desktops but can also:

- advise other staff on best practice
- incorporate the concept of personal, workgroup and corporate domains and the separation of records from other information sources into the organization of every manager's desk
- help to make the concept of organizing documents part of the working culture
- ensure that offices have fewer places where records can be lost.

Organizing electronic materials in the personal domain

Besides the contents of their paper trays, employees now have incoming messages in e-mail in-boxes and other pending or action items in word-processing or other office software files. Many different software environments may hold working documents that should be destined for capture in a records management system.

Arranging and prioritizing such documents in electronic form can sometimes be more difficult than organizing their paper equivalents. Computer applications often lack features for noting the status of work in progress, and many users simply interfile documents for action with completed work. Most e-mail systems alert users to new or unread mail but otherwise leave them to provide their own means of denoting the action status of messages. In the absence of other mechanisms users often rely on their own memory, but this can result in messages remaining unanswered and corporate records unidentified.

Although individual solutions can only be designed after an analysis of local practice, a recommended framework for managing working documents is as follows:

1 Storage systems on personal computers should be set up to include folders that replicate the action and pending trays used for paperwork. If an employee participates in a number of processes, multiple folders can be provided.
2 Action and pending folders are normally in the personal domain, but may be needed at workgroup level for collaborative processes. They should be used to hold incoming items awaiting action, unfinished drafts and working notes, but not for record storage.
3 If *copies* of records are held in personal or workgroup space for reuse as templates, the folders holding them should be distinct from those used for action and pending items.

These approaches may require significant changes to existing working methods, but if employees are encouraged to adopt them the ground will be prepared for effective records capture systems.

Collaborative working and groupware

In networked environments 'shared' directories or folders can be set up in standard operating systems or office applications, so that all members of an organization or business unit have access to a common resource. However, where team working is the norm it is likely that specific groupware technologies, designed to support collaboration and communication between members of a workgroup, will be used. At a basic level, shared access to word-processing documents may be enhanced by an online discussion forum for members of the group or by shared access to contacts data, diaries and work-scheduling tools. More complex systems may include project management and remote conferencing facilities. Access to collaborative tools is often provided through a corporate intranet.

A groupware product that focuses on the creation and use of documents is likely to offer a range of features to support their control, organization and retrieval. Users can be assigned specific rights to add documents to the shared workspace, view documents or edit them. Documents can be routed to a sequence of colleagues for review or action, and version control can be provided.

Similar features are often available in products sold as electronic document management (EDM) systems, which manage documents created and used within a variety of software platforms. Many provide integrated management of e-mail as well as imaging facilities to allow digitized copies of paper documents to be held alongside documents created digitally. Eventually the distinction between groupware, EDM and other office applications may disappear as the products converge under the influence of web technology.

Products that promote a systematic approach to organizing and sharing working documents can help users to identify those that need to be formally captured as corporate records. However, most groupware products are highly dependent on proprietary technology and few offer full records management capabilities.

Options for capture of corporate records

In uncontrolled environments records created digitally are often held on floppy disks or other removable storage media that are easily lost, or on personal computers where they are likely to be accessible only to their creator. However, if organizational records are to be accessible over time to all who need them, they must be captured into a formal records management system. To ensure this, corporate procedures and a suitable technical infrastructure are required. These are usually easier to establish and monitor where a computer network is in place. Where personal computers stand alone a higher level of user commitment may be required to achieve compliance.

If the records to be captured exist in digital form, they can be:

- printed to paper (or another analogue medium)
- captured to a secure electronic store associated with the application used to create or receive them
- captured to a secure electronic store outside the original application.

Printing to paper can sometimes be the easiest option in the short term. Printouts can be captured with other paper records by filing them in a conventional hardcopy records management system. However, some digital records are difficult to convert to analogue form: printing voicemail messages, for example, will remain impractical until voice recognition technology is much improved. As noted in Chapter 1, printing is an imperfect solution even for textual records: paper-based storage imposes limitations on records created for an electronic environment, and essential elements of the record are often impossible to capture on paper.

Capture within the applications used to create records seems attractive and may be less intrusive on the work of operational staff. Guidelines for managing records using standard office software have been published by the National Archives of Canada (1993, 1996) and the New York State Archives and Records Administration (1995). These give advice to users on matters such as organizing electronic folders, establishing naming conventions for documents, protecting them against loss and making provision for access by other users besides the creator.

However, office applications are productivity tools, not records management tools. Some are designed primarily for use with personal directories accessible only through private passwords. At the time of writing, most lack adequate features to support retention control or protect records against amendment. Almost all rely on proprietary formats, which may impede migration to new environments for continuing access. None can provide the full range of functionality needed to support a comprehensive records management system.

Capture of documentary records within their original application is usually only an interim solution. It can be especially problematic when different applications are used in a single process, as co-ordination of the records may then be difficult.

Office systems are rarely capable of providing pointers to records maintained in another electronic environment or on paper.

When an application is acquired or modified, it may be possible for records management requirements to be included in the specification and design. Often, however, the cost of this is excessive, the resources unavailable or the software unable to support what is required.

Options for capture outside the original application include the saving of e-mail messages as text files or in another format. This may provide some protection, since messages stored in e-mail applications are divorced from other records and prone to inadvertent deletion. However, it is dependent on users' willingness to save messages systematically and on the ability of the system to capture saved messages in their entirety and preserve any underlying data, including links to attachments.

The most effective solution is to capture records to a dedicated system. Some organizations design their own records management applications but more commonly a commercially available system is used. The options are:

- an electronic records management (ERM) application
- an electronic document management (EDM) application with ERM components or an acceptable level of records management functionality.

Both are available off the shelf, although some customization is often needed.

Digital records in documentary format can be captured directly to the system. Where relevant, paper records can be digitized for capture. In general, both EDM and ERM products support:

- capture
- registration, storage and indexing
- ownership and access rights
- retrieval, checkout and return of documents.

EDM applications are primarily intended to support ease of access. Their suppliers may have little awareness of a distinction between records management and information management, and most applications are focused on providing shared access to documents as information sources rather than maintaining reliable evidence of organizational activities. For this reason they are generally good at managing the content and structure of documents but their ability to handle contextual information varies. Some are designed to support the management and publication of documents as separate entities and may be unable to handle complex aggregations. Many are intended to promote dynamic reuse of document content and have little functionality to ensure the integrity of records over time. Most can handle digitized images as well as documents 'born digitally', and some can provide pointers to paper files in a hybrid system. The best have a range of security controls, such as transaction logs that provide an audit trail of changes, or the facility to make only copies (not originals) available for modification. Until recently few offered tools for managing retention and disposal, but such features are now beginning to appear.

ERM applications, on the other hand, have been designed with records management needs in mind. Currently available ERM packages are essentially EDM products that also offer a range of records management tools. Although they may be targeted at different markets, there is no absolute distinction between EDM and ERM applications and in future there may be increasing convergence between them.

The most reliable products are those that conform to published standards such as those listed in Figure 4.5. Products that comply with one or more of these standards will support the integrity of documentary records and their ongoing management both as evidence and as sources of information.

• US Department of Defense *Design criteria standard for electronic records management software applications*, DoD5015.2-STD, http://jitc.fhu.disa.mil/recmgt/standards.htm.	First issued 1997; revised 2002.
• UK Public Record Office *Functional requirements for electronic records management systems*, http://www.pro.gov.uk/recordsmanagement/eros/invest/.	First issued 1999; revision in progress 2002.
• European Commission *Model requirements for the management of electronic records*, http://www.cornwell.co.uk/moreq.html.	First issued in electronic form 2001; published in hard copy 2002.

Fig. 4.5 *Standards for ERM applications*

A reputable ERM package should be able to capture records from a variety of source applications in a variety of formats, including e-mail and voicemail as well as digital images and office documents. There should be no requirement for records to be organized on the basis of the application where they were created. Where necessary it should be possible for all records relating to a particular activity to be presented to the user in a single electronic folder.

Some ERM products support the concept of the personal domain by providing users with an area where they can hold materials outside the formal records management system. Users create a document using office software, and are then given the option of holding it in their personal domain or capturing it as a formal record in the ERM system. Documents saved in the personal domain can be amended or deleted at will; documents captured within the system can be viewed but cannot be altered, nor can they be destroyed except in accordance with agreed disposal policies.

Most ERM applications also allow authorized users to make copies of captured documents for forwarding to third parties, or for use as templates for new work. Users who have requested a working copy for editing have the option of capturing the edited copy as a new and separate record, but cannot overwrite the original.

ERM applications do not provide document creation tools of their own, but work as unobtrusively as possible alongside standard office products. The best ERM applications can be fully integrated with word-processors and other office software. Records can be captured to the ERM system from within the office suite, and office applications launched automatically when copies are requested for editing. If an ERM application shares a user interface with a standard e-mail package, this encourages the capture of e-mail messages and attachments and counteracts the mistaken but commonly held view that e-mails are informal communications to which records management rules do not apply.

ERM applications have their limitations. They are not designed to hold records in the form of data: they can store completed forms as images or text but cannot accept data records that need to be managed in a database. To varying extents they all depend on proprietary technology, and it is not yet clear how well they will manage issues of technology obsolescence when records need to be retained for many years. Their introduction can be costly, needs a high level of management commitment and may require significant changes to established working practices. Nevertheless for most records in documentary format they offer the best technical solution that is currently available.

Capturing information products in a records management system

Records and information products

As noted in Chapter 1, organizations often generate information products that need to be captured alongside records. Like records, information products may be in any medium, but are moving away from paper to digital media. Products for internal use, such as technical manuals, are increasingly published on local networks or intranets. Those intended for an external audience, previously issued as brochures or booklets, are now found on corporate websites. Documents such as these may be captured in libraries or information centres for their value as reference sources, but may also be captured as records in order to provide evidence of their creation, their transmission or publication, or their use.

Some information products are created purely for the use of an individual, but most are designed for a wider audience. A report, for example, can be prepared for a presentation or for a senior manager (in which case it is traditionally considered as a record); or sent to a group of recipients (when its status is more ambivalent); or published to the entire organization or the outside world (when it is formally recognized as an information product by librarians and information managers). For items such as reports no firm line can be drawn between transmission and publication, or between a record and an information product.

Effective records management requires the capture of context as well as content. Drafts and working papers, or instructions given to a computer, may need to be captured alongside a report to provide a complete record of its creation. Evidence of its transmission or publication may be provided by agreements, letters, delivery notes or other messages, or by the report itself.

Information products on paper

When products such as reports are on paper, multiple copies are commonly circulated, with the result that several duplicates are retained. There can be good reasons for capturing duplicate copies in a records management system, for example to provide evidence of their receipt by an individual or business unit or their role in another activity. Often, however, their capture will be judged unnecessary and records managers will wish to ensure that duplicates are destroyed at the earliest opportunity.

In an uncontrolled environment this is difficult to achieve. Usually too many copies are kept, but occasionally all copies of a report are destroyed because everyone assumes that a copy will be available elsewhere. However, if a master copy is captured in a records management system, local copies of internally circulated material can safely be destroyed when their immediate use is past. A similar strategy can be employed for information copies of minutes and meeting papers: signed minutes can be distinguished as the formal record, while unsigned copies are marked as uncontrolled duplicates. When recipients know that a master copy or original is held in a secure and accessible location, they are less likely to want to retain personal copies and it becomes possible to ensure that these are destroyed systematically.

Like reports, management directives can be seen both as records and as information products. Paper directives range from single memoranda to books of instructions for implementing policy or procedures. They are 'published' internally by sending an identical copy to each employee or business unit. Identification and capture of a master or 'record' copy is again the key to avoiding unnecessary retention. Temporary directives, giving short-term announcements or instructions, can usefully be distinguished from those that remain in force until superseded. The latter are often revised and reissued at a later date. The context of publication and any revision should be documented, and version control strategies applied where necessary.

Electronic publications and websites

As an alternative to paper distribution, information products may be made available on a network or intranet. This provides easy access, reduces copying and ensures that only the latest version is displayed to staff seeking current information. Master copies can be captured digitally from a central source. Moreover, software can ensure that any paper printouts are automatically marked as uncontrolled or 'non-record' copies, or can even be configured to prevent printing altogether.

However, for the records manager some questions remain. Digital publications are often amended incrementally: should each change be captured as it occurs? Both intranet and internet websites usually contain a variety of material, much of which would have been published separately when paper was used: is it appropriate to capture the separate components or the site as a whole? There are no definitive answers.

One strategy is to capture records from source documents when they are published to the site. This approach can be facilitated by using an EDM or web content application to manage documents for publication. The document management component of electronic publishing is then separated from the access component: documents are held in the EDM or web content application and replicated to the intranet server. The application should offer good version control and may provide a suitable basis for record capture.

Alternatively, capture of the site itself could be considered. Since websites are rarely static, a 'snapshot' could be taken at fixed intervals or on some agreed trigger: whenever the site is updated, when particular kinds of update occur or when users submit data. However, snapshots only preserve changes to the content. In order to capture the context of those changes, other evidence will be required. This might take the form of a log of changes to the site, indicating when and by whom each change was made. An ideal situation, though not easy to achieve at present, would be the ability to re-create the state of the website at any given moment in the past, together with contextual metadata about who was responsible for each part of it and what activities gave rise to its contents.

Capturing data records and datasets

Broadly speaking, a database may contain:

- data entered on a single occasion, with no further changes made
- data that are subject to addition and amendment either continuously or periodically
- data that are subject to addition but not amendment over time.

As noted in Chapter 1, most databases are used to manage current information, but some hold data that provide evidence of organizational activities. Databases of this type are used to record but not to effect transactions: they supersede the traditional paper register as a record of what has occurred. If a database is used solely to provide a record of activities over time, its contents will grow but should not be subject to amendment. Log files may be used to capture evidence of when, how or by whom the data were entered.

Provided that it can guarantee the continuing integrity of the data, a database of this kind can form an effective component of a records management system. However, if the database application lacks adequate safeguards the data must be moved or copied to a more robust environment to secure their ongoing management. They can be copied at the time of creation or transferred retrospectively.

When a database only supplies users with the latest information, data are normally overwritten when no longer current. Such data do not form evidence of external transactions, although a log of changes to a database can capture records of data entry and editing, to provide evidence of transactions made against the database itself. It is often unnecessary to maintain data of this kind once their immediate usefulness is past, but sometimes there is a need to transfer some or all of the content to a more secure or less volatile environment. This may be done when the database ceases to be amended or during its active life.

Some sets of data are created over a specific period, usually in connection with project work, and the database or dataset is then closed. If these need to be transferred to a more secure environment, this can be done when the project ends. Many databases, however, remain active for a long time and informational data may need to be secured while a database is still subject to amendment. This can be achieved by taking snapshots of the database, of specific datasets within it or of specific views of the data. Snapshots can be taken on demand if the organization needs to capture evidence of the state of the database when used as a basis for a particular decision or action; they can also be taken automatically at agreed intervals.

Like snapshots of websites, snapshots of informational data only capture content. Transaction logs are needed to provide full contextual evidence of changes made to the data. Most database applications create logs automatically to support back-up and recovery, although further configuration may be needed if these are to be used for evidential purposes.

In more complex database systems, modifiable and non-modifiable data may be found together. For example, financial systems usually provide current balances and budget forecasts (which are subject to update) as well as holding data recording individual receipts or payments (which should remain unaltered). In such cases a combination of strategies may be required. The records manager's priority should be to ensure the integrity of the transactional records.

If it is not possible to retain data securely in their native environment, reports can be printed to paper, microform or optical disc. This solution captures data content but users lose the ability to view the data in different ways. It may be preferable to copy the data to a plain text file (such as a tab or comma separated file) or to a separate database for records management purposes. For large quantities of informational data, transfer to a 'data warehouse' may be appropriate. Data warehouses provide non-volatile digital storage for data to be used in managerial decision making, but rarely provide adequate support for transactional records (Cain, 1995). Another option, likely to be increasingly employed, is conversion of the data to XML.

Capturing dynamic digital objects

A 'digital object' is any self-contained block of text, graphics or program code that can be read or processed by a computer. The capabilities of computer technology in associating one digital object with another have created new challenges for records managers. While the record of an activity refers to an event or sequence of events that is fixed in time, a record may also be associated with other digital objects that may not be static.

Technology supports different kinds of associations. An e-mail message can be associated with an attachment, just as a paper letter can have an enclosure; unlike the letter, it can also have a copy of an earlier e-mail message or another document inserted within it. In each case, by the time that the message is transmitted the object associated with it has been detached from its original computing environment. If a computer program is attached to an e-mail message, and the program is then updated at source after a copy of it has been e-mailed, the copy sent by e-mail remains unaltered. A copy of a document forwarded by e-mail is also unaffected by the fate of any copies retained by the sender. The separation of these objects from their native environment means that they are only of value to the recipient if the document can be understood, or the program made to function, in the environment where they are received. However, it also means that, if a record of the incoming message needs to incorporate these objects, their capture and ongoing maintenance will not be disturbed by any changes to their original environment.

Besides allowing a copy of one object to be inserted within another, technology also permits active links to be made between objects. Compound documents intended for online viewing often include material derived from links of this kind. For example, a report may contain links that point to separate image files. Whenever the report is viewed, the relevant images are pulled into it. If the images are deleted or their storage location changed without notice, or if the body of the document is transmitted to a different computing environment from the images, the link is broken and the images are no longer available to users of the report.

The same technique may be employed if an author intends that a compound document should be updated automatically when alterations are made to a source document. The report may be linked to a budgeting spreadsheet that is regularly updated, with the intention that whenever the report is examined the latest financial data will be displayed within it. Again, the linking technique rests on the assumption that the source components will remain accessible, as well as editable, in their original computing application. If either the spreadsheet application or the data become inaccessible in the future, the link will fail and the report will be incomplete.

Records consciously created to provide evidence of past activity are unlikely to use links to dynamic sources of this kind, but products designed to supply current information are increasingly constructed in this way. Some information products are 'virtual' documents that have little or no static content but are assembled by pulling together data from other sources in response to access requests from users. For example, a web page that appears to the user as a single document may in fact be created dynamically at the time of viewing, from databases concealed behind the website.

How can such products be captured and maintained over time? When two or more associated objects are static, it may be relatively simple to manage the objects together and ensure that the links between them are preserved. Capturing a document that is derived wholly or partly from links to dynamic objects is more problematic. A snapshot can provide evidence of its state at a particular moment but cannot re-create the functionality of the original. Snapshots taken during creation, transmission or publication will give the creator's view but may not reflect its state when viewed by a recipient. An alternative might be to capture the wider computing environment as a whole and to seek to maintain its full functionality, but this is likely to incur high overheads.

There are also automated transaction systems that derive data from dynamic sources, for example by taking details of suppliers, customers, goods or prices from a dynamic database at the moment when a transaction is made. Using databases in this way can be very efficient in productivity terms, but for records management purposes it is necessary to ensure that the system captures a static record of the transaction, in which the data are not subject to further change.

Another kind of link is one that does not pull in content, but points outwards to it: an electronic record may contain pointers or navigational links to other objects that were accessible at the time of its creation. A familiar example is an e-mail message that contains hyperlinks to addresses on the world wide web. Such addresses are often subject to alteration, and the web pages or other objects that form the destination of the hyperlinks may themselves be modified at any time. Once again it could be argued that a snapshot of the destination objects should be captured within the record.

At this point the boundaries of the record have to be defined. To what extent is a linked object part of the record? What if it contains further links pointing to yet more objects? One test is to ask whether the linked object is intrinsic to the activity represented by the record, or simply provided as background information that may be less critical.

Registering records

What is meant by 'registering' a record?

As part of the capture process, records need to be registered to provide formal recognition of their existence within the records management system. This is achieved by an entry in a 'register' of some kind, either on paper or in a database.

An essential element of registering a record is giving it a *unique identifier* that distinguishes it from all other records within the system. Unique identifiers usually take the form of a numeric or alphanumeric code. Methods of constructing them are discussed later in this chapter. Their purpose is to identify each record to those who operate and use the system and to provide a convenient and unambiguous means of citing it in speech and writing. In paper systems identifiers are also used to locate files in cabinets or on shelves; in electronic systems they serve to identify records in the software environment.

Registration is closely associated with the collection of metadata. It provides an opportunity for classifying records and for assigning them a title that is descriptive of their context and content. Normally the title complements an identifier in coded form, but where coded identifiers are not used the title itself forms the unique identifier. Registration also provides an opportunity for gathering a wider range of information about the record. This includes metadata about the registration process itself: the date when the record was registered, and details of the individuals who registered it or authorized its registration.

Registration is sometimes seen as a process concerned only with paper files, but it is also an essential part of electronic records systems. It can take place at any level of aggregation: individual items, files, folders and record series can all be registered. Registration at file level is essential if paper records are to be managed within a robust and effective records management system. Electronic systems, and some paper systems, also register each item.

Registering records at item level

Individual paper items can be registered on receipt or at the point of filing. In a centralized registry system, a unique identifier is assigned to each incoming item, and details of the sender and date of receipt are entered in a register or database. Outgoing mail, and other items created within the organization, are individually registered when a copy is inserted in the file.

Before computerization, incoming mail was often registered in loose-leaf or bound volumes, tabulated in rows and columns and kept in chronological order. The contents of a file could also be listed item-by-item on the file cover or on sheets of paper attached to the file. These registers and lists provided a useful security check but were laborious to search. In their place, a database or records management software package may be used for registering paper records.

Registration at item level supports the tracking of individual documents and thus provides a high degree of control. However, item level registration of paper records is usually labour-intensive even when a database is employed, and is often rejected as impractical. Instead, the view may be taken that 'if an item . . . is directly attached to a hard copy file, and the file is registered, this will serve as an adequate register' (Smith et al., 1995, 45).

In electronic records systems, registration at item level is essential. It is also comparatively simple to achieve: much of the process can be performed automatically, with capture and registration taking place simultaneously. When items are captured in an ERM application, for example, unique identifiers in code form can be assigned by the application without any need for user action. User input is only required if there is a need to collect metadata that the computer cannot assign automatically.

Registration also provides an opportunity for items to be authenticated. Paper records may be signed, sealed or stamped, if this has not been done at the creation stage. Electronic records may have digital signatures, digital watermarks or timestamps applied to protect their integrity.

Classifying new items

When records managers speak of *classification*, they may refer either to the activities associated with designing a classification scheme (as discussed in Chapter 3) or to those involved in applying the scheme to particular records. When records are captured, they need to be classified in this second sense of the word: a classification derived from the scheme must be assigned to them.

Sometimes creation, capture and classification occur together: if a record is created by writing an entry in a ledger, it is captured and classified as it is created. More commonly, however, a record stands alone at the point of its creation; only when captured is it linked to a larger accumulation of existing records. In paper systems the capture of an item depends on its insertion into a file. Its classification requires two steps: determining the correct file and ensuring that it is placed there. One step is intellectual and the other physical. Both are essential elements of record capture.

To find the correct file for a particular item, it is necessary first to identify the process to which the item relates, in order to discover the relevant record series. As shown in Figure 3.12 (page 86), the classification scheme can be used to determine the appropriate series and to ascertain the arrangement of the files within it. Finding the specific file that is wanted normally requires an understanding both of the arrangement of the files in the series (are they arranged by activities, subjects or attributes, or by steps within a process?) and of the item that is to be filed. If the scheme indicates that files are arranged by activities, the item must be examined to discover the activity to which it relates. Some items may already bear the unique identifier of the file in which previous material relating to the same activity has been housed: this may be given as 'your reference' on an incoming letter, or as a number on an order form. Otherwise it is necessary to search the documentation of the records system (typically, the file index or database), to see whether the new item represents a continuation of previous activity. If it does, a file should already exist and the next step is to locate it so that the new item can be attached.

These can be laborious tasks, and many organizations rely on junior clerks to find paper files and attach incoming items to them. The work of the clerks may extend beyond simple checking of indexes: in the case of client files, for example, they may need to verify addresses or dates of birth to be sure of distinguishing one client from another of the same name. There may also be rules about the sequence in which papers are to be arranged within a file. Procedural controls are likely to be needed to ensure that each item is attached to the correct file and in the correct order.

Similar issues arise if copies of outgoing paper correspondence, or other records created within the organization, are passed to clerks for filing. It is good practice for records creators to note the relevant file identifier on each item before sending it to be filed. This speeds up the filing work and helps to ensure that items are placed in the correct file. It also ensures that items can be refiled correctly if they subsequently become detached.

If new papers are to be added to a file that is in use, they may be held in a dummy folder until the borrower returns the file. Alternatively they can be forwarded to the borrower, accompanied if necessary by a coversheet giving the identifier of the file to which they relate.

In digital systems no delay or physical effort is involved in associating an item with an electronic folder. Filing clerks are not required, as records creators can in effect do their own filing. However, it remains essential that records are classified correctly. Regardless of the media used, the role of the records management unit is to ensure that all staff responsible for classifying records understand the classification rules and apply them correctly. If the resources of the unit can support a helpdesk service, staff responsible for classification can be encouraged to seek expert advice in any cases of doubt.

Registering a new file or folder

New files or folders must be opened as the need arises: depending on the arrangement of the record series, this might be when a new activity is begun or when a new client, supplier or topic is addressed. When a new file is opened it is registered: its identifier is assigned, its classification confirmed, and details added to the appropriate control list, index or database. If it is a paper file, it must also be physically constructed: a file cover is taken from stock and labelled as necessary, before the relevant items are inserted inside it. Most records management software packages can generate labels for file covers from information entered when files are registered.

Controls are needed to verify that no relevant file already exists. For example, before a new file is opened indexes must be checked or clients asked for personal details in case they are already known to the organization under a different name. In some organizations, requests to open new files have to be approved by a supervisor or by the records management unit: this can help to eliminate duplication and ensure that records are classified correctly, but approval mechanisms must not be so complex that staff seek to evade them.

Apart from the physical issues of file construction and labelling, these procedures can be paralleled in digital systems that use folders. Some software applications provide additional support for controlling the creation of folders: requests to approve new folders may be routed electronically to an authorizing officer, or the application may run an automatic validation check to see if a relevant folder already exists. In a hybrid system it may be necessary for an electronic folder and an equivalent paper file to be registered simultaneously.

Registering a new series

A record series is registered when it is added to a classification scheme. A request for a new series implies that a new process has been initiated within the organization. It is important to have procedures to manage such requests and ensure that new series are created only when there is a genuine need for them. Rules are needed to establish how new processes are assessed and who is authorized to make amendments to classification schemes.

Assigning unique identifiers

Requirements for identifiers

The chief requirements for an identifier are uniqueness and persistence:

1 *Uniqueness*: the same identifier must not be used more than once, and even when a record has been destroyed its identifier should not be reused.
2 *Persistence*: the identifier should not be subject to change over time.

Identifiers are assigned to records at all levels of aggregation, except that in paper-based systems items that are not registered individually may not have distinctive identifiers of their own. In hybrid systems, identifiers for paper records should be consistent with those assigned to their electronic counterparts.

Identifiers for files in paper systems

In a paper system, each file has a title in human language, and often a coded identifier (the 'file reference') as well. Coded identifiers may be numerical (1, 2, 3 . . .) or alphanumerical (A1, A2, B1, B2 . . .), or may use more complex combinations of letters and numbers (K23/L47/1689T). Coded identifiers are sometimes omitted from smaller paper records systems, where files are identified only by their titles; but in larger systems it is impractical to rely on titles alone. Whatever the scale of the system, the use of codes helps to ensure that records are identified consistently and to avoid possible ambiguities.

Titles should not be used as unique identifiers if there is a risk that two records may have the same title or if titles are subject to change. Personal names are rarely adequate as identifiers for files relating to clients or employees, since individuals may have identical names or may change their name, for example on marriage. Coded identifiers obviate problems of this kind.

The simplest form of code is a 'running number', where each new record is assigned the next number in a continuing sequence. However, if large quantities of records are created, such numbers become lengthy. Five- or six-digit numbers often give rise to filing mistakes: for example, a file bearing the number 117111 can easily be misfiled as 111711. Colour-coding systems, where each digit on a file cover is printed in a different colour, are often used to help overcome this difficulty.

Some coding schemes seek to limit filing errors by breaking the number into shorter elements, which are less liable to confusion. For example, the first element might be a year date: the first file opened in 2003 could be numbered 2003#1, the second 2003#2 and so on. In January 2004 the numbers would begin again at 2004#1.

Files with an alphanumerical code such as A7111 or ABC7111 are also less prone to misfiling than files with a purely numerical code such as 117111. However, the letters I, O and Z should not be used in alphanumerical systems, to avoid confusion with the numerals 1, 0 and 2.

Some coding schemes assign blocks of numbers to particular subject groupings: for example, in a series of purchasing files numbers between 4001 and 5000 might be assigned to purchases of computer equipment and numbers between 5001 and 6000 to purchases of office furniture. Such schemes are primarily intended to allow related files to be stored side by side in a paper filing system. When applied to series where new files continue to be opened these schemes require an accurate prediction of future growth; if this is underestimated, the allocated block of numbers will eventually run out.

Coding schemes for paper files also need to allow for the closure of files at agreed intervals, or when they are too full to accept further documents, and the opening of continuation files. A closed file and its continuation should each bear the same identifier, but with the addition of a further element (such as 'Part 1', 'Part 2') to indicate their status.

Identifiers at higher and lower levels

Each series should also have a unique identifier. A series should be given a title, naming the process that the series represents. In all but the smallest records systems it is also good practice to assign a numerical or alphanumerical code to each series.

Within the series, unique identifiers for files can be built on the identifier at series level, to reflect the relationship between records at different levels of aggregation. In a simple coded scheme, P1 is the first file in series P, and P2 the second file in the same series.

If there are intermediate levels between the series and the file, the scheme can be extended accordingly. For example, if series P has two sub-series they could be identified as P/A and P/B. The files within sub-series P/A could be P/A1, P/A2 and so on.

More complex schemes can be devised to meet local needs: for example, within sub-series P/A, file P/A2003#1 might be the first file opened in the year 2003. Coding schemes are limited only by the ingenuity of those who devise them, but should not be made unnecessarily complicated.

Some records managers prefer to use mnemonic codes. For example, codes containing the letter P might refer to purchasing activities (or publishing, or personnel). The advantages claimed for mnemonic codes are that they are easy to remember and that experienced users can often recognize the context of a record merely by looking at its code. The drawbacks are that mnemonic schemes are more complex to administer and that changes over time can invalidate the original significance of the codes. For these reasons mnemonic schemes have fallen out of favour in recent years.

It is possible to combine codes at one level with language-based titles at higher or lower levels. For example, a series may be identified by its title ('Equipment purchase'), while each file within the series has a code as well as a title ('file 3:

Air-conditioners'). Conversely, the series may have both a code and a title ('series 27: Copyright clearance requests'), while individual files have titles alone ('Central Television'). The determinants are local needs and the size of the system.

At lower levels, identifiers need be unique only within the context of the next level of aggregation. Thus it is possible to have two files called 'Central Television' (or two called 'file 3') if each is in a different series. To allow this, the full identifier for a file should include the identifier for the series to which it belongs: in this way the file 'Copyright clearance requests: Central Television' can be clearly distinguished from the file 'Contracts: Central Television', which forms part of another series.

If a unique identifier is also to be provided for each item within a paper file, the contents of file A1 may be individually numbered A1/1, A1/2 and so on. These numbers may be written or printed on the items concerned. Within the file, the misplacement or absence of any item will be immediately apparent from an inspection of the numbering sequence.

Identifiers for electronic records

In the electronic world, computer technology requires a unique identifier for records at item level. If a tiered folder structure is used, identifiers are also needed at each of the higher levels.

Office systems generally make users assign language-based names to electronic documents when they are first saved, and to folders or directories when they are created. The combination of document and folder names provides a 'path', which acts as an identifier for the document. In the past, names were often limited to a maximum of eight characters, but this limitation is now rare and longer and more meaningful names are usually supported. The system will reject names that are already in use and possibly names that contain non-standard characters, but generally no other naming controls are applied. In a typical office system, document and folder names fail to provide persistent identifiers, since they can be changed by users at any time.

ERM systems also support language-based naming conventions, but can be expected to provide more sophisticated features than standard office systems. They may impose controls on the form of names and restrict the ability of users to change existing names at will. They may also assign a further identifier to each record, in the form of a code. The system will ensure that such codes are fixed and non-reusable. If an existing record is copied to a personal workspace, and then amended so as to create a new record, a new unique code will be assigned.

While language-based titles must be assigned by human operators, coded identifiers can be generated automatically by electronic systems. System-generated codes are usually assigned in a running number sequence. They may be invisible to users and employed only for system purposes; or users may be asked to approve a code suggested by the system, with the option of overriding it with an alternative of their choice. If codes are entered manually, the system may check automatically for their uniqueness or their conformity to a predetermined scheme.

Meaningful and non-meaningful codes

Most coding schemes for paper records use codes that not only identify records but also indicate their relationships at higher and lower levels of aggregation. However, electronic systems in particular need not follow this model. In an automated system item 456 could belong to folder 123: their relationship can be maintained by the system irrespective of the codes that are assigned. Meaningful codes can be helpful to users and records management staff and can act as a security check for paper records, but non-meaningful codes offer the benefit that items found to have been placed in the wrong file or folder can be repositioned without altering their coding. Unique identifiers for records should not be derived from their physical storage locations (such as shelves, filing cabinets or digital storage media), since storage arrangements are liable to change over time.

Assigning metadata

What metadata may be needed?

If records are to remain usable over time, a range of descriptive and other metadata will be required. As noted in Chapter 3, classification provides one element of metadata but many others will be needed for understanding, maintaining or gaining access to records later in their lives.

Most of these metadata must be gathered and associated with each record at or before the moment of its capture. They may include:

- a *unique identifier*
- *registration metadata*: who captured and registered the record, and when
- *structural metadata*: information about the form of the record (letter, minute, report, etc.), the level of aggregation (item, file, series) and relationships to other levels or other records at the same level

- *context metadata*: classification of functions, processes and activities; details of persons, corporate bodies or other agents participating in an activity; locations, materials, goods; dates of activity including dates of creation, transmission and receipt of the record; mandate or authority for record creation; transmission or copying procedures
- *content metadata*: title; description or abstract; language of the record; version control
- *metadata to enable discovery*: subject keywords; index terms
- *location, logical and physical format* (media, data formats, software dependencies) and *extent* (number of pages, dimensions, electronic file size)
- *custodial responsibility*, in a records management system with distributed responsibilities: who is responsible for preserving the record and ensuring its availability
- *rights management information*: who may read the record (in whole or part), who may copy it, who may know of its existence, and on what terms and conditions; who or what imposes these rules, and who may change them or authorize exceptions
- *retention information*: how long is the record to be retained; what maintenance or disposal actions are outstanding; who or what determines the retention status, and who may change it.

Retention metadata are discussed further in Chapter 5 and record titles and index terms in Chapter 7.

Decisions on the selection of metadata to be gathered should be based on local needs. Their gathering is often a phased process. Some may be gathered during creation of the record but others are added at the point of capture. Some may be subject to later amendment in the light of new information or changed circumstances but the initial assignment of metadata should ideally be complete when the record is captured.

Traditional records management practices have often relied on assigning metadata at a later stage in the life of a record, but this is now recognized as unsatisfactory. Metadata captured with the record are likely to be accurate because the information is immediately to hand, and their gathering is efficient because it can be done without revisiting business activities completed in the past.

In some cases, however, metadata will be subject to revision at a later stage. For example, Chapter 5 shows that decisions about retention status sometimes need to be reconsidered. In addition, other types of metadata can only be gathered after capture of the record. These include:

- *management and preservation history*: details of movement, migration and disposal actions performed, and of changes to existing metadata; dates of these actions and who was responsible for them
- *use history*: who viewed or copied the record and when they did so.

Attaching metadata to paper records

Most metadata are applied to paper records at series or file level, because manual systems are usually too cumbersome to allow more than a minimum of metadata to be applied to individual items. At item level, metadata may be limited to information contained within the item itself, such as the names of senders and addressees. At file level, metadata may be entered on file covers, lists, registers, index cards, databases or records management software applications. Series level metadata are recorded in classification schemes and other system documentation in paper or digital form.

The application of metadata to paper records is often demanding on resources and complex to administer. Some examples are given in Figure 4.6. Many of these involve laborious manual procedures. Some, such as the entering of each client's name in a number of different places, can involve substantial duplication of work and give rise to inconsistency. Effective controls are necessary if metadata are to be employed successfully in a paper records system. A records management software application should offer the tools that are required.

Metadata required	Options for applying metadata
• Names and roles of creators or contributors	• Text written or printed on documents • Entry in manual register or database
• Date and place of receipt of incoming mail	• Rubber stamp applied to documents in the mailroom or business unit • Entry in manual register or database
• Conditions of access to records	• Entry in classification scheme • Label on shelf or cabinet • Label on box or file cover • Entry on file list or index card • Entry in database
• Names of clients	• Label on file cover • Name written or printed on documents in the file • Entry on file list or index card • Entry in database

Fig. 4.6 *Examples of how metadata may be applied to paper records*

Attaching metadata to electronic records

Electronic records systems make the gathering of metadata easier and their use more efficient. All the metadata can be managed together in a single electronic environment. Metadata can be applied at item level as easily as at higher levels, since no cumbersome manual processes are required to attach them. Duplicate data entry should be unnecessary, as metadata can be reused wherever they are needed.

Electronic systems may be configured so that users are prevented from creating or capturing a record until certain metadata have been supplied. Typically, before creation or capture can proceed users are presented with an electronic form (often called a 'profile'), which must be completed in whole or part. The fields on the form correspond to those elements of metadata that the user is expected to provide. Other metadata can be system-derived: for example, a workflow application might automatically collect metadata about the steps in a process where records are created or captured, while the date and time of creation or capture can be obtained from the system clock. Information about technical dependencies can also be gathered automatically.

Profile forms for electronic documents are provided in many standard office applications, although they may gather only a limited range of metadata. Their use is normally optional and most users of office software ignore them. Profiles in office applications are also prone to error: for example, some applications attempt to identify authors of documents automatically, often by populating the profile from the password or other identifier used to log on to the system, but errors may arise if users do not log on separately, if existing documents are used as templates or if collaborative authoring takes place.

Most ERM applications employ profiles to gather a wider range of metadata and restrict automated features to those where there is no scope for error. The use of profiles for documentary records is normally obligatory in ERM applications, although there is a risk that users will be reluctant to devote time to completing a profile when other pressing tasks await them. Ideally, metadata collection should impinge as little as possible on business activity, but in practice this is not always possible. However, ERM systems assist users by providing authority files and 'inheritance' techniques.

1 *Authority files* hold frequently used terms that can be inserted into individual profiles when required. Check boxes or drop-down lists may be employed where the range of choice is small. Data entry then becomes quicker, and consistent terminology is ensured.

2 *Inheritance* depends on the principle, set out in Chapter 3, that metadata should be applied at the highest level possible. For example, if a whole series has the same confidentiality rule, users need not enter this information for every item in the series: instead, each item inherits the rule from metadata entered previously at series level.

Many ERM applications also allow profiles to be created for paper records, so that information about all records can be held in a single environment. In a hybrid series, some elements of metadata will be common to paper and electronic media, while others (such as location and physical format information) will be distinctive. If a single environment is used to hold all the relevant metadata their management becomes much easier.

In ERM applications, metadata collected in profiles are normally held in a database where they can be searched when required. Further features are usually provided to control the quality of metadata content. Fields on profile forms can be made mandatory, to ensure that they are not left empty, or can be subject to validation, so that metadata are automatically tested against preset criteria and rejected if they fail to conform. Most systems permit records management staff to check, amend or augment the metadata supplied by creators of records. Some systems bypass creators by sending all new records to a trained indexer to add the necessary metadata.

Automatic classification tools for electronic documents have recently begun to appear in the ERM market. Intended for use when records are to be classified on the basis of their subject content, they rely on pattern recognition and neural-network technology to assign subject metadata to electronic records without human intervention. As yet, however, they remain relatively untested.

Records created in data-centric applications do not require the use of separate profiles to collect metadata. Instead, records managers should seek to ensure that contextual and other information required for records management forms part of the data gathered by the application in the course of business. Since data-centric systems are frequently used for well-defined routine processes, it may be possible to configure them so that much contextual information is collected automatically. However, it cannot be assumed that all such systems are capable of collecting a full range of metadata: their suppliers are rarely aware of records management requirements, and it is usually necessary to specify additional functionality beyond the standard configuration of the system (Bantin, 2001; Giguere, 1997). Moreover, especially in customer-facing processes, some records of the process may be created as data while others take the form of electronic or paper documents;

in such cases it will be necessary to determine the most appropriate environment for holding contextual metadata. Such issues may not be easy to resolve, but the deciding factors are likely to be the technical capabilities of different systems, the availability of resources and the need to ensure that pointers between related records are maintained.

Metadata standards

Publicly available metadata standards have been promoted and used for many years by information professionals concerned with interoperability and the sharing of data beyond the confines of a single organization. For records managers too, standardization of metadata is valuable, not least because published standards provide a benchmark of systematic best practice.

Several detailed specifications for records management metadata structures have been formulated in recent years. They include:

- the *Reference model for business acceptable communications*, developed by David Bearman at the University of Pittsburgh, USA, www.archimuse.com/papers/nhprc/meta96.html
- the *Recordkeeping metadata standard for Commonwealth agencies*, published by the National Archives of Australia, www.naa.gov.au/recordkeeping/control/rkms/summary.htm
- the *VERS metadata scheme*, published by the Public Record Office Victoria, Australia, www.prov.vic.gov.au/vers/standards/pros9907/99-7-2toc.htm
- the *SPIRT recordkeeping metadata schema*, developed at Monash University, Australia, http://rcrg.dstc.edu.au/research/spirt/deliver/index.html.

Each of these provides a generic set of metadata elements to support the effective management of records, and guidelines for their interpretation and use. Some may be too detailed for use in smaller organizations, but all offer insights on metadata issues that are relevant to an organization of any size.

Other metadata standards that may be of value to records managers include:

- the *INDECS (Interoperability of Data in E-commerce Systems) metadata model*, a specification of descriptive and intellectual property rights metadata for e-commerce transactions, developed with funding from the European Community, www.indecs.org/
- the *UNTDED trade data elements directory* (ISO 7372), a set of standard data

elements for documenting parties, goods and modes of business in international trade, www.unece.org/trade/docs/tded.htm
- the *AGLS (Australian Government Locator Service) metadata set*, designed to facilitate discovery of records and information products published on government websites, www.naa.gov.au/recordkeeping/gov_online/agls/user_manual/intro.html (*AGLS* metadata are derived from the Dublin Core metadata set, http://dublincore.org/, with additional elements to support records management)
- *ISAD(G): general international standard archival description*, adopted by the International Council on Archives as a standard for retrospective description of records in archival custody, www.ica.org/biblio/com/cds/isad_g_2e.pdf.

References

Bantin, P. C. (2001) The Indiana University electronic records project: lessons learned, *Information Management Journal*, **35** (1), 16–24. Also available as Bantin, P. C. (2001) *Strategies for managing electronic records: lessons learned from the Indiana University electronic records project*, at www.indiana.edu/~libarch/ ER/NHPRC-2/rmarticle2.pdf.

Bearman, D. (1994) *Electronic evidence: strategies for managing records in contemporary organizations*, Archives and Museum Informatics.

Bearman, D. (1995) Archival issues in a computing environment. In Yorke, S. (ed.) *Playing for keeps: the proceedings of an electronic records management conference hosted by the Australian Archives, Canberra, Australia, 8–10 November 1994*, Australian Archives.

Cain, P. (1995) Data warehouses as producers of archival records, *Journal of the Society of Archivists*, **16** (2), 167–71.

Dollar, C. (1992) *Archival theory and information technologies: the impact of information technologies on archival principles and methods*, University of Macerata.

Giguere, M. D. (1997) *Metadata-enhanced electronic records.* Available at www.phila.gov/records/divisions/rm/units/perp/pdfs/ieee.pdf.

Hedstrom, M. (1997) Building record-keeping systems: archivists are not alone on the wild frontier, *Archivaria*, **44**, 44–71.

McDonald, J. (1995) Managing records in the modern office: the experience of the National Archives of Canada. In Yorke, S. (ed.) *Playing for keeps: the proceedings of an electronic records management conference hosted by the Australian Archives, Canberra, Australia, 8–10 November 1994*, Australian Archives.

National Archives of Canada (1993) *Managing your computer directories and files*, National Archives of Canada.

National Archives of Canada (1996) *Managing shared directories and files*, National Archives of Canada. Also available at www.archives.ca/06/docs/5shared.pdf.

New York State Archives and Records Administration (1995) *Managing records in automated office systems*. Available at ftp://ftp.sara.nysed.gov/pub/rec-pub/state-rec-pub/autofice.pdf.

Public Record Office (1999) *Management, appraisal and preservation of electronic records*, Vol 2, [UK] Public Record Office. Also available at www.pro.gov.uk/recordsmanagement/eros/guidelines/.

Reed, B. (1997) Metadata: core record or core business?, *Archives and Manuscripts*, **25** (2), 218–41. Also available at http://rcrg.dstc.edu.au/publications/recordscontinuum/brep1.html.

Smith, P. A. et al. (1995) *Introduction to records management*, Macmillan Education Australia.

5
Managing appraisal, retention and disposition

In records management, *appraisal* is the process by which an organization identifies its requirements for maintaining records.

Records managers have developed appraisal techniques primarily to support decisions about retention: which records can be destroyed at an early stage, and which merit longer-term or indefinite retention? However, appraisal can also be used to support other decisions. According to the Australian records management standard, appraisal seeks 'to determine which records need to be captured' into a records management system as well as 'how long the records need to be kept' (AS 4390.1-1996, clause 8.1). Other uses might include decisions on what records should be created, or identifying those that require special measures for protection or security. In a comprehensive records management programme a range of appraisal decisions may be required.

This chapter examines different theories of appraisal and considers how appraisal techniques can be applied to control the retention of records. Effective retention management demands a system which ensures that records are retained for as long as necessary and that those no longer required are eliminated. This chapter discusses three components of the system: methodologies for making appraisal decisions; documentation of decisions; and operational measures for their implementation.

The need for retention controls

Records, whether paper or digital, cannot all be retained indefinitely. Storage and maintenance over time is often expensive and, as the volume of records grows, access becomes slower and more difficult.

In practice some kind of appraisal occurs even where no records management programme exists. In the absence of formal controls, retention decisions are made on local initiative. Usually nothing is done until cabinets or servers are full, then someone makes a decision on what to do about it: paper records are moved to another storage area, a bigger server is acquired, or records are moved offline or destroyed. Such decisions are often arbitrary: redundant records are kept, thus incurring unnecessary expense, or records still needed are destroyed prematurely.

A records management programme aims to ensure that retention decisions are made rationally. One of its key justifications is protection of the organization against legal action. Besides retention of records needed for legal defence, this includes the ability to show why any particular records were destroyed. Irregularities in destruction procedures can bring suspicion, if an organization is taken to court or if there is an access request under freedom of information laws, that records may have been destroyed with intent to suppress embarrassing evidence. The existence of a structured retention system allows the organization to prove that any destruction took place as part of normal business practice. In many countries, systematic records retention and destruction procedures are also needed for compliance with privacy or data protection legislation.

Besides supporting accountability and defence against litigation, efficient retention systems:

- make it easier to retrieve records which are needed by removing those which are redundant
- help to avoid inadvertent destruction
- eliminate the cost of storing and maintaining unwanted records.

Appraisal decisions must take account of the organization's requirements for records for business use and accountability. Decisions about retention may also acknowledge cultural interests, or the interests of external users, to ensure the preservation of corporate or societal memory. In practice, the wider needs will carry greater weight in some organizations than in others. In the private sector, an organization may choose to keep only those records needed for its own purposes. In a democracy, public sector bodies and some private ones can be expected to take a wider view.

The development of appraisal: theory and practice

Acknowledging the problem

Jenkinson (1956, 149) recognized 'the necessity for decreasing by selection of some kind the intolerable quantity of documents accumulated by modern administration . . . a disagreeable necessity . . . because . . . there can be no absolutely safe criterion for Elimination'. The lack of a 'safe criterion' raises many difficulties: acknowledging the impossibility of finding a risk-free system of appraisal, records managers have continued to debate what strategy should be adopted.

'No theoretical question is more perplexing . . . than what should be the basis of appraisal'. For all the thinking, 'no theory of appraisal has yet been . . . generally accepted as the foundation of methodology and practice' (Eastwood, 1992, 71).

Schellenberg's taxonomy of values

Traditional approaches have focused on the perceived 'values' of records. In the mid 20th century, faced with the problems posed by bulk of official records of the US government, Schellenberg devised a system of record values (see Figure 5.1) to be used as the basis of appraisal. He wrote that 'public archives have two types of value: a primary value to the originating agency and a secondary value to other agencies and non-government users' (Schellenberg, 1956, 28).

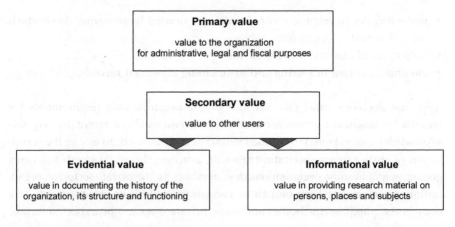

Fig. 5.1 *Schellenberg's appraisal taxonomy*

To Schellenberg, *primary value* represented the importance of records to the organizations where they originate. He divided it into *administrative value* to support the ongoing business of the organization, *legal value* to establish obligations and protect legal rights, and *fiscal value* to document the receipt and use of funds.

By *secondary value*, Schellenberg meant the value to users outside the organization where the records originate. While mentioning the possibility of a value to 'other agencies', he saw secondary value mainly in terms of use by historians and other scholarly researchers. He identified two types of secondary value in records:

1 *Evidential value*, concerning 'the organization and functioning of the agency that created them'. He suggested that, in assessing evidential value, the appraiser aims to select records containing 'significant facts on how the agency was created, how it developed, how it is organized, what functions it performs and what are the consequences of its activities' (Schellenberg, 1956, 139–40).

2 *Informational value*, derived 'from the information that is in public records on persons, places, subjects and the like with which public agencies deal' (Schellenberg, 1956, 148). He suggested that informational value often resides in case files, and that the interest lies in the content rather than the context of the records. When considering informational value the appraiser tries to assess the value of the records to researchers interested in particular topics, and values records according to the uniqueness of their content, the uses to which it might be put and the number of users it might serve.

Schellenberg's taxonomy of values – primary and secondary, evidential and informational – was widely adopted as an appraisal framework in the USA in the second half of the 20th century, and became increasingly influential in many other parts of the English-speaking world.

Jenkinson and the Grigg appraisal system

In contrast with the North American tradition, the classic European approach to appraisal emphasizes the view that the authenticity of records derives in part from their interrelationships, and that any artificial selection adversely affects those that remain and impairs their impartiality as evidence. Instead of attributing different values to records, European theory sees each record as unique in its context and of equal value.

This approach derives from long-established ideas about the nature of archives and antedates the recognition of records management as a professional discipline. In the early 20th century it was articulated in the UK by Jenkinson, who saw archivists as unconnected with the business interests of organizations and believed that their role was not to select records but to act as unbiased custodians. In his view, if selection must occur only those who use records in an administrative role

149

have legitimate authority to undertake it. 'For the Archivist to destroy a document because he thinks it useless is to import . . . an element of his personal judgment . . . but for an Administrative body to destroy what it no longer needs is a matter entirely within its competence and an action which future ages . . . cannot possibly criticize as illegitimate' (Jenkinson, 1937, 149).

Jenkinson's views were reflected in UK central government policy in the report of the Grigg Committee, constituted in 1952 to examine the management of government records. Its proposals (1954) included new procedures for the appraisal and transfer of non-current files. These were to be divided into two categories: those concerned with policy, legal, financial or other general matters, and case files or particular instance papers. The Committee recommended that:

- files in the first category should be reviewed by departmental staff five years after their closure, using the criterion of continuing departmental need
- a further review of the remnant should be held 25 years after the opening date of the file, using historical criteria
- files in the second category should usually be scheduled for destruction at the earliest opportunity
- files in both categories selected for long-term preservation should be transferred to the UK Public Record Office before they reach a certain age (originally 50 years, but later reduced to 30 years).

These proposals sought to minimize the involvement of Public Record Office staff in the appraisal process. The two-tier review system mirrors Schellenberg's distinction between primary and secondary values, but also assumes a close link between continuing administrative relevance and cultural significance. It recognizes that records may need to be reviewed more than once during their life and that on each occasion different criteria will have prominence.

Besides the Public Record Office, many other organizations adopted the two-tier review system, often combining it with elements of value attribution derived from the writings of Schellenberg. The system remained largely in place in UK central government until the late 1990s, when it began to be replaced by archival acquisition and operational selection policies (Simpson and Graham, 2002).

Limitations of the traditional solutions

Schellenberg's taxonomic approach and the Grigg review system originated in an era when there were fewer records, all on paper. The Grigg system in particular relies on file-by-file appraisal, which is feasible only if the bulk of records does not overwhelm the appraiser. Appraisal strategies now need to take account of the quantity of records produced by contemporary organizations and the predominance of computers in the workplace.

Jenkinson's views on appraisal are widely recognized as intellectually coherent but impractical in the modern world. However, Schellenberg's 'value' system has been increasingly criticized, not merely as anachronistic but on the grounds that it is flawed and confused. In particular, his discussion of evidential value has been attacked for its focus on factual content and its alleged failure to recognize the importance of authentic evidence to support business needs and organizational accountability.

Schellenberg was writing in the 1950s, when accountability was a less significant issue than it is today. He acknowledged that records provide 'proof of . . . stewardship of responsibilities' and that 'materials containing evidence . . . have value for the current and future functioning' of an organization. However, he also stated that he did not consider evidential value as 'the value that inheres in public records because of the merit of the evidence they contain . . . [or] the sanctity of the evidence', but rather as 'a value that depends on the importance of the matter evidenced' (Schellenberg, 1956, 139–40). The body of his discussion (1956, 140–8) confirms that he saw evidential value largely in terms of facts about the functions, activities and structures of the organization that would provide a source of data for historians.

A further criticism of his model is that it fails to reflect the full complexity of the issues that it addresses. It assumes that organizations have no interest in records beyond their use for administrative, legal and fiscal purposes, and that external users have only cultural interests: neither assumption is necessarily correct. Moreover it sees informational and evidential values only as components of 'secondary' value. In practice, both evidence and information can be sought by internal and external users alike.

New approaches: macro appraisal

More recently, new approaches have been sought. It has been recognized that file-by-file review and the emphasis on Schellenbergian values are not only increasingly impractical in an electronic age, but have also tended to decontextualize records by encouraging appraisers to focus on their content. Many professionals now agree that appraisal should be based on analysis of organizational purposes and the systems that support them, thus moving the focus from the records to the broader contexts in which they are created.

As Cook (1992, 46–7) suggests, this involves asking questions such as:

- How, why and by whom are records created (rather than what information do they contain)?
- How are they used by their creators (rather than how might they be used by future users)?
- What functions and processes do they support (rather than what internal structure and physical characteristics do they have)?
- What should be documented (rather than what documentation should be preserved)?

Cook indicates that this approach requires an understanding of the complexity of forces at work in contemporary organizations. The broad purpose of an organization is articulated in the interaction of function and structure. Sub-functions and sub-structures are established to carry out the organizational purpose. These require further systems to organize and supply the documentation that they need, and through these systems records are produced. In appraisal 'primacy is given to the creator, not the records, and . . . provenance . . . [is] rooted in the conceptual act of creation rather than in the physical artifact of the record eventually created' (Cook, 1992, 47).

As noted in Chapter 3, in practice records managers have preferred to focus on functions rather than administrative structures, not least because functions are more consistent over time. Functional analysis provides a robust basis for appraisal because it offers a stable link to the context in which records are created. Whereas the older methods operate from the bottom up, the new approaches are top-down, looking first at functions and only later at records.

Because the new approaches focus initially on appraising functions or structures at a high level, some writers refer to them as 'macro' appraisal. One example is the Dutch PIVOT methodology, developed in the early 1990s, which focuses appraisal on the organization and its environment. The evidential value of records is seen as deriving from the value of the function, and functions rather than records are analysed and appraised (Hol, 1996). Decisions about the retention of records are based on the importance of the function.

In considering records kept for cultural purposes, macro appraisal focuses on society, as reflected in organizational functions and structures. Its primary goal is to articulate 'the most important societal structures, functions, records creators and records-creating processes . . . which together form a comprehensive reflection of human experience' (Cook, 1992, 41). Macro appraisal may be particularly applicable where cultural purposes are seen in terms of reflecting the interaction between citizen and state, and has been adopted in several national records and archives services.

A further development of macro appraisal for cultural purposes is the 'archival documentation strategy', which is 'a plan to assure the adequate documentation of an ongoing issue, activity, function or subject' (Abraham, 1991, 48). The concept of the documentation strategy was designed for archival institutions seeking to acquire records whose business use has expired. Documentation strategies are usually inter-institutional and share the expertise of records creators, users and archivists to identify priority areas for acquisition.

Macro and functional appraisal were originally devised and used to support selection for cultural purposes, but have also been adapted as a basis for decisions about records kept for business use and accountability.

However, macro appraisal is not without its critics. In its most acute form it makes no provision for records managers or archivists to look at records at all: decisions are taken purely by defining and assessing the context of record-creating activities. Thus the objection can be raised that macro appraisal distances records managers from the records for which they are responsible. Moreover, in focusing on analysis of functions and systems, macro appraisal can lose sight of the user. It correctly emphasizes the role of records as evidence but overlooks the fact that users also employ records for their informational content.

Many macro appraisal methods remain dependent on assessing and prioritizing value (although this is often disguised by using words such as 'importance' or 'significance'). Proponents of macro appraisal often expect appraisers to ask questions such as: which record creators are important? which functions are vital to an organization? which are significant to the wider society? Critics argue that questions like these cannot be answered objectively, since there is no external standard of 'importance' against which the answers can be measured. To meet this difficulty, in recent years some records managers have moved away from a focus on value or importance and have sought to consider other factors such as the needs of stakeholders, the costs of keeping records and the risks incurred if they are not kept.

Appraisal strategy: a framework for decision making

Effective appraisal has several facets. It often requires an assessment of both context and content of records. It must also recognize that it is not always possible to reach a final decision all at once, and that the focus of appraisal may vary over time.

Traditionally, all appraisal decisions were made by looking at records when some

time had elapsed after their creation. When file-by-file review was rejected as impractical, records managers examined records created in the past and sought to
identify *series*, and then proposed retention rules that could be applied to the existing files in each series and to others that might be created in the future. However,
this approach still obliged appraisers to reconstruct contextual information after
the event, instead of collecting it when it was immediately available. A better
approach is to make the initial decisions at an earlier stage, when the records management system is designed. The framework given here assumes that retention
requirements can be built into the system from the start. Decisions can then be
based on first-hand knowledge of the context of the records.

An analysis of the environment in which an organization operates, and of its
business functions and processes, is a prerequisite for appraisal. Methods of collecting and mapping the necessary information have been outlined in Chapter 2.
Only when functions and processes have been identified is it possible to consider
how long the records of a particular function or process should be retained, and
whether or when they should eventually be destroyed.

Sometimes, especially if the outcome is focused on societal purposes, a single
decision can be made at the macro level of the function. However, where organizational requirements are to be met, it is rare for the same retention period to
be assigned to all the records of a particular function: appraisal at lower or micro
levels is usually needed. Retention decisions thus descend to process level.

If records are classified on functional principles, as discussed in Chapter 3, each
process corresponds to a distinct record series. Appraisal at system design stage
is likely to focus on processes and the series arising from them. Functional classification schemes are usually the most appropriate framework for appraisal
because they provide a firm connection between records and the context of their
creation. Initial retention decisions can be made as a classification scheme is
developed. For example, it might be decided to apply the same retention period
to all records of the recruitment process. These records form a single series (see
Figure 3.5, page 81). Retention metadata can be assigned to the series and inherited by lower-level records as they are captured.

Because a single retention decision can often be applied to all the records within
a series, the series is usually seen as the key level of control for retention management. However, it is sometimes appropriate to make decisions at lower levels.
For example, within the series of recruitment records in Figure 3.5, a different retention period could be agreed for each of the three sub-series (advertising, shortlisting
and interviewing), if it is felt that records of one sub-process are needed for
longer than those of another.

If the grouping of records below series level is not derived from a logical model of a process, retention decisions at levels below the series become less straightforward. As noted in Chapter 3, many series are divided into instance or subject groupings. Some of these may need to be kept for longer than others, but this cannot be assessed at system design stage unless there are known attributes of likely instances or subjects.

For example, some of the hospital patient records in Figure 3.9 might relate to patients with genetic diseases. It is possible to predict that some patients will have this attribute (i.e. that some genetic diseases will occur), and a decision could be made at system design stage that these records are to be kept longer than records for other diagnoses. Series are sometimes divided into attribute groupings, but this is not a prerequisite when attributes are to be used as a basis for retention control; instead, those responsible for assigning retention metadata can be told that when a particular attribute occurs (for example, when a patient has a genetic disease) a particular retention rule should be applied to the records concerned.

If retention decisions are not based on predictable attributes or on process, they cannot be made at system design stage but must be left until individual records are available for examination.

Appraisal criteria

Finding a basis for assessment

For decision making to be effective, adequate appraisal criteria will be required. 'The basis for evaluation is ultimately a consideration of use' (Eastwood, 1992, 83). While respecting the need to evaluate records in terms of their innate qualities, appraisers will fail in their task if they forget that records are kept so that they can be used. The model proposed here looks first at the *needs of users*, in terms of the uses of records and the characteristics that users seek in them.

As noted in the Introduction to this book, there are three broad reasons for using organizational records:

1 Records are used for *business purposes* when they are used to support administration, regulation, public or professional service, economic activity or dealings between individuals and organizations.
2 Records are used to support *accountability* when there is a need to prove that organizations or their staff have complied with legal or regulatory requirements or recognized best practice.

3 Records are used for *cultural purposes* when they are used as a means of acquiring or augmenting an understanding of an organization or of aspects of society or the wider world.

Internal and external users both have an interest in the availability of records. Each group may use records for business, accountability or cultural purposes, although the balance of their interests is likely to vary. In practice, the criteria for deciding what records are to be *created* and *captured* are usually limited to the organization's own needs for business and accountability. External stakeholders are only likely to be considered insofar as some records may be created or captured to meet the needs of external regulators. However, when decisions are made on *retention periods* for captured records, cultural purposes and the needs of a wider range of external users may also be taken into account.

To this picture must be added the characteristics of records as evidence and as information sources:

1 *Evidence*: records may be needed because they form evidence of the activity in which they were created. They are used in this way when *proof* is required that a particular activity took place or that it took place in a particular manner.

2 *Information*: records may be needed because they are sources of information. They are used in this way when users seek *facts* or *knowledge* (about the structure, operations or working methods of the organization or about other subjects, persons or places).

Evidence and information are to some extent intermixed. Facts about parties, places or goods involved in a transaction, which can be viewed as information at one level, can be viewed at another level as contextual data or metadata supporting the evidential qualities of the record. Moreover, users seeking evidence may want not only proof that something was done, but knowledge of what was done, who did it or when it occurred.

The information content of records can be (and often is) copied to a database, abstracted, transcribed, aggregated or sampled. When this has been done, it may be preferable to retain the information in this form if the original records are not required for evidential purposes. If the information is available in more than one form, retention decisions can take account of the duplication of information and its relative accessibility in one form or another, but the original records may still be required if doubts arise about the credibility of the information. Records place information in the evidential context of the activities where it was originally collected or employed.

Although this book uses the words *evidence* and *information* in a slightly different sense from Schellenberg, it follows him in referring to them as *values* of records. They are values that users seek in records and thus form part of the complex picture that appraisers must take into account. In addition there is a third value:

3 *Artefacts* or *objects*: records may be used because they are physical artefacts. They are used in this way when users are interested in their aesthetic qualities, tangibility, physical form, associations or saleroom value.

The use of records for their value as artefacts is rare when records are new. Such use typically occurs with paper records long after their creation. Records may be kept because they are unusual or visually pleasing, or for symbolic reasons arising from their association with a particular individual or event.

Needs of internal users

Records are normally kept in the first instance for use within the organization. They are used by those who created them, their successors, other employees of the organization and agents acting on the organization's behalf. Figure 5.2 compares internal users' interests in the values of records with their purposes in terms of business, accountability and cultural use. Darker shading represents heavier demands. Business and accountability needs predominate; cultural use may also occur but is much less prominent.

		PURPOSE OF USE		
		Business use	*Accountability*	*Cultural use*
VALUES SOUGHT	*Evidence*			
	Information			
	Artefact/object			

Fig. 5.2   *Internal use of records*

Business use embraces both evidence and information: for example, evidence to prove that a customer owes money to the organization or to support legal action asserting the organization's rights; information content to provide the facts needed for a range of operational tasks and managerial decisions.

To meet business requirements the records manager must assess the period for which the creator, the business unit or the organization as a whole needs the records for ongoing administration and operation. In principle, while there is a business need for records they should not be destroyed. In practice it can be difficult to identify the period of time for which business needs persist.

The first step is to assess how long the activity supported by the record may continue. This may extend for many years: records of employee pension contributions and entitlements, for example, may be needed for 80 or 90 years.

The next step is to assess any period for which records may be needed for business purposes after the completion of the original activities to which they relate. Even when activities are believed to be complete, records may be required for a further period in case the matter is revived or a need arises for action against third parties who have defaulted on their obligations or infringed the organization's rights.

In addition, the record of one activity may be needed to support another activity in the future. The compilation of an annual report, for example, may require access to records of many different activities (AS 4390.5-1996, clause 6.4.2). Long-term retention may be required if a record is used repeatedly in other activities. In many organizations the records most likely to be used in this way are those arising from creative activities such as the management of core functions and the development of policies, procedures and precedents.

Records originating from a creative activity can be used in other creative activities or in routine activities. When records are used to support routine work records managers can use process analysis to assess retention needs: how far back does a typical instance of a routine process need to refer to the records? However, as noted in earlier chapters, process analysis is unsuited to creative processes, whose requirements are often harder to quantify; and even in routine environments there will be exceptional circumstances when an older record is needed in a particular case.

Besides using them in business as evidence and as information sources, organizations sometimes keep records for business purposes because of their value as artefacts. An organization employs older records as artefacts when it uses them for advertising, marketing or public relations.

To support *accountability* records managers must assess the needs of the creator, the business unit and the organization for records to provide evidence that it has acted correctly and in accordance with its rights and obligations. This encompasses:

- compliance with the law and internal and external regulations
- auditing requirements (financial audits, quality audits and other internal and external inspections)
- response to challenge (legal defence and handling of internal and external grievances or complaints).

Sometimes it is easy to identify specific retention requirements in terms of years. Laws and regulations may stipulate an exact retention period for particular records (in the UK, for example, the Companies Act 1985 requires accounting records of public limited companies to be kept for six years, and private companies for three years). Chapter 2 has discussed how records managers can identify relevant legislation and external regulations. They must also take account of the organization's internal regulations.

Audits and inspections usually take place at predictable intervals. They are normally governed by laws or other regulations and it is usually easy to identify the records that the auditors will require and the time for which they are likely to be needed for auditing purposes.

In other areas, determining retention can be more difficult. In some jurisdictions, data protection legislation states that records relating to a named individual must be destroyed as soon as their retention is no longer required, but identifying the appropriate moment for destruction is not always straightforward. Many other laws require the keeping of records but do not specify a time period for which they must be retained.

Limitation laws do not usually mention records, but specify time limits within which legal actions may be brought. Such time limits can provide a basis for retention periods, but it may not be easy to identify the records that might be needed for legal defence. A further difficulty is that the limitation period runs from the moment when an injured party can reasonably be expected to be aware of injury, which sometimes can be many years after the event.

Where no exact period is prescribed by legislation or other external authority, a local decision must be made. A cautious organization or one whose work is highly sensitive may choose to retain substantial quantities of records of all kinds, while organizations that are confident of being able to meet legal challenges may choose to retain much less.

Records are rarely created with *cultural use* in view. In practice, however, organizations frequently use their records for cultural reasons (to support corporate memory and perhaps in a formal written history) and these needs may be taken into account in retention decisions. For cultural purposes there may be a particular need to retain records that provide evidence of or information about high-level decision making, key functions, policies and procedures, the external involvement of the organization, research activities and changes and developments over time.

Needs of external users

In some organizations, the availability of records to external users is limited to those who have a formal right to see them (regulators, or members of the public exercising legal rights); in others, records are made available more widely. Figure 5.3 indicates that, where records are available to external users, they are used chiefly for accountability and cultural purposes. Retention criteria depend to some degree on the breadth of access that the organization seeks to provide, either in-house or by transferring records to an external archives service at a later stage in their life.

		PURPOSE OF USE		
		Business use	Accountability	Cultural use
VALUES SOUGHT	Evidence			
	Information			
	Artefact/object			

Fig. 5.3   External use of records

External accountability faces two ways: the organization needs to show that it has acted correctly and mandatory or advisory regulators need to verify that organizations have fulfilled their obligations. Inspections and audits may be held by funding bodies or by statutory or sectoral regulators; they may be wide-ranging or limited to checking compliance with particular laws, regulations or standards. Records are needed to provide evidence of the existence of appropriate policies and procedures and of compliance.

Members of the public may also need records for accountability purposes, typically to exercise their rights under freedom of information or data protection laws, both of which are discussed in Chapter 7.

Most other external use is for cultural purposes. Many users seek information from organizational records to support personal or academic research or in the course of education. Other users may be interested in the physical representation of a record as an artefact. Some have very specific requirements (for particular records or closely defined topics) but others may seek a range of records to study trends over time.

Some external users may wish to use the records for business purposes of their own, but organizations may not always welcome such use if they see it as detrimental to their own interests.

Balancing the competing interests

It is rarely easy to make a retention decision that encompasses the business, accountability and cultural interests of both internal and external stakeholders. Often the longest retention period takes precedence, but this may have cost implications. In some organizations, commercial pressures or best value policies may put records managers under pressure to keep retention periods as short as possible.

One way of balancing the different interests is by assessing the risks of not having records that might be needed. A key question is: what level of risk will the organization accept? To assess risk, the possible consequences of the absence of records should be identified and their severity matched against the likelihood of their occurrence. The consequences could be financial (fines, damages arising from inability to initiate or defend a legal action, disruption or loss of business) but could also be measured in terms of loss of opportunity, amenity, reputation, prestige or goodwill. A risk assessment seeks to judge how far the absence of particular records would be likely to incur such consequences, and how serious their impact would be. The highest risks are those where both impact and probability are greatest (see Figure 5.4).

The risks of destroying records must be set against the costs of maintaining them. Costs include accommodation, equipment and the services of records staff or contractors. As Figure 5.5 shows, risks attached to retention and costs of destruction may also be taken into account.

A further factor is the organization's attitude to the interests of external users. Most internal business needs are ephemeral and will expire at some point. However, especially in the public sector, the political or social benefit of retaining records may determine longer retention periods. The need to protect the interests of citizens may justify higher costs, although the balance between cost and benefits of retention after organizational needs have been met must still be weighed.

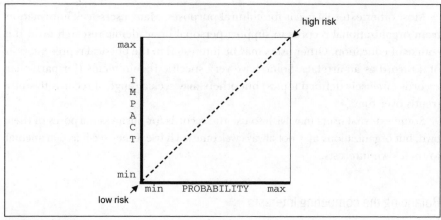

Fig. 5.4 *Risk assessment*

Many people are likely to be involved in making retention decisions. Representatives of business units can advise on what records they need to carry out their business. Lawyers, insurers, financial and tax experts, auditors and quality assurance or compliance advisers can help assess risk or advise on financial and legal requirements, standards and best practice. Historians and representatives of cultural interest groups can advise on cultural needs. Records managers and archivists can analyse the organization's overall needs for records and advise on retention practices. Many organizations use a specialist committee to bring these experts together.

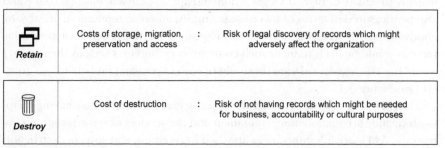

Fig. 5.5 *Costs and risks*

Documenting and applying retention decisions

Retention schedules and metadata

The results of appraisal are decisions about the maintenance of records. These decisions must be documented, and this has traditionally been done by creating a *retention schedule*, which provides practical and consistent guidance for managing records through their lives.

'The retention schedule has long been accepted as one of the principal foundations of any records management programme' (Bailey, 1999, 33). In its paper form it is a list of the various series of records, specifying how long the files within each series or sub-series are to be retained, the reasons for setting this retention period and the actions proposed when the period expires. As shown in Figure 5.6, the retention period consists of two elements: a starting point or trigger, and a period of time. Other information may also be included in the schedule, such as who is responsible for each series and for seeing that the necessary actions are performed.

	starting point	time period	action	authorization
Series A	end of current month	+11 months	destroy	Board meeting 1/3/2001
Series B	end of current financial year	+6 financial years	destroy	Financial rules 1998
Series C	termination of contract	+10 calendar years	destroy	etc.
Series D		keep indefinitely		etc.

Fig. 5.6 *Retention schedule (1)*

Abbreviations (such as CM for 'current month') are often employed in retention schedules, but these are not user-friendly and need explanation if the schedules are to be applied by operational staff rather than records management specialists. Operational staff may also find it helpful if series are identified in language that is familiar to them: *Garage Books* may mean more to them than the formal *Series N123: Testing of vehicles*, although the formal title indicating the business process should appear beside the informal title on the records manager's copy of the schedule.

If records are to be retained for more than a short period they may require transfer to alternative storage, a different medium or another software environment. Instructions for such transfers (which are discussed more fully in Chapter 6) are often included in retention schedules. Figure 5.7 shows an expanded schedule incorporating details of storage transfers.

Retention schedules were traditionally drawn up on paper; often the records manager prepared a separate schedule for each business unit or functional area. The metadata provided on the schedule dealt only with the later stages in the life of the records, following traditional practice where records managers had little or no concern with records creation. However, in a comprehensive programme that

	starting point	time	action	time	time total	action
Series E	file closure	+1 year in current store	move to records centre	+5 years in records centre	6 years	destroy
Series F	file closure	+3 years in current store	move to archives	keep indefinitely		
Series G						
Sub-series G1	folder closure	+1 year online	move offline	+3 years offline	4 years	destroy
Sub-series G2	folder closure	+1 year online	destroy			

Fig. 5.7   *Retention schedule (2)*

manages the creation and capture of records as well as their ongoing maintenance, retention information can be linked to classification schemes and other metadata in an integrated control system. A classification scheme, as described in Chapter 3, provides a basis for organizing records to reflect the processes and activities that give rise to them. As the key source that identifies and defines the various record series, it provides an appropriate framework for documenting retention decisions.

In a database, classification and retention metadata can be managed together. Electronic records management applications, like automated systems for managing paper records, usually provide a database environment where information about retention decisions can be linked to a range of other metadata about records throughout the organization. Use of a database makes it easy for records managers to analyse retention data when planning storage, security or migration requirements.

Authorization and updating

Retention decisions must be approved by the senior executives of the organization, since they are ultimately responsible for records management policy and compliance. Schedules are usually prepared by records managers on the basis of expert recommendations and then submitted to senior managers for approval. They typically require the authorization of the chief executive and other senior staff such as legal, financial or planning directors. Schedules for approval need not give details of storage arrangements, but simply state the recommended retention period and final disposition of the records, together with reasons for the recommendation. As evidence of authorized appraisal decisions, the approved schedules should be retained for the life of the organization.

Appraisal decisions must be checked periodically to ensure their continuing validity. When significant organizational changes occur, structural or functional analysis may need to be repeated. Laws and regulations are frequently amended and records managers must ensure that retention policies reflect current requirements. When a retention decision is to be changed, approval from senior management must again be sought and operational databases or retention schedules updated as necessary. Records of superseded decisions should be retained for evidential purposes.

Making the schedules available

Schedules are a key operational tool and should be available to all who need to know about retention. If details of retention decisions are held in a database, printed reports can be distributed or different views of the database made available to users throughout the organization. Output from a database might include a summary schedule giving senior managers an overview of retention requirements, and process-based schedules to enable co-ordinated retention actions when different parts of a series are created in different business units. If responsibility for implementing retention decisions is split between operational and records management staff, departmental views of schedules might give information only about current requirements, after which responsibility transfers to the records manager.

When schedules are updated, version controls are required together with mechanisms for recall and replacement of old versions. Electronic delivery, typically on an intranet, ensures that only current versions are available to users and can also link schedules to electronic forms and online classification schemes or other sources of advice and good practice.

Assigning retention status to newly created records

Older records management approaches separated retention control from records creation and capture. Retention management has traditionally been left to a later stage in the life of records, when they are compared with a retention schedule to identify the actions required. This often makes schedules difficult to apply, since the existing records do not always match the categories in the schedule. However, if retention decisions are linked to series level entries in classification schemes, each file or folder can be assigned its retention status at the same time as it is created, classified and allocated to a series.

ERM applications and automated systems for managing paper records may allow metadata defining the retention status of newly opened files or folders to be automatically inherited from metadata entered previously at series level. In ERM applications, individual items may likewise inherit their retention status from higher levels of the system, at the point when they are assigned to a folder. In a wholly electronic system such inheritance can be fully automatic, requiring no human intervention. However, where records are on paper, manual action may be required to annotate file covers or other documentation with words such as 'Destroy on completion of audit' or 'Destroy 10 years after closure', so that users are made aware of the status of each file.

If the trigger for destruction of a file or folder runs from the moment of its closure, the calendar date for destruction must be calculated when the file is closed. ERM applications and automated systems for paper records can perform the calculation and update metadata automatically, but where destruction dates need to be noted on file covers or paper documentation this too must be done manually. A simple code such as D2018 (for 'Destroy in 2018') can be employed. Usually this is best done at the moment of closure, but if closed files are subsequently moved to alternative storage it can be done when they are transferred.

Reviewing retention decisions after the creation of records

This chapter has recommended that initial appraisal decisions should be made when classification schemes are designed, and should be applied to records as they are captured. Undertaking initial appraisal at a later stage is less effective, because appraisers are likely to have less knowledge of the processes that led to the creation of records. It is also likely to be more laborious, especially for electronic records, which may be difficult to assess after their initial capture.

However, the advisability of making a single irrevocable decision at system design stage remains open to debate. As noted above, organizations give different weight to different claims when making retention decisions: business and cultural use, requirements for evidence and information, internal and external needs. In general, the more weight that an organization gives to *evidential* criteria, the more feasible it is to make retention decisions at system design stage, by appraising functions and processes before records are created. Some *information content* can be predicted and assessed in advance but much can only be assessed once the records have come into existence. Homogeneous information (such as might be found in bank statements or patient healthcare records) can sometimes be assessed at system design stage, but records that are expected to contain heterogeneous information (for example, senior managers' correspondence) may need to be assessed after creation if their information content is relevant to determining retention.

All these factors have an impact on a related question: who should be responsible for applying the appraisal decisions to the records? When records are created in a routine process, it is often possible for operational staff, or an automated system, simply to apply the rules agreed at system design stage. Where necessary, supervisors or records specialists can monitor the actions taken by operational staff: for example, by checking that newly classified records have been assigned to the correct series and given the retention status indicated in the schedule or classification scheme.

Often, however, retention management systems must recognize that initial decisions may need to be reviewed at a later stage. This applies especially to the records of creative processes, since they are more varied and less predictable. To provide the necessary flexibility, mechanisms may be required to allow:

- overriding of appraisal decisions made at system design stage in order to apply longer or shorter retention periods to particular records at the moment of their capture
- altering the retention status of records during their active life, if an ongoing activity evolves so that its outcome seems likely to differ from what was envisaged when the file was opened.

Both of these situations can be expected to occur from time to time in relation to particular files or folders within a series. One arises when an exceptional activity is begun which requires a retention period that differs from the rule for the series as a whole. The other may arise when an activity originally thought trivial assumes greater complexity: for example, when a response to a standard enquiry turns into a major investigation, or when a patient's life-threatening disease only becomes apparent as diagnosis proceeds. In both cases, a variation of a previous decision is required.

Such variations at file or folder level may be inevitable in some series, but separate retention periods for different items within a file should be avoided wherever possible. Normally the whole file should be retained for the longest period required by any of its contents, in order to preserve contextuality.

Where such variations are necessary, creators of records or their line managers can be authorized to set or change retention periods for individual files, or the decision may be referred to records management specialists. If the nature of an activity changes after the opening of a file, other previously gathered metadata such as the file title, index entries or details of access rights may also have to be altered.

Retention decisions for older records often have to be reconsidered when business needs that were thought to have expired become current again. For example, if an abandoned road-building project is revived and the road is to be built after all, the project records will again be needed for business purposes. Changes to legislation or regulatory requirements, or the use of records in a legal action, can also mean that the original retention period must be amended. New retention periods may be assigned to a whole series or to one or more files within a series. Users, legal advisers and records management staff must work together to ensure that such changes are made when required.

In all these cases, alterations to previous retention decisions are *reactive*: they are made in response to events that occur unexpectedly. A *proactive* option is to plan in advance that retention decisions will be reviewed at an agreed point in the future. This should be seen not as a way of postponing appraisal, but as recognition that it may not be possible to consider all relevant factors at the initial stage. Cultural requirements or artefactual values in particular may only become apparent later in the life of a record. A planned review at a late stage may consider business or accountability issues that have emerged since creation, but more commonly focuses on retention to meet cultural needs.

Planned reviews must have an action date attached to them. Like other action dates in retention planning, this is calculated as a period of time after an initial trigger. Figure 5.8 shows how a planned review can be built into a retention schedule. Reviews are often timed to coincide with transfers to alternative storage.

	starting point	time	action	responsibility for action
Series H	end of project	+12 years	review	records manager and head of unit

Fig. 5.8 *Retention schedule (3)*

When the review takes place, possible outcomes are decisions to:

- keep indefinitely
- destroy immediately
- destroy at an agreed point in the future
- review again at an agreed point in the future.

The action that is decided on could be applied to a whole series or sub-series, or the review could be conducted at micro level with a separate decision made for each file. When a review is planned, account must be taken of the staff time and other resources that will be required, especially if review at file level is envisaged. File-by-file reviews should be avoided unless they are essential.

When previous appraisal decisions are altered, or new decisions made at a planned review, the agreed actions must be documented and existing metadata updated where necessary. If micro-level changes are made in a paper-based system, file covers, lists and indexes may all need amendment or annotation. In automated systems updating of metadata is generally easier but procedures must still be in place to ensure that it is not overlooked.

Retention of 'legacy' records

In the early stages of a records management programme a strategy is also likely to be needed for managing the retention of records that were created outside the formal programme, or before its establishment, but have subsequently come within the records manager's purview. These are often called 'legacy' records. It is rare to find that such records have been classified on the basis of functions and processes, or that systematic decisions about their retention have been already been made. Sometimes they may be in considerable disorder. In these circumstances retention decisions are rarely easy.

One option is to reclassify the records using a functional classification scheme. Initial retention decisions can then be made as reclassification proceeds, using the methods and criteria discussed earlier in this chapter. However, reclassification demands intensive resources and may not be cost-effective for older records that are no longer in regular use.

Where reclassification is impractical, it may still be possible to appraise the functions and processes to which the records relate, and seek to match the records to particular processes in order to determine their initial retention status. If the records are in good order, it should be possible to identify coherent sets of records that resemble (and may even be known as) a series. Although there can be no guarantee that each 'series' will be found to correspond to a single process, there is often sufficient correlation to allow the records manager to apply appraisal decisions based on functional analysis.

However, this is not always easy. Functional analysis only captures the state of an organization at a specific moment: for legacy records, a view of changes over time is needed and it may be necessary to combine the results of analyses undertaken on a number of occasions in the past. If no such analyses are available it can be difficult to find a substitute, especially if functions or processes have been discontinued or substantially changed. An understanding of former processes can often be gained by examining their records or by interviewing long-serving or retired staff, but it is rarely feasible to conduct a detailed analysis.

The information content of legacy records is usually easier to assess. If the records constitute a series, or have some other form of coherence, a review of a sample can often indicate the type of information that they contain. However, if legacy records are in disorder, retention decisions based on systematic functional analysis and on sampling are both likely to be difficult. File-by-file review may be the only option. Nevertheless, decisions should be based on whatever evidence is available about the context of the records, and not merely on their content. All the criteria discussed earlier in this chapter are relevant, although some will be difficult to apply to poorly organized legacy records.

Assessing a large quantity of legacy paper records requires knowledgeable staff or expert contractors, and space where they can work. Besides access to retention policies and procedural guidelines, they will need shelving to house the records while work is in progress, trolleys for moving records and generous desk space where records can be spread out for examination. Assessing legacy electronic records is less demanding on working space, but is often more time-consuming if computer files have to be examined individually.

As with planned reviews, possible outcomes are decisions to keep records indefinitely, to destroy them (immediately or at a future time) or to assess them again later in their life. Unless immediate destruction is proposed it may be necessary for legacy records to be transferred to appropriate storage, and this is often arranged as retention decisions are made.

Disposition

Records managers use the terms *disposal* or *disposition* to refer to the actions that are associated with implementing decisions about the retention or destruction of records. These may also include migration and transfers of records to new storage locations, custodians or owners (ISO 15489-1:2001, clause 3.9; AS 4390.1-1996, clause 4.9).

While most retention decisions are made at series or other high levels, disposal actions are normally carried out at a lower level (usually file level in the case of paper records). A diary system must be in place to ensure that actions are carried out promptly. ERM applications and automated systems for managing paper records can provide reminders when actions are due. Where records are kept in electronic form, systems can also be programmed to carry out some disposal actions automatically. However, before records are destroyed or transferred, it is usually wise to check that there have been no changes to retention requirements and that the action noted against each record still applies.

If records are in the custody of the records management unit, responsibility for disposal normally rests with the records manager. If records are in other custody, responsibility may rest with operational or information technology staff. Formal consultation between the parties is sometimes necessary before disposal action occurs, but sometimes one party is authorized to take action as soon as the agreed retention period has expired. Where responsibility rests with the records manager, it is usually sufficient to inform the relevant business units that destruction or transfer will be carried out after four weeks unless they give notice to the contrary.

Destruction of records must be undertaken confidentially and certificates of destruction required from any third party contractors. The choice of method will be determined by security needs, costs and environmental impact. Paper records can be destroyed by shredding or more securely by pulping or incineration. The use of standard waste bins or other non-secure facilities is not acceptable. Electronic records can be erased by reformatting, degaussing or physically destroying their storage media. 'Delete' functions in standard operating systems and office suites do not erase records: they only remove access paths or index links and leave records vulnerable to recovery. It is important to keep track of back-ups and other copies (in any medium) so that these can also be destroyed.

Some records are not destroyed, but retained indefinitely. This may be taken to mean that they will be kept permanently, but it is perhaps more correct to say that no limit on their retention has been set. It remains possible that they will be reassessed at some time in the future.

Quality control and documentation

As the Australian records management standard recommends (AS 4390.5-1996, clause 8), appraisal programmes should be monitored and documented to provide evidence of compliance with policies, procedures and regulations. Independent audits should include regular checks that:

- appraisal analyses and decisions are approved and up to date
- records are retained in accordance with appraisal decisions
- destruction and transfer of records are managed and documented appropriately.

When disposal actions take place, documentation must be created or updated to provide evidence of what was done and how it was authorized. In an automated system it should be possible to maintain metadata about destroyed records as well as those that remain. In a manual system, lists or indexes must be annotated when files are destroyed, and the date and authority for the action noted. Organizations must be able to account for their records, and documentation enables them to prove that destruction occurred in compliance with agreed policy. It also enables records managers to justify their actions to colleagues, successors and executive staff, and allows future users of records to know what was destroyed and what was retained. Such documentation should be kept for a number of years; in many organizations it is kept indefinitely.

References

Abraham, T. (1991) Collection policy or documentation strategy: theory and practice, *American Archivist*, **54** (1), 44–52.

Bailey, S. (1999) The metadatabase: the future of the retention schedule as a records management tool, *Records Management Journal*, **9** (1), 33–45.

Cook, T. (1992) Mind over matter: towards a new theory of archival appraisal. In Craig, B. L. (ed.) *The archival imagination: essays in honour of Hugh A. Taylor*, Association of Canadian Archivists.

Eastwood, T. (1992) Towards a social theory of appraisal. In Craig, B. L. (ed.) *The archival imagination: essays in honour of Hugh A. Taylor*, Association of Canadian Archivists.

Jenkinson, H. (1937) *A manual of archive administration*, 2nd edn, Lund Humphries.

Jenkinson, H. (1956) Modern archives: some reflexions, *Journal of the Society of Archivists*, **1**, 147–9. Reprinted in Ellis, R. H. and Walne, P. (eds.) (1980) *Selected writings of Sir Hilary Jenkinson*, Alan Sutton.

Hol, R. C. (1996) PIVOT's appraisal of modern records: a 'floody' tale from the Dutch experience, *South African Archives Journal*, **38**, 5–15.

Report of the Committee on Departmental Records (Grigg report) (1954) Cmd. 9163, HMSO.

Schellenberg, T. R. (1956) *Modern archives: principles and techniques*, F. W. Cheshire.

Simpson, D. and Graham, S. (2002) Appraisal and selection of records: a new approach, *Comma, International Journal on Archives*, 2002– 1/2, 51–6.

AS 4390-1996 *Records management*, Standards Australia.

ISO 15489-1:2001 *Information and documentation – records management – part 1: general*, International Standards Organization.

6
Maintaining records and assuring their integrity

A fundamental element of records management is ensuring that records remain secure, intact, accessible and intelligible for as long as they are needed. This chapter considers the strategies that are required to maintain the integrity of records over time.

With paper records, the main emphasis is on storing the physical media and protecting them from loss or damage. Electronic records require a different approach: the physical carriers are likely to be short-lived, but the records must be maintained over time and probably across several generations of storage media. While preservation of paper records is costly in terms of space occupancy, electronic storage media are compact and relatively inexpensive but costs are incurred in ensuring that records remain accessible.

Storage systems for paper records

Centralized or decentralized?

Storage of records can be centralized or decentralized. In a fully centralized system, records for the whole organization are stored together. A central store offers a high degree of control and security, and optimizes the use of space by employing bulk storage equipment. In a decentralized system, records are held closer to where users work, but controls may be more difficult to achieve.

Some organizations centralize all their paper records storage, but this is increasingly rare. More often, following the lifecycle model in Figure 1.2 (page 6), decentralization of some or all current records is combined with a centralized facility for records deemed to be semi-current or non-current.

Most organizations recognize that standard procedures and access controls for paper records are easier to enforce in a centralized system, where specialist records staff can be employed; but when records are required frequently or urgently the convenience of local access usually takes priority and decentralization is preferred. Current records are likely to have high referral rates. Records that have passed beyond the current stage are rarely required at very short notice, so local accessibility is less important.

Besides speed of access, decentralization provides a sense of ownership by records creators and users. Decentralized storage is often the day-to-day responsibility of the business units where records are created, as central records staff rarely have the resources to service decentralized paper files. In some organizations the central records manager may not be expected to have any participation in the management of decentralized systems. However, all records should be subject to the same rules, regardless of their location: those in decentralized storage are not exempt from the records policy of the organization. Since few staff in business units can be expected to have records management skills, there is likely to be a role for the records manager in training and advising staff as well as in systems development and monitoring of local practice.

Current paper records systems

Centralization of current paper records is typical of (and perhaps only feasible in) 'power' and 'role' culture organizations where there is little local autonomy. Centralized systems have often been associated with the mailroom and registry services described in Chapter 4: current records are stored in the registry area, and registry staff are responsible for retrieving and replacing files as well as registering incoming and outgoing correspondence. It is also possible to have a centralized storage and retrieval system that is unconnected with the mailroom: in this case, central records staff manage and store records at file level but do not usually register individual items.

Decentralized systems offer a range of possibilities in terms of scale and diversification. As a variant on the single store for the whole organization, each business unit or operating site may have its own central storage area. This can allow a broadly centralized system to be delivered through a small number of local registries. Elsewhere, records storage may be devolved further, with each section or workgroup having its own defined storage space. In general, the fewer the number of devolved systems, the easier it is to ensure good records management practice. Where storage is highly diversified, systematic procedures can be hard to implement and monitor.

Individuals, especially those who have sole responsibility for an activity or process, may seek to store files at their desks or in the immediate vicinity. Some organizations have opted for this extreme form of decentralization for all their records, but such systems quickly become chaotic, uncontrolled and unaccountable. Individuals who store their own records often see them as their personal property rather than a corporate resource. For these reasons, individual storage should normally be limited to those items that can appropriately be held in the personal domain, as discussed in Chapter 4.

It is not always easy to decide between central and local storage for current paper records. Particular tensions can arise when different parts of an organization participate in different stages of a single process. For example, purchase orders may be received in one business unit and passed to another for fulfilment; the treatment of patients in a hospital may involve numerous steps undertaken in different departments. Good records management practice requires the maintenance of a unified record of the process as a whole. If there is no central registry and each department keeps its own record of the steps for which it is responsible, the record of the process is fragmented. Centralized systems can maintain unified records but complex procedures are often required for moving active files from one department to another.

For many organizations, a mixture of centralized and decentralized storage is appropriate. Decisions about which current records should be stored and managed centrally, and which locally, should normally be made at series level. Centralized systems are sometimes used for series that are felt to be particularly important, such as those that record policy decisions or precedents, where a higher degree of control is required. When this model is followed in UK government agencies, series held centrally are known as 'registered' file series: those held locally are not considered to be formally registered, although they should still be fully documented so that they can be managed effectively over time.

Other key issues in deciding whether to recommend centralized or decentralized storage are use and the need for access. Even if only one business unit is involved in creating a series, it should be stored and managed centrally if staff from more than one unit need to use it regularly. When only one business unit needs access the case for local storage is stronger. If paper records are needed frequently and urgently they must be housed where they are easily accessible.

Establishing and managing a records centre

What is a records centre?

Centralization may be easier to achieve for paper records that are infrequently required for current business, as operational staff usually want to move such records out of their working areas. In uncontrolled systems, older records are usually dumped in disorganized basements or other substandard accommodation. In a well-ordered system, records that need to be retained for a further specified period are systematically transferred to a centralized storage area, often known as a records centre. Benedon (1969, 258) defined a records centre as 'a low cost, centralized area for housing and servicing . . . records whose reference rate does not warrant their retention in office space and equipment'. Records centres promote efficiency and economy in the use of space and other resources. They are mainly used for paper records, although they can be used for any media. They are likely to be significantly cheaper than office space since they use high-density storage equipment and are often sited away from city centre locations. The regular transfer of records from office areas or registries ensures that space throughout the organization is used efficiently. A records centre also provides a dedicated location where records are made accessible and where maintenance procedures and disposal actions can be managed systematically.

Records centres are usually controlled and operated by a central records management unit, but ownership of records transferred to the records centre often remains with business units, which will want assurances of confidentiality and access restricted to authorized personnel. Local records centres, including those based in or provided for a single business unit, are also possible; but the most efficient use of resources is usually achieved by having a few large centres rather than many small ones.

A records centre should be a defined area that can be physically secured to protect records from unauthorized destruction or access and from natural disasters and human threats. It may be on-site, within a building or complex of buildings used for the substantive functions of the organization, or at an off-site location. Off-site records centres may be managed in-house or a commercially managed facility may be used. If an off-site records centre is chosen, there is usually a need for a small on-site store where records can be held while awaiting collection.

In-house records centres

Figure 6.1 sets out some of the issues to be considered when planning an in-house or directly managed records centre.

Available on-site accommodation is often unsuitable for a records centre. All too frequently, when on-site accommodation is sought, unusable spaces are suggested: basements with service pipes liable to flooding or overheating, awkwardly

- **Storage area**: The optimum size of a records centre can be difficult to estimate, since quantities of records for storage are subject to change over time, but approximations can be obtained from records survey projects. Besides overall capacity, calculations and plans must be made for ceiling heights, shelving dimensions and layout, and ease of access for trolleys or carts. Floors must be capable of bearing the weight of the shelving and the records. There may also be a need for specialized storage areas for non-paper media, with appropriate environmental controls.
- **Transportation and delivery**: Are records to be moved to and from the records centre by portering staff, or will motorized transport be required? Doors must be wide enough to handle the expected size of consignment. A loading bay and freight lifts between floors may be needed.
- **Reception area**: Working space is likely to be needed for processing incoming records and returns of borrowed records.
- **Destruction area**: Space, separate from the reception area, is needed for processing records due for destruction.
- **Office accommodation**: Whether records management staff are based in the records centre or only visit periodically, space must be allocated for their work and for storing stationery and other supplies. Cleaning and washing facilities must also be available.
- **Reference area**: Although most users will want records delivered to their desks some may need to consult records on-site. If so, reference facilities should be provided, with tables, chairs, adequate lighting, copying facilities and computers or microform readers if required. Records centre staff may need similar facilities to search for records or information wanted by users.
- **Media conversion**: Space may be required for staff and equipment for microfilming or digitization.

Fig. 6.1 *Records centre planning issues*

shaped or low-ceilinged rooms that cannot take high-density shelving, storerooms scattered around the building or inaccessible lofts that are cold in winter and hot in summer. However, if on-site storage space with a suitable specification is available, its proximity to office areas will encourage use of the records centre and facilitate access to the records housed there.

Off-site accommodation has many advantages. Records centres can be situated in low-cost locations such as warehouse areas or industrial parks. They can be purpose-built or existing buildings can be converted. Disused premises such as warehouses or factories may already be owned by the organization and be suitable for conversion. Higher levels of security and larger capacity can often be provided if records centres are located off-site.

The main disadvantage of off-site records centres is their distance from users. Transport for incoming and outgoing records must be provided, at additional cost. Requests from users can sometimes be met by sending copies by fax or e-mail, or by providing a telephone enquiry service; but when users want original records delivered a time delay is inevitable. Some distributed organizations successfully manage national or regional records centres, which are typically 75–150 km (50–100 miles) from their users. However, most organizations find that 30 kilometres

(20 miles) or one hour's travelling time is the maximum practical distance. An off-site records centre may also incur higher costs of building maintenance. Dedicated staff are needed, appropriate to the level of service delivered, but staff may be reluctant to work at an isolated location especially if there are few amenities in the area.

Outsourcing

Commercially managed storage can be used to supplement or replace an in-house facility. An organization can contract out the management of its own records centre or rent space in a building owned by a contractor. Rented storage facilities range from self-service to fully serviced; suppliers range from general ware-housing companies to companies that provide specialist records storage and consultancy services. They may be employed if there is a management preference for outsourcing or on cost or convenience grounds. Rented storage is often cheaper and almost always more flexible than using in-house storage areas. Outsourcing is also useful if in-house records centres are full and an overflow store is required, if large quantities of records need storage at short notice or if there are too few records to justify an in-house records centre.

These advantages must be balanced against the loss of control that outsourcing can bring. Much depends on the reliability of the chosen contractor. Standards vary widely, and the cheapest suppliers may not provide an acceptable quality of service. Before entering into an agreement, it is wise to inspect the facilities closely and make a thorough investigation of the level of service provided. Figure 6.2 provides a checklist of issues for consideration.

In addition, any contract must specify precisely what is expected of the supplier, and what penalties will be incurred if the supplier defaults (for example, if requests for records are not met on time). The contract should include a probationary period, and the notice required for termination should be clearly stated together with any termination charges. Ownership of metadata and other documentation (whether provided to the supplier by the customer or created by the supplier while performing the contract) should be vested in the customer. The terms of the contract should also stipulate what documentation the supplier is to create. If documentation is not available when the contract ends, it may be impossible to transfer the records to another supplier or resume in-house management.

Building and storage areas
- Are they of sound construction, clean and well-maintained, with a stable environmental record and space for present and likely future needs?
- Do the storage areas have suitable robust shelving and safe handling devices, with specialist facilities for non-paper media if required?
- What security checks are in place?
- Are each organization's records stored in defined areas which are inaccessible to staff from other organizations?
- Are storage boxes anonymous (marked only with codes)?
- Are the storage areas adequately protected against fire, flood and other hazards (*see* Figure 6.6, pages 208–9)?

Services
- How are transfers arranged? Do the supplier's proprietary storage boxes have to be used?
- What retrieval services are provided for customers? Can individual files be retrieved or only complete boxes? Will the supplier search for information in the records?
- What transportation is used? How quickly can deliveries be made? Is there an express service for urgent requests? What are the normal hours for delivery? What happens out of hours? What back-up services are available?
- Can customers access records at the records centre? Can they authorize access for third parties?
- What are the tracking systems for records? How is misfiling prevented?
- If the supplier is to be responsible for carrying out disposal actions, how are these to be notified? What destruction facilities are used?

Staff
- Are the staff trained and knowledgeable about records management procedures and standards?
- Are they responsive to customers' needs?
- Have they been security vetted?

Costs
- What are the standard charges? What do these include?
- Is insurance provided? Does it cover the risk of losing the evidence and information in the records, rather than just the cost of the storage media? Would additional cover be needed?
- What charges are made for retrievals or other services?
- What are the costs of removing records at or before the termination of the contract?
- How often are charges reviewed?

Fig. 6.2 *Commercially managed storage: checklist*

Choosing a suitable option

A requirements specification should be drawn up, to provide a basis on which to plan an in-house records centre or negotiate with commercial contractors. The choice between the various options depends on a number of factors including the availability of space in buildings owned or occupied by the organization, the quantity of records to be housed and the types of storage media in use. Other factors are the frequency and urgency of retrieval requests, the level of service required and the methods available for transporting records to and from the records centre. The costs of each option may be set against any saving on space, equipment or staff time.

Transfer of records to the records centre

Business units often wait until they have no more space for paper records and a storage crisis is imminent before transferring records to the organization's records centre. However, an effective records management programme should ensure that there is a regular flow of records from business units or registries to the records centre. If regular transfers are combined with the systematic application of retention controls, backlogs need never arise. It can be useful for each business unit to have an agreed annual transfer period, when records for transfer are identified and forwarded.

Many organizations impose a rule that files relating to ongoing business should be closed at agreed intervals (perhaps at the end of the year, or at a fixed period after opening) and continuation files opened to house new items. It is also good practice to close files when they become too large (more than 25 mm or 1 inch thick). After an appropriate period, closed files can then be transferred to alternative storage.

Procedures should be established for business units to follow when transferring records. If a commercially managed records centre is used, it is generally best for all transfers to be co-ordinated by an in-house records manager, rather than allowing each business unit to make separate contact with the commercial supplier.

It is usually the responsibility of operational staff to place files in boxes for transfer and to provide a transfer list of the contents of each box. The records centre supplies suitable boxes and guidelines on filling them. These should include instructions to remove files from hanging folders and pack files in their original sequence. Each box must be marked with a unique identifier, which is either preprinted on the box or added by the business unit at the time of packing. Box identifiers might use a consignment code (for example, HR02/4/10 is box 10 of the fourth consignment from Human Resources transferred in 2002) or a simple running number system (15950 is the 15950th box supplied to business units, or 03/265 the 265th box supplied in 2003).

The records centre also supplies blank forms for compiling the transfer lists that accompany the boxed records. For each consignment, the form asks the business unit to provide the following information:

- name of business unit
- consignment number (optional)

- date of transfer
- box identifiers
- series and file identifier, title and covering dates of each file transferred
- contact details of sender.

If paper forms are used, they should be self-duplicating or photocopied after completion: one copy of the transfer list is kept by the records centre and the other returned to, or retained by, the business unit. If a commercially managed records centre is used, a third copy may be required for the in-house records manager. When boxes arrive in the records management unit, records staff check their contents against the lists before the boxes are shelved or forwarded to the commercial storage facility. If an automated system is used for managing paper records in the records centre, the data from the transfer list are added to it. In a networked environment, business units can have access to electronic forms allowing them to enter the relevant information directly into the automated system. Records centre staff then add other data, including the date when the consignment was received and processed, the name of the person responsible and the code for the shelf location assigned to each box.

Business units often see the task of listing records for transfer as a low priority, and as a result the lists that they supply are frequently inadequate. However, if full descriptive metadata are collected at the time of creation, as recommended in Chapter 4, these can be reused at the point of transfer: metadata assigned when records are created are likely to be of higher quality than metadata collected retrospectively. If metadata are held in an automated records management system while records are current, it should be possible simply to alter the location data in the automated system when the moment of transfer arrives.

One of the key responsibilities of in-house records centres is ensuring that disposal actions (destruction, review, transfer to archival custody) are carried out when due. Commercial facilities may also undertake these tasks if required. Records centres therefore need metadata relating to retention decisions and outstanding disposal actions. In traditional records systems these are supplied by the transferrer or added by records management staff, after comparing the transferred records with an agreed retention schedule. Chapter 5 has suggested how retention metadata can be assigned to records at an earlier stage in their life; it is then necessary to ensure that the existing metadata accompany the records when they are transferred.

Dates when disposal actions are due must be noted on each box or in an external control system. However, the boxing of paper records adds a tier of complexity: retention decisions are normally made at series level and retention metadata are then applied to files within the series, but transfer boxes often contain a variety of files with different disposal actions outstanding. Ideally, all records in each box would have a single disposal action due on a single date, but this is not always possible. In practice the action date for a box may have to be the latest date applicable to any of its contents.

Options for electronic records

The models described above for paper records have their counterparts in electronic records systems. Where computers are networked, the storage of online electronic records can be centralized or decentralized: they can be stored on central servers or distributed between local servers in different parts of the organization. The choice is determined not by issues of accessibility as in the paper world but by the architecture of the organization's computer systems and the extent to which responsibility for information technology is managed centrally or devolved to business units.

These options broadly correspond to the use of central or distributed registries for storing paper records. Online storage by individuals, using the hard disks on their personal computers, corresponds to the storage of paper records at users' desks and should be discouraged for the same reasons. In a networked environment, online storage should be restricted to corporate servers so that appropriate control systems can be maintained.

The transfer of less frequently used paper records to alternative storage can also be paralleled in an electronic system: digital records whose usage rate has declined can be moved from online to offline storage. Servers have limited storage capacity, and computing specialists see transfer to tape or offline disc as a way of moving older files to less expensive media. From the records manager's viewpoint, moving records offline may provide an opportunity to transfer them to media that are more durable or more stable, although access is slower when records are held offline.

The period for which digital records need to be kept online may vary from one series to another. Records of routine processes can often be moved offline fairly quickly; records of creative processes may have to be kept online for longer as they are more likely to be needed for ongoing business. Following the model for paper files, electronic folders can be closed at agreed intervals to facilitate transfer to offline storage.

When offline transfer is controlled or supported by relevant software, it is often called 'hierarchical storage management' by computing specialists. An ERM software application should support the designation of records for offline transfer, by:

- checking records against agreed timetables and prompting the movement of those due for transfer
- identifying records that have not been viewed for a certain period and offering them for transfer
- allowing records management staff to transfer records on demand.

When records are held in databases, the database will eventually grow large as its content accrues. Older records from databases can similarly be retired to offline storage. Co-operation between records managers and database administrators will be needed to ensure that data records are retired systematically and remain accessible when they are offline.

Discs and tapes holding offline records are sometimes stored in the organization's records centre. Human intervention is then required to deliver them to users. If faster access is wanted, they can be stored adjacent to a server on an automatic loading device or robot system (sometimes referred to as a 'jukebox'). Robot systems extract discs or tapes from storage and mount them into a drive in response to a user's request. To users the delay appears minimal, but such systems 'are best described as providing "near-line" access . . . since . . . access times are . . . measured in seconds rather than the milliseconds associated with true online access' (Saffady, 1993, 74).

Managing archives

Some of the organization's records will almost certainly be kept indefinitely, whether for business or cultural reasons. These constitute the organization's *archives*, and their management requires particular care. Guidance on accommodation and facilities for the maintenance of archives is given in BS 5454:2000 *Recommendations for the storage and exhibition of archival documents* and in other texts listed in the Bibliography at the end of this book.

Responsibility for archival records is rarely assigned to business units, whose focus on current operations makes it unlikely that they will wish to make provision for long-term preservation of records. Responsibility may be assigned to the records management unit, a separate in-house archives unit or an external archives service. Where electronic records are to be retained indefinitely, both archival and technical expertise must be available.

If archival records are kept by the records management unit or by an in-house archives unit that is closely linked to it, artificial division of the organization's records can largely be avoided. However, where long-term retention is primarily for cultural reasons, some organizations prefer to pass responsibility to an institution that has a specific mission to acquire and maintain archives for cultural use. For some organizations the choice between in-house retention and transfer to an external archival authority may be determined by legislation. In the case of transfer, adequate metadata or other documentation must accompany the records.

Selecting and using storage media and equipment

Paper: file covers

Covers used for paper files need to be robust and clearly labelled. Within the cover, papers should be secured with fasteners to reduce the risk of their becoming detached or disorganized. To avoid rust, inert plastic fasteners are recommended.

Commercially produced paper and file covers usually have an acidic content that will eventually cause them to degrade, but should suffice for records that have been assigned a short retention period. There should be little difficulty in keeping most paper materials for up to 30 years in a well-ventilated storage area where the temperature does not exceed 27°C (80°F) and the relative humidity is below 60% (National Archives of Australia, 2000). Paper can often survive for much longer in these conditions but for long-term storage a temperature around 16°C (60°F) and relative humidity between 45 and 60%, with minimal fluctuation, is usually recommended (BS 5454:2000, clause 7.3). This means that in temperate climates special environmental controls are unlikely to be needed for paper records with a short lifespan. For records designated for indefinite retention, environmental conditions should be monitored and creators should be encouraged to use paper conforming to ISO 11108:1996 *Information and documentation – archival paper – requirements for permanence and durability*, which will remain stable over a long period.

Boxes

The standard box used in a records centre should take common sizes of records comfortably. Such boxes are usually about 375 mm (15 inches) deep, 300 mm (12 inches) wide and 250 mm (10 inches) high, with an integral or separate lid and hand holes at each end. When fully packed, they weigh about 12 kg (26 lb); larger or heavier boxes may be difficult or unsafe for staff to handle. Boxes for archival records are often smaller and have higher standards of specification including acid-free board and brass staples.

Cabinets and shelving

In choosing equipment such as cabinets and shelving units, the first step is to define the requirements. Figure 6.3 provides a list of relevant questions.

Choosing storage equipment for records

- Is the equipment for an office area (where it may need to match décor or other furniture) or for space dedicated to records storage such as a registry or records centre?
- How much space is required for existing records and for future growth?
- What media will be stored (e.g. paper files, drawings, computer printout, tape, discs, microfilm)? What is their typical size and shape?
- How frequently and how urgently do users need access? How many people need access at one time? Do different series have different requirements?
- Do the records need high levels of security or environmental protection?
- What space is available in the storage area? Are conditions imposed by the shape of a room, maximum floor loading or ceiling heights?
- What budgetary limits apply?

Fig. 6.3   *Storage equipment: checklist*

When requirements have been agreed, the range of equipment (see Figure 6.4) can be considered and a shortlist drawn up, matching the organization's needs to the available options. The equipment chosen should be suited to the space (not all floors can carry bear the weight of mechanized units or mobile racking) and to the records being stored (if shelving is chosen, its depth and width should take standard boxes or files and fit them efficiently). It should also meet security needs, allow safe and easy access for the expected number of users and be cost-effective to purchase, install, maintain and use.

Electronic media

There are two main classes of electronic storage media: *magnetic* (widely used in computing since the 1950s) and *optical* (introduced in the 1980s). In recording on a magnetic storage device, such as a hard or floppy disk, magnetic fields are generated to alter the magnetic state of the device. As well as disks, magnetic recording can use tapes, which may be enclosed in a cassette or cartridge or wound on an open reel. Optical storage uses light generated by laser beams to change the optical properties of the device. Most optical storage products are in disc form: optical tape has been developed but is little used. There are also magneto-optical (MO) discs, which combine magnetic and optical recording.

Optical and MO discs can be purchased in various sizes (measured by the diameter of the disc). They offer storage capacities (measured in megabytes or gigabytes) that are considerably greater than magnetic disks of comparable physical size. At the time of writing, three types of optical discs are available: rewritable, write once

Type of equipment	Characteristics of use
• Filing cabinets	Probably the most common type of current file storage, they are useful for small quantities of records where only one user requires access at any one time. They are lockable but wasteful of space: the backs of drawers are often left empty, and in front of each cabinet a large floor area is required where drawers open and users stand.
• Rotary or carousel units	Shelving units which rotate around a central shaft can be used for small quantities of paper records in ring binders or lever-arch files.
• Lateral cabinets	These are shelved cupboards with doors or roller shutters and are often used in office areas. They use floor space efficiently and can be installed singly or in rows. They can be accessed by more than one user at a time, have adjustable shelving and can provide storage for several types of media in one unit. Roller shutters provide security but can flex or jam. Safety steps may be needed for access to the top shelves.
• Static open racking	A cheaper form of lateral shelving, static open racking is not secure unless installed in a locked area. In offices it may look out of place but in records centres and other less visible areas it provides cost-effective storage. Racking up to 2.5 metres (8 feet) high can be reached from safety steps. Taller racking is possible, but special ladders, catwalks, mezzanine floors, fork lifts or mechanical picking devices will be needed to retrieve records. Where multiple rows of shelving are installed, aisle width is determined by the space required for ladders and other equipment, but should be at least 1 metre (3 feet).
• Mechanized conveyor units	Computer controlled vertical units are designed for use by a single operator, who stays still while the conveyor brings the required shelf within reach of the operator's workstation. They make good use of floor space and ceiling height and can handle large capacities needing frequent retrieval. Security is high but installation and maintenance are expensive, and retrieval is impossible in the event of mechanical breakdown or power failure.
• Mobile racking	Mobile racking is sometimes used for current records, but more commonly for older records. Since only one row or aisle can be accessed at any one time, it is unsuitable for records with high retrieval rates. It provides efficient use of space where large quantities are to be stored, although long rows and tall racks are not possible. It can be mechanically operated or power assisted, and provides some extra security since it can be locked shut.
• Specialist units	Specialist storage units such as plan chests and microfilm cabinets are available in various sizes, but usually have to be purchased from specialist suppliers.

Fig. 6.4   *Cabinets and shelving: the main types*

and read only. Figure 6.5 summarizes the characteristics of each type. There are mass-market consumer formats – CD (compact disc) and DVD (digital versatile disc) – as well as more specialist formats for business use.

Magnetic and optical media can both be used for online and offline storage. Online storage devices are usually chosen by computing specialists, and the need for fast and simultaneous access normally means that fixed magnetic hard disks are employed. In a networked environment, there is usually an array of hard disks attached to a central server. Newer options include *network attached storage*, where the disks are installed in a dedicated storage appliance connected to the network and usually

Type of disc	Characteristics	Examples
• Rewritable	Discs are erasable and reusable. Contents can be modified.	CD and DVD rewritable MO rewritable
• Write once	Discs are non-erasable. Despite their name, further recording is possible if there is unused space on these discs, but existing contents cannot be altered.	WORM (write once, read many times) CD and DVD recordable (CD-R, DVD-R) MO write once (CCW or CC-WORM)
• Read only	A publishing medium. Users cannot write to discs, but can only read the published contents.	CD-ROM, DVD-ROM

Fig. 6.5   *Optical discs*

accessed through a web browser. Storage is also available from remote providers using the internet, but at the time of writing this is an immature market offering few guarantees of stability.

Records managers are more likely to be concerned with the choice of offline media. From a records management viewpoint, speed of access is usually less important than the reliability of the media themselves and of the drives that are needed to write to and read them. New storage devices appear almost every year, but untried products should generally be avoided: it is better to wait until their reliability is proven.

Capacity may also be an issue, especially if images are to be stored. An image of a documentary record may require more than ten times as much disc space as the same document stored as text characters. Although each new generation of storage media offers greater capacity, numerous discs or tapes may still be required if there are large quantities of records.

Longevity is a further factor, but available information on this subject is based only on laboratory tests by manufacturers and not on experience in the real world. Manufacturers have claimed that rewritable optical discs will last between 10 and 40 years, while CD-R and CD-ROM are often claimed to have a life expectancy of 100 years or more. In practice the accuracy of such predictions may be immaterial, since it is unlikely that equipment to read these discs will still be available in 50 or 100 years' time and the records will need to be copied to another storage device long before this.

Magnetic tape also has an expected lifespan of several decades. Compared with most optical media, it can offer high capacity at lower cost. Its reliability is known and its continuing availability may be less subject to the vagaries of the marketplace. However, it is vulnerable to high humidity and fluctuations in temperature, and may be corrupted if exposed to other magnetic fields. Unlike discs, tape only allows serial access, which is likely to be slow. It is almost always suitable for back-up copies of records held online, but its suitability for records formally retired to offline storage may depend on the urgency of users' needs for retrieval.

Optical discs are rarely suitable for the highest storage volumes, but provide faster access than tape and higher capacity than magnetic disks. Although they may be prone to abrasion and scratches from careless handling, they are unaffected by magnetic fields and less vulnerable than tape to extremes of temperature and humidity. The choice between different optical formats is not easy: write once or read only formats are often preferred because they offer protection against alteration of records, but WORM discs are expensive, while the complex process for producing read only discs means that records for transfer must be sent to a specialist production unit. At the time of writing CD-R discs are cheap, easy to use and widely available, but may be less robust than read only or WORM discs.

Digital storage is an area of rapid change but up-to-date information may be found on the websites of trade associations such as the Computing Suppliers Federation, www.csf.org.uk/, or the Optical Storage Technology Association, www.osta.org/.

Any storage device that is chosen should be tested before use. As a further precaution against failure of a storage device it is wise to keep duplicate copies of electronic records, perhaps using discs or tapes from different manufacturers. Discs and tapes should be housed in inert plastic cases, tightly closed to keep out dust particles and stored vertically on shelving or in metal cabinets. Optical discs should be labelled on their cases: attaching labels or writing on the discs themselves should be avoided. The contents of each disc or tape should include an internal label so that it can be identified if its physical label becomes detached.

Storage location control

When storing paper records, a system for location control must be devised. This requires every file or box and every storage location (cabinet, drawer, shelf or other unit of storage space) to be labelled with a unique identifier. As noted in Chapter 4, the identifier of a file may be a title or a numeric or alphanumeric code; for boxes and shelves the identifier must be a code.

Decisions are needed on the order in which the files or boxes are placed on the shelves or in the cabinets; the identifier is the key to their physical arrangement. Similar decisions are needed about the order of papers within a file cover.

In each case the sequence can be chronological, numerical, alphabetical or random. Papers within a file are often stored in chronological order, to show the sequence of activity, while current files are often stored in numerical or alphabetical order within each series.

Storing files in *numerical or alphanumerical order of coded identifiers* normally means that newly opened files are housed together at the end of the sequence, and this in turn concentrates filing activity in one part of the storage area. A variation on the standard numerical sequence is *terminal digit filing*, where (typically) six-digit numeric codes are divided into three pairs of digits and the primary filing order is determined by the last pair (Kallaus and Johnson, 1992, 183–7). Congestion is reduced because sequentially numbered records are distributed rather than stored together. Terminal digit filing is less practical with alphanumeric codes.

Storing files in *alphabetical order of file titles* requires a set of *alphabetical filing rules* to determine areas of potential ambiguity, such as whether the filing sequence is letter by letter (*Newcastle* before *New York*) or word by word (*New York* before *Newcastle*), and the handling of hyphenated words, abbreviations and complex personal or corporate names. Standards for alphabetical filing include ISO 12199:2000 *Alphabetical ordering of multilingual terminological and lexicographical data represented in the Latin alphabet* and ANSI/ARMA 1-1997 *Alphabetic filing rules*. Filing alphabetically by file title is rarely ideal, since newly opened files have to be inserted in the middle of an existing sequence, which often necessitates readjusting the contents of cabinets or shelving units to make space for accruals.

Storing records in *random physical order* is possible provided that the logical order is maintained in system documentation. Records to be shelved are assigned the next available space and location information is maintained in a database, usually in association with barcode technology for rapid data entry: barcoded identifiers on records are matched to barcodes on the shelves by swiping each barcode with a portable scanner. When a record is borrowed its storage location may be reallocated and a new location assigned to the record on its return. Using random storage, reshelving is much faster than when an alphabetical or numerical sequence is used. Random storage is also more efficient in its use of space, and there is no need to adjust shelving arrangements when accruals arrive or when existing records are removed or destroyed. Random order is sometimes used for current paper files but is more commonly used for boxes in records centres, as an alternative to storing each consignment together. It has the advantage of anonymity and thus offers security from unauthorized access, but it can make stocktaking difficult and legitimate browsing impossible.

If a single storage area is used to house more than one record series, or records from more than one functional area or business unit, finding aids are needed to point users to the relevant locations. When files within a series are arranged in alphabetical or numerical sequence, users who know the unique identifier of a file can then find its exact location fairly rapidly. If some other sequence is used, users will require a finding aid to discover the location of a particular file, and retrieval is necessarily slower. Finding aids may take the form of a location list, register, index or database, and may also be integrated with classification schemes or other metadata about the records. Finding aids in records centres match shelf location identifiers with box identifiers and may be integrated with other manual or automated tools for records centre management.

Paper records of abnormal size or shape may have to be stored separately from the main sequence. When an item is stored separately from the file to which it logically belongs, a cross-reference should be placed in the file concerned; files stored separately from the rest of a series can have a marker on the shelf or in the cabinet. In both cases the special storage arrangements should also be indicated in the finding aids for the relevant storage areas or in the metadata systems used to document physical and logical relationships.

The issues discussed in this section are chiefly relevant to paper records. In the electronic environment software applications normally take care of location control without any need for human intervention. Although a set of retrieved records will be presented to users in a given sequence this does not reflect the underlying storage arrangements, and the sequence of presentation can normally be re-sorted at will. Records staff do not need to maintain manual data about the location of records, unless they are held on offline discs or tapes that need to be physically retrieved from storage.

Conversion to an alternative medium

Why convert?

An organization may have a number of reasons for deciding that records created in one medium should be converted to another. Conversion can eliminate mixed media retention systems, enhance durability or improve the security of records. It can also facilitate access to their information content or reduce the space that they occupy.

Converting from paper

Organizations have used microform (microfilm and microfiche) as an alternative to paper since the 1920s. Microfilming is a well-established technique, and with careful storage 'archival' silver-gelatin film has a long life (though probably not as long as the best quality paper). Microform copies typically occupy 2% of the space required for paper storage, and it is easy to make further copies if required. However, access tends to be slow and microform is often disliked by users.

During the 1990s digitization developed rapidly as an alternative to microfilming. To convert paper records to digital form, flatbed scanners are normally used. A digital camera may be used if records are of unusual size or shape or if bound volumes are to be digitized. Digitization creates a bitmapped image, which can be stored on computer media and viewed on screen. However, the computer cannot recognize the textual content of the image unless optical character recognition (OCR) techniques are employed.

In comparison with microform, digital imaging offers faster and more sophisticated retrieval, facilitates the sharing of images between users and often provides better image quality. It can also be undertaken earlier in the life of a record. While microform conversion is best done when record-creating activity has ceased and no further papers are to be added to existing files or series, digitization is possible at the point of capture: if desired, records can be scanned individually on receipt or on completion of the business activity, as an alternative to bulk digitization later in life. The chief disadvantage of digital imaging is its level of dependence on rapidly changing technology.

It is also possible to combine microform and digital solutions. When paper records are digitized *en bloc* it is relatively simple to add a further process that makes additional copies on microform for security purposes or as a possible safeguard against technology obsolescence. Microform to digital conversion is also available, either in bulk or by converting individual microform images on demand.

Microfilming and digitization incur high initial capital costs, which must be weighed against benefits expected later:

1 If space saving is the objective, conversion decisions for paper records should take account of agreed retention periods. When records are to be retained only for a short time, the cost of conversion is almost certain to be higher than the cost of storing the originals. When records are to be retained indefinitely, the substitution of copies for the paper originals may prove mistaken if the copies use inferior media and do not survive, or if their long-term accessibility is compromised. Media conversion is often most appropriate for paper records that are to be retained for a medium term rather than those with continuing long-term value.

2 If conversion is proposed for access purposes, the reference requirement must be shown to justify the cost. When space saving is not at issue, the originals need not be destroyed after conversion: there are often accountability or cultural requirements for preserving original paper records even when business needs are met by microform or digital copies.

Converting from digital formats

Media conversion is also possible for records that are 'born digital'. As noted in Chapter 1, the low-risk strategy of transferring electronic records to paper has many limitations but still has its place, especially for organizations that do not have the technical skills or infrastructure to guarantee preservation of access to digital media.

Other options used in larger organizations are *computer output microform* (COM) and *computer output to laser disc* (COLD). Both are used primarily for handling large quantities of output from data-centric computer systems. They take online data that no longer need to be computer-processable and commit them to microform or optical disc in report format. Where the volume of data is sufficient to justify the initial outlay on equipment, they provide a cost-effective alternative to paper printout. COLD offers superior retrieval features in the short term but COM is usually recommended if the data are to be retained for more than ten years (Stephens and Wallace, 1997, 18).

Policies and procedures

If a case is made for media conversion, some policy decisions are required. Questions to consider include:

- Which records are to be converted?
- At what stage in their life does conversion take place?
- Which new media are to be used?
- Are the originals to be preserved after conversion?
- How long are the copies to be retained?

These decisions can be documented in a separate policy statement or the relevant metadata can be incorporated into a retention schedule or classification scheme. A decision is also needed on whether to employ an external bureau or an in-house facility. Outsourcing requires a careful choice of supplier and a tightly worded contract. In-house conversion usually provides better security and quality control, but may cost more. The British Standards Institution has published BS 6660:1985 *Guide to setting up and maintaining micrographics units* and PD 0016:2001 *Guide to scanning business documents*, which offer useful guidance.

In any conversion it is essential that the context of records is preserved as well as their content. Digitization at the point of records capture allows contextual information to be collected when the records are classified, as discussed in Chapters 3 and 4. When conversion takes place at a later stage, the records will already be classified and the existing metadata and any file or folder structure must be carried over. Conversion also provides an opportunity to verify the existing metadata and rectify any errors or omissions. Additional metadata will also be required: the authority for conversion, the date, the individuals responsible for the work, details of the new media, the physical state of the original records at the time of conversion and technical metadata on the conversion process. The unique identifier of the records converted must be noted and a new identifier assigned to the copy. Operational procedures and quality control measures should be logged as they are carried out; other metadata may be assigned when the work is complete.

Legal issues

Media conversion usually focuses on the preservation or use of the *information* that records contain. The microfilming or digitization of a paper record substitutes a copy for an original and diminishes its value as *evidence*. Nevertheless, as noted in Chapter 2, copies are increasingly admissible as *legal evidence* in courts of law. In many judicial systems copies are normally admitted unless it can be shown that a litigant possesses the original but has failed to produce it. On the other hand, opponents in legal disputes may challenge the conversion process, claiming that those responsible for it have inadvertently or maliciously failed to create true copies of the originals.

Well-documented conversion programmes help to ensure that copies will be given due weight as legal evidence. Good practice requires organizations to maintain evidence of:

1 *Corporate policy on media conversion.* If conversion forms a regular part of a records management programme, it should be possible to demonstrate that copies were made in the normal course of business. Even for one-off conversion projects, the existence of a written policy makes it easier to show that there were good reasons for making copies.
2 *Trustworthy operational procedures.* If an imaging unit employs trained staff who have no direct interest in the business activities that gave rise to the records,

and maintains full documentation of the conversion process, 'it should be relatively easy to persuade the court that the imaging facility is above suspicion' (Smith, 1996, 73).

3 *Random or comprehensive quality checks,* perhaps by an independent third party, to show that nothing has omitted or falsified. Certificates verifying that images are complete and accurate can be filmed or scanned along with the records, but the trustworthiness of images cannot truly be judged while imaging is still in progress. A final certification should be made when imaging is finished.

In many cases, organizations wish to destroy the originals when conversion is complete. Few jurisdictions prohibit the destruction of originals after copying, but the courts may seek proof that it was done without any intention to conceal potentially damaging evidence. The existence of an agreed retention and disposal policy, and of documentation showing that original records were destroyed in accordance with that policy, will be usually be accepted as providing a satisfactory reason for producing a copy in court.

Some authorities (such as Hamer, 1996, 25) recommend that originals should be retained in cases where the law requires transactions to be in writing. Depending on the jurisdiction, such requirements may relate to contracts for goods over a certain value, credit transactions or purchases of land or shares. In most jurisdictions the meaning of 'writing' in this context has not been fully tested in the courts; but while 'writing' generated digitally may be acceptable, records that have been converted from one medium to another are perhaps more likely to be rejected. It may also be wise to keep originals that are of poor quality (to show that a poor quality image accurately represents the original) or contain amendments or alterations that are indistinct on the copy.

Besides taking advice from legal experts, organizations can follow published guidance, such as the UK standard BS 6498:2002 *Guide to preparation of microfilm and other microforms that may be required as evidence* or PD 0008:1999 *Code of practice for legal admissibility and evidential weight of information stored electronically.*

Preserving electronic records over time

Challenges of maintaining electronic records

Digital storage media are likely to deteriorate much more quickly than traditional media such as paper and microform, and discs and tape should be inspected and read at intervals to check for any signs of decay. They can easily be damaged by exposure to dust, direct sunlight, chemical gases or traffic fumes. BS 4783:1988 recommends a constant temperature between 18 and 22°C (64–71°F), and constant relative humidity between 35 and 45%, for the long-term storage of digital media. Failure to observe these recommendations may shorten the life of a disc or tape, but in practice transferring records to new media is often easier than maintaining precisely controlled environmental conditions.

Such transfers can be seen as a further form of media conversion, but they must be distinguished from the conversions discussed in the previous section. With a paper record, the medium and the record are inseparable, and media conversion creates a copy that is intrinsically different from the original object. A digital record is not a physical object but a set of electronic signals that can be moved from one medium to another: the medium and the record are separable. If a copy is made, it is likely to be indistinguishable from the original. Such copying is sometimes known as 'refreshing' the storage media. If it is done in the course of an established records management programme, it should carry minimal risk to the evidential value of records.

The rapid rate of change within the computing industry also makes digital media liable to obsolescence. The width of a standard floppy disk, for example, was progressively reduced from 8 inches to 3.5 inches between the 1970s and 1990s, and disk drives for the older sizes became difficult to obtain or use within a few years of each change; records stored on older disks thus became inaccessible on most computer systems. For all these reasons, effective management of digital records requires systematic procedures for transferring them to new media before the old media become unusable.

However, effective preservation of electronic records requires more than a systematic approach to managing hardware dependency. Even if the correct hardware is available records will not be readable without a software application that can understand them; yet software technologies are even more subject to obsolescence than hardware. Most new software releases are superseded within two or three years of their first appearance. 'The general rule is that the longevity of storage media is greater than the longevity of the storage media drives, and that the longevity of the . . . drives is greater than that of the software' (Dollar, 1999, 86).

Short-term solutions

Suppliers of commercial software products commonly provide a degree of *backward compatibility*: a new version can accept files from previous generations of the software and read them in the current version. This is an acceptable access route while manufacturers maintain support, but is not robust in the longer term. Commercial pressures lead manufacturers to phase out support for older software formats, in order to promote sales of their latest products.

Suppliers also provide increasing levels of *interoperability*: some software products can interpret records created in current or earlier versions of another application designed for a similar purpose (for example, one word-processing package may be able to read records created in another).

Backward compatibility and interoperability can be used to provide access in the short term, but neither is reliable for more than a few years, and both can sometimes distort or lose elements of structure, formatting or content. To maintain accessibility in the longer term, other techniques are needed.

Electronic document management and electronic records management packages usually provide *generic viewers* or *browsers*, which allow a user to view documents in their native format without launching an application. These tools purport to read documents in almost any widely used format. They can often handle documentary records created using mainstream commercial software ten or more years previously; but they are usually unsuitable for records that take the form of data rather than documents, and should probably not be relied on for documentary records created using less well-known software or whose retention period extends into or beyond a second decade. Generic viewers are themselves subject to obsolescence and must be upgraded as new software formats appear on the market.

Seeking a longer-term strategy

Short-term accessibility tools will suffice for recently created records, but do not address longer-term issues of preservation and access. There are several possible approaches to the problem of technology obsolescence for electronic records that are to be retained for an extended period of time. Some currently proposed strategies seek to preserve intact the streams of electronic signals ('bitstreams') that ultimately underlie all electronic records, while providing access by maintaining or imitating original technologies; others rely on the migration or reformatting of records to use new technology.

None of these strategies is risk-free; all require maintenance and resources over time. The choice between them depends on the requirements and capabilities of the organization and the nature of the records: how many different types of records there are, the length of time for which they are to be kept, the hardware and software environments in which they were created, the extent to which users want to preserve or re-create the original experience of seeing and using records as they were when newly created, and the extent to which they want to take advantage of new technology to gain access to records and exploit them in innovative ways. At the time of writing, the most affordable and effective strategies are largely restricted to records created using simpler technologies or those with a relatively short lifespan; for records that depend on more complex technology, long-term solutions remain elusive.

Maintaining or imitating original technology

At the simplest level, *technology preservation* seeks to maintain working instances of hardware and operating systems and of the software applications in which records were created. The maintenance of computer 'museums' is widely recognized as impractical as a long-term solution because of the growing range and complexity of technology that would have to be kept running when specialists with appropriate technical knowledge are unlikely to be available. However, technology preservation could be viable in the short term, for records whose agreed retention period does not extend beyond the time for which old technology can be expected to remain in working order.

A more sophisticated approach is *emulation*: the writing of programs that allow the behaviour of specific outdated hardware, operating systems or software to be mimicked on current platforms. Of these, the most viable is probably emulation of hardware to run original software and operating systems (Rothenberg, 1999). Like technology preservation, emulation preserves the original 'look and feel' of records, but relies on scarce skills and is expensive to develop and maintain. It also depends on access to the specifications of the original technology, which are proprietary to, and may not be released by, the manufacturers (Bearman, 1999). Emulation has not been fully tested as a records management solution and is unlikely to be a practical option for most organizations.

Preserving electronic records through migration

At the time of writing, the most practical preservation strategy is probably *migration*: the transfer of records 'from one hardware/software configuration to another, or from one generation of computer technology to a subsequent generation' (Waters and Garrett, 1996, 6). Migration modifies the bitstreams of electronic records so that they can be interpreted by current software. Records are maintained initially in their native computing environment, then moved to new platforms in response to technological change. Migration offers the advantage that it is a concept widely understood by computing professionals, although they usually perceive it in terms of migrating particular computer systems with their associated data, rather than migrating records that derive from defined processes but may have been created in diverse computing environments.

At its simplest, migration is achieved when a software application takes records from previous versions of the software (using backward compatibility), or from another application with which it interoperates, and saves them in its current version. Alternatively, records can be exported to a common interchange format such as Rich Text Format (RTF) and then imported into a current application. For more complex migrations, a commercially available migration program may be used; if no adequate program exists, a special program must be written. A migration program should read records in their present format, analyse differences with the proposed new format, report any risk of mismatch and provide documentation of the completed migration process; but commercial programs often lack some of these features (Wheatley, 2001). While simple migrations are usually easy to perform, successful migration of records created in complex or unusual computing environments is much more difficult.

If a migration strategy is chosen, records will need to be migrated at intervals throughout their life. At each migration some degradation is inevitable, and any links or other features not supported in the new format will be lost. The risk is that after repeated migrations the integrity of records may be difficult or impossible to demonstrate. To reduce the risk, the fidelity of the migration process should be tested on a sample of records before any non-migrated copies are destroyed. A further precaution is to keep records in both migrated and non-migrated form. In addition, the existence of migration policies and documented procedures will allow future users to discover why and how migration was carried out. A migration *Risk assessment workbook*, produced by a team at Cornell University, is available at www.clir.org/pubs/reports/pub93/AppendixA.pdf.

Migration can be employed in two modes: 'evolution' in which records are migrated at frequent intervals as technological developments occur, and 'leapfrog' in which records are held in old formats until they are almost obsolete and then moved forward to a leading edge technology. 'Evolution' can be costly, but 'leapfrogging' is risky if migration is left too late. In either case, it is often difficult to identify the optimum timing. Organizing migration may be relatively easy for records of routine processes, since these are typically carried out within a single software environment, but more difficult for records of creative processes that employ a range of software products. If records generated using different software applications are stored together to reflect their common functional origin, migration strategies are complicated because some records are likely to require migrating before others.

Metadata about records needing migration should be maintained in association with retention metadata, to ensure that records that are to be retained are migrated when required and that resources are not wasted on migrating records whose retention period has expired. Migration schedules can also be combined with timetables for the refreshing of physical storage media.

Using standard logical formats

Migration does not necessarily shift records into dependency on newer versions of the software used to create them. It is often preferable to select a small number of standard formats and to move each record into one of these formats for preservation. Where possible, such formats should be platform independent and non-proprietary. Ideally, proprietary formats should be used only if they are 'open' formats whose specification is in the public domain. Non-proprietary or open formats are subject to obsolescence, but usually at a slower pace than most commercial formats.

Conversion to a standard format may occur at capture, when records are moved offline or when they are transferred to an external agency such as an archival institution. Records in standard formats should require fewer migrations, and these should be less complex to administer because fewer formats are involved. Costs are reduced, especially if the scheduling and initiation of migration can be automated; and over time there is a lower risk of degradation from repeated migrations.

Different formats will be needed for textual and non-textual records. For textual records, the choice of a standard format may depend on how far their visual presentation needs to be preserved as well as their context, content and logical structure. Plain text files, typically using the ASCII or Unicode character sets, provide one option but are rarely ideal: they are stripped of all proprietary control codes but at the cost of a loss of structure, formatting or other functionality that is often unacceptable. Records in the form of data can be converted to plain text in comma separated files, but for documentary records it may be necessary to choose a proprietary but semi-open format such as PostScript or its display-oriented derivative Portable Document Format (PDF). For bitmapped images, the recommended format at the time of writing is Tag Image File Format (TIFF); this was also developed as a proprietary format and has been released in numerous versions, but substantial parts of its specification are publicly available.

A non-proprietary solution for some textual records is provided by Extensible

Markup Language (XML), which can be used with plain text files to capture logical structure and associated with a stylesheet to maintain visual presentation. XML is not a file format but an encoding language supported by the World Wide Web Consortium, www.w3c.org/, which is committed to its ongoing maintenance and platform independence. Unfortunately the assignment of XML markup to existing records is often a complex task. It may be relatively straightforward for record series where each item is homogeneous and consistently structured, but is likely to be prohibitively expensive for records whose structure does not conform to a defined pattern.

Applying open formats for records retention may become easier in future if technology suppliers make more use of recognized standards in the software products employed for records creation. The use of XML, for example, is greatly simplified if it can be applied during the creation process rather than retrospectively. This is likely to become increasingly feasible for records in the form of data, as XML-compliant databases are introduced and XML is adopted as a standard for electronic commerce and for data capture using electronic forms. In addition, XML editing tools are often used to create procedural and technical manuals. Web pages are usually created using HyperText Markup Language (HTML), which is related to XML but is a more volatile standard and may be less suitable for longer-term preservation. For most other documentary records, creation in XML or other non-proprietary formats is usually impractical at present; but this may change if open standards become more widely supported in word-processing and other office applications.

Sometimes it can be appropriate to preserve more than one copy of a record using a different format for each copy: for example, both a plain text file and a digitized image might be kept. Separate preservation and viewing formats may also be needed. In the case of images, uncompressed formats such as TIFF should be used for preservation but are generally unsuitable as delivery formats, while compressed formats may be employed to provide users with accessible copies.

Metadata and preservation

Whichever preservation strategy is adopted, metadata about the technological dependencies of each record will be needed; if a migration strategy is chosen, these must be supplemented by metadata about migrations scheduled and carried out. Systematic collection of preservation metadata requires appropriate planning when records management systems are designed. For example, acceptable standard formats for each series can be designated and documented when classification schemes are drawn up, provided these are updated regularly to take account of any necessary changes.

As well as the records themselves, the metadata that support their maintenance, interpretation and use must also be preserved and accessible over time. Whether records are digital or in paper form, the relevant metadata must remain associated with them through any changes to their storage arrangements. Moreover, the threats to digital records from technological obsolescence apply equally to metadata held in digital form and appropriate countermeasures are essential: the best precaution is often to hold metadata in, or ensure their convertibility to, plain text or XML. Full contextual information must be preserved for the life of each record; if contextual information about digital records depends in part on an electronic folder structure this too must be preserved when records are migrated.

Most digital objects carry some descriptive information of a technical nature, and some digital formats allow the embedding of additional metadata by the user; but most formats do not provide internal support for the range of metadata needed for records management, and such metadata often have to be stored separately from the records to which they relate. However, there is then a risk that the link between records and metadata may be broken, particularly when records are transferred from one computing environment to another. If this happens, records become unmanageable or unusable.

Object-oriented technology can largely eliminate this risk by allowing records and their associated metadata to be bundled or encapsulated in a single container. The Public Record Office Victoria, Australia, is experimenting with this approach: XML metadata and electronic records in native or PDF format are encapsulated within an XML wrapper (Heazlewood et al., 1999). In the USA, the National Archives and Records Administration is investigating the use of XML and object-oriented strategies to preserve records by transforming them to persistent self-describing objects (Thibodeau, Moore and Baru, 2000). These initiatives have a wider aim than simply ensuring that metadata and records are tightly bound. If successful, they may overcome many of the limitations of existing methods of preservation.

Protecting records against loss, misplacement or alteration

The need for appropriate safeguards

Records must be protected against long-term loss or temporary misplacement. To ensure their integrity, appropriate measures must also be taken to protect them from unauthorized alteration.

Physical security measures for storage areas and computing infrastructures are discussed later in this chapter (see Figure 6.6, pages 208–9). They can offer protection against natural disasters and against unauthorized access or damage by unlawful intruders, but not against malicious acts or carelessness on the part of staff or others who have legitimate access to records.

Various options are available for securing records against misplacement, loss or alteration by individuals who have access to them. High levels of assurance can be expensive and an assessment of costs, risks and benefits is likely to be required. The degree of protection afforded to the records of each function or process will depend on the needs of the organization and the level of risk that it is prepared to accept.

Protecting paper records against loss or misplacement while in use

Steps to avoid temporary misplacement or long-term loss are linked to procedures for documenting borrowers and users of paper files, and for ensuring that records are replaced correctly on their return. Whenever a file or box is removed from storage, whether for borrowing or for rapid consultation and immediate return, the loan should be documented. Loans are normally initiated by the completion of a record request form, on paper or electronically, giving details of the requester, the unique identifier of the file or box required and the date of the request. Records staff may key the data from paper request forms into a database or records management software application; electronic forms may submit data directly to the database.

When records are removed from storage it is good practice to obtain the signature of the person who will take responsibility for their safekeeping. Records management applications may generate delivery notes, which can be signed by users on receipt of records. Alternatively, users may be asked to sign a copy of the paper request form.

The movement and return of records must be tracked effectively so that they can be found whenever they are required. Manual methods include:

- charge-out registers or file movement cards, where entries are made on the dates of borrowing and return
- tracer cards or request forms left on shelves or in boxes or filing cabinets in place of borrowed records; these also ensure that returned records are replaced in the correct location.

Request forms can be created in duplicate so that, when records are removed from storage, copies of the completed forms can travel with them. If a label addressed to the borrower (with wording such as 'Please return this file to the registry when you have finished using it') is securely attached to all records on loan, the risk of loss is reduced.

Records removed from storage may be passed from one user to another, and these movements should also be tracked. Users can be asked to complete a transfer form when records are passed on, and to send it to the records staff so that the charge-out documentation can be updated. To enforce this procedure, users must be made aware that they are formally responsible for the safekeeping of records issued to them until a transfer form has been completed to assign responsibility to another user.

There are broadly three models for the return of records to storage:

1 Users (or secretarial assistants) personally replace the records they have borrowed.
2 Users return records to dedicated filing staff who then replace them in storage.
3 Filing staff visit offices and workstations and actively seek records which users no longer require.

The employment of dedicated filing staff usually means that fewer records are misfiled. Where necessary, checks can be made to ensure that the contents of each file are in good order before it is replaced in storage. Regular visits to users help to ensure prompt returns but are labour-intensive.

Whichever model is chosen, there should be a formal mechanism for following up borrowed records after an agreed period. Recall notices can be sent to users listing each file or box which is overdue, with a request that it should be returned if no longer needed; users can also be given the option to confirm that they still have the file or box and to indicate how long they want to hold it, or to identify another user to whom it has been passed.

Records staff can also provide a 'bring forward' service, where a diary system is maintained to allow users to request records for follow-up action at a future date. A service of this kind can encourage users to return records to storage rather than keeping them at their desks until the action is complete.

Manual systems have often worked well in the past and can still be used, but in a paper records system of any size it is now usual for these tracking procedures to be supported by a records management software application. Such applications can register the issue and return of records, and can help to keep track of their movement from one user to another. Details of authorized users and their access rights can be managed within the application, and 'bring forward' dates and other reminders can be generated automatically. Searching and reporting tools can provide information about records issued to particular users, records issued or returned on particular dates or within a range of dates, or records that have not been returned or are overdue. When a records management application is used in association with barcoding technology, issues and returns are recorded by swiping barcodes and keyboard entry is minimized. Many of these features are identical to those found in library loan systems. Unlike library systems, however, records management applications often need to handle loans at different levels of aggregation: they must support the loan of an entire box or a single file from within the box.

Even when a records management software application is in use, tracking procedures must be followed meticulously if paper records are not to be lost. Misfiling is easy if staff are careless, and it is common for records not to be returned when they are finished with, or for files to be passed to colleagues without updating the charge-out information. To check for misfiled or missing records, regular stocktaking of storage areas is usually needed. This can be reinforced by periodic 'desk audits' of records on the desks of operational staff. Barcode scanning is often used to speed up stocktaking in storage and office areas. An alternative is to use radio frequency tagging technology: files are fitted with transponders so that their location at any given moment can be displayed on a computer screen.

Protecting paper records against alteration

Tracking procedures offer safeguards against the misplacement of paper files but cannot prevent users from losing individual items within files or making illicit alterations to them. Paper items have traditionally been hard to amend without detection, but the advent of digital photocopiers has made such tampering relatively easy. The removal of an item from a paper file, whether intentionally or inadvertently, is even easier.

Limited countermeasures are available. Items with signatures, stamps or seals are more difficult to alter undetected than those which consist only of typescript or computer printout. Protection against counterfeit is also possible using holograms, but in practice this is only suitable for a small number of record types such as certificates and licences. Detailed listing of file contents and sequential numbering of pages within a file can offer some protection against the removal of individual sheets, although these methods serve to detect rather than prevent such losses. Stronger measures such as providing access only under supervision, or issuing users with surrogate copies in place of original records, are not always feasible but are usually effective.

Ensuring the integrity of electronic records

In contrast with the paper environment, where the physical handling of records means that most systems are necessarily insecure to some extent, a well-planned digital system can offer high levels of security. Offline storage media handled by users need to be tracked in much the same way as paper, but when electronic records are accessible online the problems associated with tracking paper files are eliminated. Online records can be viewed by authorized users without the need to move physical objects from one location to another. They can be routed among users, or viewed simultaneously by multiple users, without any risk of misplacement.

Electronic systems can also combine ease of user access with appropriate guarantees against unauthorized amendment or deletion. Software applications that are not designed to support records management may provide few controls, but when records management features are designed into an electronic system the degree of protection is normally much higher than in the paper world.

A simple approach used by many systems is to have *software controls* that allow end-users to access records but not edit or delete them, while records management staff may destroy records but not edit them. Such controls can sometimes be circumvented by skilled or determined users but are sufficient in many situations.

This approach may be combined with the use of an *audit trail*. Audit trails automatically log the date and the identity of the operator when records are captured or metadata assigned, and may log similar information whenever records are accessed. When any changes are made (for example, when metadata are edited or records deleted) these too are logged so that it is possible to show that only authorized changes have occurred.

An audit trail is a record and audit log files must themselves be rendered noneditable. Especially with workflow systems, such files can quickly become very large: retention requirements for audit log data must be assessed and retention periods set for them.

If further security is required, *non-rewritable optical storage media* can be used. Write once and read only optical discs are designed to allow users to consult stored materials without being able to modify or delete them. Some write once discs rely on software tools to disable editing commands, but these are less secure than discs that make physical changes to their surface when recording occurs so that further alteration is impossible. Use of such media effectively freezes records at the point of capture. This solution works equally for records 'born digitally' and for those that have been converted using digital imaging techniques.

Non-rewritable media remove the risk of tampering but loss, concealment or theft of a whole disc remains a possibility. Authorized destruction can also seem problematic: one approach is to store records with different destruction dates on separate discs, since it will be impossible to remove records from a single disc at different times. A simple alternative is to copy the records that are still needed onto a new disc so that the disc containing the obsolete records can be destroyed.

The integrity of electronic records can also be protected by using *cryptographic techniques*:

1   At a basic level, it is possible to apply mathematical algorithms to the bitstream that underlies an electronic record, in order to derive a *hash value* or *checksum* that is effectively unique to the record concerned. If the record is modified in any way, a different hash value will be generated when the algorithm is reapplied. This does not prevent alterations to the record, but it does provide a mechanism for detecting changes after the event.

2   A stronger solution is to encrypt the hash value using *asymmetric cryptography*. Two linked keys, known as 'public' and 'private' keys, are employed and each key decrypts what has been encrypted by the other. The private key is kept secret but the public key is made freely available. The use of the private key to encrypt the hash value creates a digital signature, which can also serve to prove that the encryption can only have been undertaken by the holder of the private key.

Asymmetric cryptography is used for security in electronic commerce, where it relies on trusted third party services known as certification authorities, which register public keys and certify the identity of their owners. There are also trusted third party services that issue time and date stamp certificates, and digital notarization instruments, which can be applied to records where absolute evidence of dating or witnessing is essential. Digital time stamping may be critical for records such as contracts or agreements that are to remain in force for a number of years, if these are to be kept in electronic form.

If cryptography is used to support the integrity of records, the cryptographic tools must themselves be preserved over time. The services provided by certification authorities rarely take account of longer-term needs for key retention. Records managers are likely to have to make their own provision for preserving public and private keys and details of algorithms used to calculate hash values. These need to be maintained in conjunction with the records, but for security purposes they should be stored separately from the records to which they relate.

It is also possible to encrypt the text of the record itself. Records of confidential transactions often need to be encrypted at the point of creation or transmission. The textual content of other records can be encrypted for security in storage, but this is not recommended because encryption adds to the problems of long-term retention by introducing an additional layer of system dependency: 'the record will become inaccessible unless a decrypted version (or the means to obtain one) is available' (Public Record Office, 1999, 47). When records are encrypted at creation, it is often best to remove the encryption as soon as the immediate need for confidentiality has passed.

A further difficulty with the use of hash values and encryption techniques (and of alternatives such as fragile digital watermarking, where invisible marks are embedded in the record in such a way that they will be disturbed or destroyed if the record is modified) is their incompatibility with migration strategies. Since these techniques are intended to be sensitive to any change in the bitstream underlying the record that they seek to protect, while migration is intended to alter the bitstream to conform with developing technologies, each inhibits the other. The long-term use of cryptography in records management is likely to remain problematic until effective alternatives to migration are developed.

An alternative use of the concept of the trusted third party is the employment of *independent agents* to store records under tightly controlled conditions of access. Such agents could then provide impartial testimony that the records in their custody are complete and uncorrupted. An in-house records management unit could provide a service of this kind but the impartiality of an external agent would be less open to challenge.

Protecting the integrity of metadata

Metadata are also at risk from accidental loss or unauthorized alteration. Paper lists and indexes can be mislaid, damaged, tampered with or concealed. In electronic systems, metadata can be manipulated or pointers to records removed. The techniques available for protecting metadata are broadly similar to those used to protect the records themselves, although any solution that is adopted must allow authorized records management staff to edit metadata while the records remain unaltered.

Measures are also needed to ensure that any unauthorized persons who succeed in obtaining access to metadata are inhibited from using them to gain access to the records themselves. In paper systems, lists and indexes can be kept in a lockable room that is separate from the record storage area, while files or boxes are marked only with coded identifiers. Electronic systems can also store records and metadata in separate secure repositories. However, there is often a tension between the need for security and the need to ensure that the links between records and their metadata are not broken. While some ERM systems focus on security, partitioning storage in order to restrict unauthorized access, others give a higher priority to eliminating the risks from detachment. Encapsulation systems take the latter approach and may even use cryptographic techniques to bind each record to its metadata.

Threats and hazards: risk assessment and reduction

Record storage areas, server rooms and computer installations are all at risk from natural hazards and from a range of human threats, as are the buildings where they are housed. Only when the various risks have been assessed can appropriate precautions be taken. Figure 6.6 describes the main risks that need to be assessed and suggests ways in which the risks can be minimized.

Risk	Assessment	Actions to reduce risk
Fire	Fire risks can arise from the behaviour of staff and visitors and from the construction of the building and adjacent premises. Wild or forest fires are a risk in some regions.	Store records away from inflammable materials and smoking areas. Remove old or faulty wiring or electrical installations. Install fire-resistant doors and heat or smoke detection systems which are constantly monitored. Maintain adequate fire extinction equipment, ideally both an appropriate automatic suppression system and handheld extinguishers. Ensure that buildings comply with regulations regarding fire alarms, exit routes and emergency lighting. Hold regular fire drills. Ensure that access to records and storerooms is not compromised in the event of an evacuation. Seek advice from fire authorities and brief them about special requirements for records.
Flood	Water damage to records can result from water used to extinguish fires, as well as tidal waves, flooding from rivers or lakes and water from storms, burst pipes, faulty drainage, gutters or roofs.	Avoid locations subject to flooding. Ensure that water pipes do not pass through or over storage areas and that drains, roofs and gutters are well-maintained. Since flood damage is minimized if water has easy means of drainage, consider providing automatic pumps in basement areas. In regions where cyclones occur, install a high capacity drainage system and ensure that all roofs are pitched for water run-off. Do not store records on the floor or the tops of shelves and keep bottom shelves well clear of the floor.

Fig. 6.6 *Risks to records*

Risk	Assessment	Actions to reduce risk
Pest infestation	Pests may include birds and animals as well as insects.	To deter pests, identify and block all points of likely entry. Screen windows, ventilators and chimneys. Ensure that the premises are cleaned regularly. Ban eating and food in storage and work areas. Use sticky traps for insects so that any infestation is discovered at an early stage.
Unauthorised intrusion	Theft, malicious damage and arson are all potential threats, both during and outside normal business hours.	Use intruder alarms linked to police or security services. Block windows or secure them with bars or grilles. Fit internal and external doors with metal shutters or secure locks. Issue keys or codes to the smallest number of people. Maintain procedures to ensure that windows and doors are locked shut and keys secured. Install closed circuit television or other surveillance. Ensure that the perimeter of buildings is adequately lit, with deterrent planting of trees and bushes provided that this does not impair surveillance. Vet all personnel carefully, including contractors, cleaners, and temporary staff. Seek advice from crime prevention officers.
Computer system failure or sabotage	Threats include hacking, virus attacks, and careless behaviour by users. Computer systems are also at risk from internal failure.	Run regular back-ups (of metadata as well as records). In networked environments, use RAID (Redundant Array of Independent Disks) configurations for fault tolerance in online storage devices and ensure that there are multiple routes to each device. Train staff not to reveal passwords or leave desktop computers running when unattended. Maintain robust external firewalls and regular updating of virus protection. Aim at compliance with ISO/IEC 17799:2000 *Information technology — code of practice for information security management.*
Explosions and bomb threats	Explosions can be caused by faulty gas supplies or vehicle impact as well as enemy attack or criminal activities.	Where possible, avoid storing records in heavy industrial areas, near airport runways or at major road or rail junctions. Organizations based in high-risk areas (e.g. those targeted by terrorists) or with high-risk operations (e.g. testing on animals or developing genetically modified foods) need to take additional preventative measures.

Fig. 6.6   *Risks to records (continued)*

Business continuity planning

If disaster occurs . . .

Disasters can strike an organization at any time. They can range from civil unrest, earthquakes, fires or floods, which threaten organizational viability, to relatively minor events such as power failures or computer breakdowns, which may cost lost business in the short term. The purpose of business continuity planning is to reduce the likelihood of disaster and ensure that, if the worst happens, business can be restarted with the minimum of interruption. Although expensive to develop and maintain, business continuity plans are a form of insurance. Potential risks are identified and plans made so that the organization is ready to react if a disaster occurs and is able to recover as quickly and smoothly as possible.

Records are often a casualty in a disaster, yet without access to records organizations will quickly cease to function effectively. Records managers should contribute to organization-wide business continuity plans, but may also develop a separate or subordinate plan for protection of records. The first step is to establish a planning team, with representatives from the records management and computing units, from facilities and security management, and where appropriate from other interested parties such as archives services and libraries. The scope of the team's responsibilities should be clarified: most business continuity plans focus on responding to the risks from fire and flood, but these are unlikely to be the only risks that records face. Sometimes the risk assessment and reduction exercises in Figure 6.6 have already been undertaken when the team is formed; if not, these should be the team's first responsibility.

Duplication and dispersal: vital records

An additional precaution to those suggested in Figure 6.6 is to copy records and store the copies at sufficient distance from the originals to make it unlikely that both will be affected by a single disaster. Copies can be stored at off-site records centres, in other buildings occupied by the organization or in rented storage space. If online electronic records are routinely backed up it is often possible for some or all of the back-up copies to be housed off-site. Copies of electronic records that have been moved offline should be dispersed in the same way.

Electronic records can be copied cheaply and quickly but duplication of paper records can be expensive: photocopying, scanning and microfilming all incur significant preparation as well as duplication costs. For this reason, records managers often choose to concentrate resources on those records whose loss would put the organization at greatest risk, or those without which it could not continue to function. These are often referred to as *vital records*. Taking expert advice as necessary, the business continuity team should seek to identify vital records of the various functions of the organization, both substantive and facilitative. Vital records of substantive functions (those relating to the core business) will vary from one organization to another, but among records of facilitative functions it is likely that many personnel, financial and legal records will be designated as vital. These include records that prove the organization's assets and obligations (such as accounts payable and receivable, payroll, pension, tax and insurance records, as well as contracts, title deeds, patents and evidence of copyrights and trademarks). Designation of vital records is a form of appraisal, and should be monitored and reviewed periodically.

Vital records probably constitute only 2–10% of organizational records. Some, such as patents and trademark records, are likely to have long or indefinite retention periods; many others may be kept only for a short time. Vital record status often changes during the course of an agreed retention period: for example, accounts payable and receivable are vital records only until payment has been made, although their retention period is likely to extend for several years. Records of obligations outstanding or rights in force, or those that contain current information, are most likely to have vital record status.

Operational procedures are needed to govern the designation of vital records, and when and how they are to be duplicated and dispersed. Since they are likely to have a high priority in the business continuity plan, secure storage is needed for originals and duplicates alike. In cases where duplication and dispersal are impractical or excessively costly (for example, where additional items are regularly added to paper files), vital records require an even higher level of protection, such as storage in steel safes with known and tested fire resistance.

Preparing for an emergency

Besides identifying potential risks and developing means to minimize them, records managers need to plan for the eventuality of a disaster happening. Duplication and dispersal of records is only a part of the solution: if an emergency occurs it will almost certainly be necessary to rescue records from the disaster site, while computer and other systems are likely to break down. The business continuity team should develop and write a plan for a swift and effective response.

The plan should establish the lines of authority in the event of an emergency. It should give 24-hour contact details of staff members who are trained in emergency procedures and list police, fire, ambulance and other contacts such as pest controllers, plumbers, electricians, building maintenance and security services. Contracts should be negotiated in advance with providers of specialist services such as refrigeration and drying facilities and emergency conservation work, and their contact details should also be listed.

The plan should also make advance provision for temporary alternative premises, in case the main building becomes unusable. A standby site for electronic systems must be able to provide a computing infrastructure that can be made operational with minimal delay. Alternative premises for paper-based records systems may also be required.

Emergency stores should be established, each containing items that will be needed quickly in the event of a disaster, including protective clothing and footwear, emergency lighting and mobile communication equipment, trolleys, plastic sheeting, and a range of containers and cleaning supplies. Electrical equipment may include fans, pumps, dehumidifiers, waterproof extension cables and portable generators. All should be kept in working order. The business continuity plan should list the equipment and supplies and indicate where they are held and where further supplies can be obtained. Emergency personnel will also need access to keys, floor plans and staff lists. Up-to-date copies of these should be held in more than one location to ensure their accessibility during an emergency.

The plan should also outline the response and recovery procedures. A senior person should be given responsibility for carrying through the plan and for deciding priorities in the event of a disaster. Each staff member with responsibilities for disaster response should have a copy of the plan at home and at work and be trained regularly in the procedures. The plan should be tested in a simulated disaster and all staff briefed on its contents.

Response and recovery

If a disaster occurs, the first step is to assess its nature and extent. The team leader will take advice from emergency services before salvage procedures are begun. As soon as it is safe to enter the storage areas, action should be taken stabilize the condition of the records, minimize further damage and enable maximum recovery. Rescue of metadata should always be a priority, since records recovered from a disaster will be of little use if they cannot be identified or understood.

Fire causes physical damage to records but this may be made worse by water used to extinguish fires. Records suffering water damage need quick treatment, especially in hot or humid conditions. Computer tapes and discs should be given priority unless undamaged duplicates are known to exist. They should be removed quickly from standing water, including any that has collected in boxes or canisters, and rinsed with distilled water. Paper records should be removed to a dry and clean working area and then dried out, beginning with the wettest, those scattered on the floor or those whose loss would put the organization at greatest risk. When there is extensive damage, wet paper records should be sent for freezing in order to stabilize them and allow time for repair priorities to be assessed. Mud, sewage or chemical contamination must be washed off by a trained person. The records should then be wrapped in freezer bags or plastic, packed into crates and transferred to a refrigeration facility. They may subsequently be freeze dried or vacuum dried. Computer media must not be frozen but, like small quantities of paper records, can generally be air dried without freezing; in cases of doubt, professional advice on drying should be obtained. Water-damaged microforms should be kept in clean water and transferred to a specialist bureau for recovery.

It will probably be some time before a paper-based records management system is fully operational following a disaster. However, electronic systems can often be restored without undue delay, provided that back-up copies of records have been made regularly and kept off-site together with copies of programs and system documentation.

After recovery from a disaster, the business continuity plan should be reviewed in the light of the experience. The scale and impact of the disaster and the speed with which the organization was able to resume normal operations should be assessed in order to identify any changes needed to the plan. In any event, business continuity plans should be checked regularly to ensure that they continue to reflect current circumstances and that contact details are up to date.

There are many general textbooks and websites on disaster management and business continuity planning. Further specialist advice for records managers is available on the websites of the US National Archives and Records Administration, www.archives.gov/records_management/publications/vital_records.html, and the State Records Authority of New South Wales, www.records.nsw.gov.au/publicsector/rk/guidelines/counterdisaster/toc.htm.

References

Bearman, D. (1999) Realities and chimeras in the preservation of electronic records, *D-Lib Magazine*, **5** (4). Available at www.dlib.org/dlib/april99/bearman/04bearman.html.

Benedon, W. (1969) *Records management*, Prentice Hall.

Dollar, C. (1999) *Authentic electronic records: strategies for long-term access*, Cohasset Associates.

Hamer, A. C. (1996) *A short guide to the retention of documents*, ICSA.

Heazlewood, J. et al. (1999) Electronic records: problem solved? A report on the Public Record Office Victoria's electronic records strategy, *Archives and Manuscripts*, **27** (1), 96–113. Also available at www.prov.vic.gov.au/vers/published/am.pdf.

Kallaus, N. F. and Johnson, M. M. (1992) *Records management*, 5th edn, South-Western Publishing Co.

National Archives of Australia (2000) *Guidelines for environmental conditions and safety and protection levels for storage*. Available at www.naa.gov.au/recordkeeping/storage/ tables/ 30less.pdf. Also available as State Records Authority of New South Wales (2000) *Standard on the physical storage of state records. Appendix A: short term temporary value records*, at www.records.nsw.gov.au/publicsector/rk/storage/app01.htm.

Public Record Office (1999) *Management, appraisal and preservation of electronic records*, Vol 2, [UK] Public Record Office. Also available at www.pro.gov.uk/recordsmanagement/ eros/guidelines/.

Rothenberg, J. (1999) *Avoiding technological quicksand: finding a viable technical foundation for digital preservation*, Council on Library and Information Resources. Also available at www.clir.org/pubs/abstract/pub77.html.

Saffady, W. (1993) *Electronic document imaging systems: design, evaluation, and implementation*, Meckler.

Smith, G. J. H. (1996) PD 0008: a lawyer's view of the legal admissibility of document images, *Records Management Journal*, **6** (2), 71–4.

Stephens, D. O. and Wallace, R. C. (1997) *Electronic records retention: an introduction*, ARMA International.

Thibodeau, K., Moore, R. and Baru, C. (2000) Persistent object preservation: advanced computing infrastructure for digital preservation. In *Proceedings of the DLM-Forum on Electronic Records, Brussels, 18–19 October 1999*, Office for Official Publications of the European Communities. Also available at http://europa.eu.int/ISPO/dlm/fulltext/ full_thib_en.htm.

Waters, D. and Garrett, J. (1996) *Preserving digital information: report of the Task Force on Archiving of Digital Information*, Commission on Preservation and Access. Also available at ftp://ftp.rlg.org/pub/archtf/final-report.pdf.

Wheatley, P. (2001) Migration – a CAMiLEON discussion paper, *Ariadne*, **29**. Available at www.ariadne.ac.uk/issue29/camileon/.

ANSI/ARMA 1-1997 *Alphabetic filing rules*, ARMA International.

BS 4783:1988 *Storage, transportation and maintenance of media for use in data processing and information storage*, British Standards Institution.

BS 5454:2000 *Recommendations for the storage and exhibition of archival documents*, British Standards Institution.

BS 6498:2002 *Guide to preparation of microfilm and other microforms that may be required as evidence*, British Standards Institution.

BS 6660:1985 *Guide to setting up and maintaining micrographics units*, British Standards Institution.

ISO 11108:1996 *Information and documentation – archival paper – requirements for permanence and durability*, International Standards Organization.

ISO 12199:2000 *Alphabetical ordering of multilingual terminological and lexicographical data represented in the Latin alphabet*, International Standards Organization.

ISO/IEC 17799:2000 *Information technology – code of practice for information security management*, International Standards Organization.

PD 0008:1999 *Code of practice for legal admissibility and evidential weight of information stored electronically*, British Standards Institution.

PD 0016:2001 *Guide to scanning business documents*, British Standards Institution.

7
Providing access

Records are kept so that they can be made available to authorized users when required. Users may include the staff of the business unit where the records were created, other business units within the organization or authorized users from outside the organization.

At the time of their creation, records are normally accessible only to their creators and perhaps to other members of a workgroup. When they are captured into a records management system, they normally become more widely accessible: capture is often the moment when the existence of the records is publicized, although it may also be the point at which formal access controls are applied to protect confidentiality.

Since most organizations hold large numbers of records, systems must be in place to allow different users, and records management staff, to ascertain what records exist and to find those that are relevant to a particular need. Along with access control mechanisms, these need to be planned when records management programmes and systems are set up. This chapter examines the issues and offers some solutions to the questions of records retrieval.

Meeting the needs of users

Users and their requirements

In order to design effective retrieval systems, records managers need an understanding of user requirements. Users articulate requests for retrieval in a variety of ways. For example, they may state that:

- a particular *record* exists, and they want to see it
- a particular *process* or *activity* took place in the past, and they want to find evidence or information about it

- they are gathering information about a particular *topic* to support the activity that they are currently engaged on
- they are undertaking *broadly based research*, and want to see if the records contain material that may be relevant.

Most of these requests allow several degrees of uncertainty. Some users may know that a record exists and be able to identify it precisely; others may seek the same record but be ignorant or uncertain of its title or location. Users may know that an activity took place but have varying degrees of uncertainty about when it occurred, who participated in it or what records it gave rise to. Access mechanisms must be able to satisfy a range of users, including those who have little or no prior knowledge of the records.

In addition, retrieval systems must be able to handle records at different levels of aggregation. Records management staff need to be able to identify what record series exist within the organization and, if custody and storage are decentralized, who is responsible for each series and where it is held. They may also need the facility to make searches across multiple series of records. Staff outside the records management unit may also need access to information about records at series level although they may not require, or be allowed, access to all records throughout the organization. Managers and policymakers are particularly likely to need occasional access to records from many different series, and retrieval mechanisms must be sufficiently flexible to meet their needs. On the other hand, operational staff are often concerned only with a single series that they use every day: they do not need a formal mechanism to identify the series, but they require an effective means of finding individual records within it.

In paper systems, delivery operates at file level (or sometimes at box level, if files are stored in boxes in a records centre). Users identify the file or box that they require and it is delivered to them as a unit. If they require specific items within a file, the whole file is delivered and they rely on the order of the items within the file to enable them to find the item that is wanted. This approach is necessary because manual systems are usually too unwieldy to allow the separate identification of individual items within a file. Moreover, if the file is maintained as a unit the risk of loss or misplacement is reduced, and for this reason users are strongly discouraged from removing individual items from the files in which they are housed.

In electronic systems, metadata to support retrieval can be applied at any level. Delivery is not limited to file level: users can retrieve a single item and can generally be given the facility to retrieve records at any level they wish.

Providing access to paper records

When a user requires access to a paper file, a number of actions must take place: first it is necessary to identify the file that is required; then its physical location must be ascertained; if it is in store, it must then be removed from its storage location to the place where the user is to examine it. Any or all of these actions may be undertaken by the user in person or by an intermediary who has been trained in the operation of the records management system.

In an uncontrolled environment users may be able to browse through the stored records and remove whatever they like. However, if records are not to be lost or misplaced, it is essential that their removal from the storage area is monitored in some way. If access is restricted to authorized individuals, further controls are needed to ensure that records are not examined or removed by anyone who lacks the necessary authorization.

Broadly speaking, there are four models for controlled systems:

1 Users have direct access to the stored records and may borrow what they like; they are trusted to provide evidence of their borrowing by completing a charge-out document or making an entry in a loans database.
2 Users have direct access to the stored records but may not remove records without going through an intermediary who is responsible for checking them out.
3 Users must ask an intermediary to retrieve the records for them; once the intermediary has checked the records out, the user may borrow them.
4 Users must ask an intermediary to retrieve the records for them; they may only inspect the records under supervision and nothing may be removed from the controlled area.

Mixed models are also found. For example, some users may be allowed direct access while others are required to go through an intermediary; or some records may be removable from a controlled area while others are not.

Sometimes intermediaries are also responsible for verifying the user's right of access, or for assisting the user in identifying the file that is required. They are often, though not always, employed by the records management unit. When records are stored in a central registry or records centre, it is usual for specialist staff to handle access requests, and these staff normally form part of the records management team. When specialist staff operate decentralized filing systems in particular business units they are often employed by the business unit concerned.

Users may express a preference for direct access to paper records; a system that obliges them to go through an intermediary may seem unnecessarily bureaucratic.

Unless the intermediaries maintain 24-hour cover, difficulties are also likely to arise when records are required urgently outside normal working hours. Nevertheless, intermediaries provide a number of important benefits:

1 If storage areas are at a distance from business units, personal visits may be difficult and intermediaries are often needed to arrange transport of the records to those who require them.
2 The employment of specialist records staff is almost essential if there is to be a guarantee that procedures will be followed systematically. Besides ensuring that records are checked out on removal and that no unauthorized access is given, records staff can ensure that storage areas are kept in good order. In the longer term, an unstaffed facility almost inevitably means that records will be lost, misfiled or damaged. If trained staff are employed to return files to storage after use, the risk of misplacement can be substantially reduced.
3 Where there are no intermediaries, users must identify for themselves the records that they require. Regular users may have little difficulty, particularly if they are seeking records that they themselves have created, but other users may not find it easy to identify or locate the records that they need. Some users may have difficulty in formulating their requirements, and specialist staff can be trained to elucidate user needs as well as operate the finding systems.

In the past, when retrieval tools were themselves paper-based and often difficult to use, the employment of specialists was frequently the only option for effective retrieval. Now, if an online database is used as a replacement for the paper lists and indexes, operational staff can be encouraged to search the database at their desktop and may have less need to seek assistance from intermediaries. Nevertheless, particularly in more complex records systems, there is still likely to be a role for specialist staff in supporting users who have been unsuccessful in their own searches.

Providing access to electronic records

Delivering electronic records to users is much less labour-intensive. If records are held in a shared online environment and users have access to software that is capable of rendering them, they can be delivered using the standard mechanisms provided by the network or intranet. Where web technology is used, information to support retrieval can be accessed via the web browser, with direct links from the user interface to the repository of records. Copies of key records can also be published on an intranet, or on the world wide web if a wider audience is sought.

In an electronic system there is no need for a human intermediary to retrieve and return records, except for those stored offline on tapes or discs that cannot be mounted automatically onto a server. Measures to prevent unauthorized users from gaining access to records can also be designed into the system, thus obviating the need for manual verification of access rights. All these benefits can be applied to digitized images of paper records as well as records that are 'born' digitally.

User services and records management staff

The services provided to users by records management staff will depend on organizational needs and the range of media employed. Where records are kept on paper or microform, services may include:

- retrieving records that users are able to identify precisely
- identifying relevant records from more limited information provided by users.

Users increasingly expect to be able to find electronic resources for themselves, without needing to seek assistance from intermediaries; but in practice they cannot always find everything they require. Services offered by records management staff may include:

- providing a helpdesk to assist online users in finding the records that they need
- handling enquiries from those who do not have online access (for example, external enquirers)
- retrieving electronic records stored offline.

In addition, some records management units offer a research service, producing summaries or statistics or writing reports using information derived from the records. Any or all of these services may be limited to internal users or may include external enquirers where appropriate.

When records management staff are responsible for retrieving records from storage, mechanisms are needed for communicating user requests to the staff concerned. If the storage area is close to hand, users can make personal visits to borrow or refer to the records; but records staff may also need to respond to requests made by telephone, by internal mail or electronically. When records centres or other storage facilities are at a distance from business units, mechanisms for handling requests from remote users are essential. If a commercially managed records centre is used, in-house records staff may take responsibility for communicating such requests to the records centre and for monitoring the speed and accuracy of its response.

With paper records, the procedure is broadly as follows: the user makes a request, staff employed in the storage area find the relevant file or box, and the user takes it away or it is delivered to an agreed collecting point or to the user's desk. Records centres that are distant from business units typically offer a same day or next day service as well as an express service for urgent requests.

If records have been converted to microfilm or microfiche, delivery may be to a viewing area supplied with microform readers. Offline digital storage media may be delivered directly to users, or to a central computing facility where they can be mounted on a server. Users may need to be notified of the procedures that they must follow when records are ready for viewing.

Approaches to retrieval

Using a known identifier

The approaches to the retrieval of records are the same, regardless of whether records are retrieved by users or by records management staff or contractors acting on their behalf. The ideal starting point is to have prior knowledge of the unique identifier of the record that is sought. For example, if customer numbers are used as unique identifiers, and customers can be persuaded to quote their number when communicating with the organization, retrieval of their records is greatly simplified.

As noted in Chapter 4, the unique identifier may be a language-based title but is more commonly a numeric or alphanumeric code, assigned to the record when it is registered. If codes are used as identifiers, a concordance is required for users who know a title but need to discover the code. For example, a member of staff may know a customer's name but not the number of their file. In the past, alphabetical card indexes were often used to enable staff to ascertain the identifiers of paper files, but the use of a database is now the normal practice.

In paper systems, retrieval depends on the ability to track the physical locations of records. First, the location of the series may need to be discovered, using a list or database that provides information about the storage areas used for each series across the organization. When the location of the series is known, individual files can be traced by virtue of their physical arrangement within cabinets or on shelving units. Storage arrangements should ensure that identifiers are easily visible: for example, if files are stored on shelves, their identifiers should be positioned on the outside edge of file covers and each shelf should be clearly labelled. In larger storage areas a plan or map may be needed. Sometimes the file that is wanted is on loan to another borrower; the procedures set out in Chapter 6 for protecting files against loss or misplacement also serve to track files that are already in use when requested by a second user.

Unlike their paper counterparts, electronic records can be viewed simultaneously by a number of users. Electronic systems employ random storage that is designed to make optimum use of the capacity of the server or other storage medium. When a user knows the identifier of a record that is stored online, the record can be requested and the software application locates and assembles it for delivery to the user. Manual tracking is unnecessary and delivery is normally instantaneous.

When older records have been moved offline or transferred to a records centre, while current parts of the same series remain online or in a current paper filing system, the location of each file or folder can be traced only if it is appropriately documented. For each series that is divided in this way, pointers to individual storage locations must be maintained, either in a manual locations list or more efficiently in an automated system.

Browsing and searching

If unique identifiers are in the form of a code, users (or records staff acting on their behalf) either know the identifier of the record that is wanted, or are ignorant of it and must be helped to discover it. If the identifier is a title, there is a third possibility: users may be able to provide an approximation of the title while being unable to quote it exactly. When identifiers are unknown, or imperfectly known, browsing or searching tools are needed to support discovery. These tools are also required when users have more general questions; for example, when a user does not know of the existence of particular records but is seeking information about precedents, past activities or topics of interest.

Searching is usually more focused than browsing. Search tools enable users to look for a specific term, or a range or combination of terms, which they believe will lead them to records relevant to their enquiry. Browsing is typically employed when users' needs are less well defined; for example, when they are unsure what they are looking for or what search terms to use. Browsing and searching techniques can be applied directly to the records themselves, or indirectly to metadata about the records.

At its simplest, *browsing* is an unstructured foray into an accumulation of records: in a disorganized paper system, users may have no option but to look through the contents of filing cabinets, shelves or boxes in the hope of finding what they want. At a more sophisticated level, users can browse by reading a classification scheme or file list (on paper or on screen). Chapter 3 has discussed the need for structured classification schemes to be documented and maintained by records management staff. If records have been classified according to a logical model of functions, processes and activities, users can browse the documentation of the records system in a structured manner, following the hierarchical levels of the classification scheme. For example, a user may consult a list of series titles to discover a number of record series that appear to be relevant, and then browse more detailed lists of the files within those series.

Browsing is sometimes seen as less important in the world of electronic systems, because of the wide range of search options that is available; but it still has a role to play. For users who cannot formulate a precise request, or who say that they will not know what records they want until they have found them, navigation through the levels of a classification scheme remains the best approach.

Users may also choose to search a database for broad terms and then browse through their search results. A further feature of the electronic environment is that search results presented to the user in one sequence can easily be re-sorted into a different order to simplify browsing.

While browsing is still widely used, *search tools* are now the most heavily promoted means of access to records, especially in automated systems. At the simplest level, a list of records may be held as an electronic document, and searches for particular words or phrases can be made using the basic finding tools in a standard word-processor. More sophisticated searches can be made if relevant metadata are held in a database application, preferably one that is designed to support retrieval of textual information. Database technology has largely replaced the card index as a retrieval tool for paper records and microforms, and is also widely used to provide access to digitized images. An integrated database is an essential component of most records management software applications.

Even more powerful search techniques are available for retrieval of electronic records. A range of search options can be provided using structured metadata, while full-text searching can look for words or phrases in the records themselves. Software applications that support electronic records management may use both of these techniques.

Full-text searching

A basic method of full-text searching is for the computer to scan each document sequentially to find all occurrences of the word or phrase that is sought. This can be slow, especially if a large amount of text is to be searched. The most common alternative is for the application to create an inverted index file, which notes the occurrence and position of every word in the text, or all except certain stop words (such as *a, an* or *the*). When a search is requested the computer checks the index rather than the text of each document, and thus the search is performed more quickly.

Full-text searching cannot be used for visual or sound records, or for voice or video clips embedded in text documents, although speech recognition technology and content-based image and video retrieval systems may eventually fill this gap. For text records, however, full-text searching is now well established. As well as records 'born digitally', it is also possible for digitized images of paper records to be searched in this way if they are converted to electronic text using OCR techniques.

Users may be attracted by full-text searching because it appears very simple. Online records can be searched on demand, and since there seems to be no need to create metadata for retrieval no additional resources are required at the input stage. However, the results of a full-text search are often less helpful than the results of a search performed using structured metadata, and thus the burden of effort is placed on the searcher rather than the creator of the record. Full-text search engines cannot distinguish between different meanings of the same word, nor can they generally do much to help users find different words or phrases that have similar meanings. For example, a word such as *induction* has exact meanings in the fields of obstetrics, logic, science and mathematics, but is also used to denote an introductory training course for newly appointed staff. A full-text search cannot normally distinguish between these usages and will find all occurrences of the word regardless of the sense in which it is employed.

Search devices and techniques

Several techniques are available to allow users to narrow their searches. Searching for a phrase (*induction course*) rather than a single word (*induction*) is often beneficial. Other techniques include 'Boolean' searching (requesting a search for *induction* **and** *course* will narrow the search, while a request for *induction* **or** *course* will widen it); 'adjacency' searching (looking for the word *course* immediately adjacent to the word *induction*); and 'proximity' searching (looking for the word *course* within, say, five or ten words of the word *induction*). Not all search engines provide these options, but where they are available they can help to overcome some of the limitations of full-text searching.

These devices (apart from the Boolean '**or**' search) all seek to focus the search more closely: that is, to increase its *precision*. Other search devices have the opposite aim, and seek to ensure that a wider range of material is retrieved: in the language of text retrieval, these are said to increase *recall*.

Some search engines achieve this by using 'fuzzy' searching algorithms, which attempt to find partial as well as exact matches: for example, a search for *induction* might also find words such as *inductive, indication* or *introduction*. Fuzzy searching varies in its capabilities but can be helpful, since records that contain the word *inductive* may be of interest to someone concerned with the logician's use of *induction*, while those that mention an *introduction* may be relevant to a searcher looking for *induction* among personnel records. Fuzzy searching can also be useful in finding mis-spelt words.

Truncation is a further device that may be useful: a search for the truncated term *induc** would find *induct, induction* and *inductive*, as well as the possibly less relevant *inducement*. Another variant is the 'wildcard' search, where a search for *ind*ct* would find both *induct* and *indict*. These techniques improve recall, but also tend to increase the volume of irrelevant material retrieved.

Reliance on full-text searching alone is rarely sufficient: for example, none of the approaches discussed above will find records that refer to induction courses only as *preliminary training programmes*, yet these may be the very items that the searcher requires. Some full-text engines use semantic analysis techniques to provide more 'intelligent' searching, but most of these are still in their infancy. In general, full-text searching can be helpful when users need *information*, as a number of sources may provide the facts that they require; it is often less useful when searching for *evidence*, because the user's needs can only be met by finding the specific records that offer authentic proof of a past activity.

Earlier chapters of this book have shown that classification metadata are essential to support users' understanding of the context of records. In practice, contextual metadata serve a double purpose: they assist with interpretation but can also be used effectively in retrieval. Classification schemes often provide the best means of focusing a search. Users can search contextual metadata, or browse through the text of a classification scheme, to identify relevant accumulations of records; if they wish, they can then use full-text searching to find individual items. Since the full-text search is restricted to a subset of records that is known to have some relevance, it is likely to be easier and more successful.

Structured searching

The alternative to full-text searching is 'structured' searching, in which users begin their search by identifying elements of data, or indexes of selected terms, where they can look for a word or other search term of their choice. For most records in documentary form, structured searching depends on the existence of appropriate metadata that are external to the records themselves. For records that are not available as online electronic text – including records on paper or micro-form, audiovisual records and images not susceptible to OCR – metadata provide the only practical search option.

Such metadata may refer to functions or processes (as described in Chapter 3). Metadata that take the form of name, place, date or subject terms may also be required when users' search needs are not fully met by function or process meta-data. In a typical automated system, searches of structured metadata are undertaken using a search engine associated with a database application. Different elements of metadata are held in dedicated fields in the database and the engine can be asked to search a particular field or a defined combination of fields, thus focusing the search to achieve precise results. Database applications for use with textual meta-data usually provide search devices that are broadly comparable to the full-text devices discussed above.

The process of assigning metadata to support the retrieval of records is often referred to as *indexing*. As noted in Chapter 4, this normally requires additional work on the part of creators of records or the employment of specialist indexers. Considerable intellectual effort may be needed to ensure that the metadata are correct. The use of metadata for retrieval incurs costs at the input stage, and there is often a time delay at that stage while the metadata are assigned.

Some important exceptions must be mentioned. Electronic records created using database software or an electronic forms interface may need fewer metadata since each record contains its own structured data, which can be searched in a sys-tematic fashion. Forms recognition software can use OCR tools to read appropriately designed paper forms and transfer structured data from the form into a database, thus minimizing human intervention and reducing input costs. Records created in or converted to XML can contain markup tags that identify and define partic-ular searchable elements within the body of the text.

Using controlled language

When capturing data for use in retrieval, some form of *language control* is usually beneficial. Language control refers to the use of agreed and consistent terminology to represent the names of persons, corporate bodies, places, subjects, functions, processes or other concepts. It is needed because:

- a person or organization may have variant names; users may be aware of only one name (for example *Pope John Paul II*; the *BBC*) but are likely to require access to records that refer to that individual or organization under other names (*Karol Wojtyla*; *British Broadcasting Corporation*; *British Broadcasting Company*)
- a place may have names in different languages (for example, *Dunkerque* in French is often *Dunkirk* in English) or there may be variants within a single language (*Beijing* and *Peking* are both English versions of the same place name)
- many other terms also have synonyms (for example, *diskettes* and *floppy disks* refer to the same objects; *human resources* and *personnel* denote the same function in an organization).

In a controlled language, a 'preferred term' is specified for each entity, with a defined grammatical form, an exact spelling and a precise order of words. Examples of preferred terms might be *reassurance* (not *reassuring* or *re-assurance*); *Netherlands* (not *Holland*); *Gates, William* (not *Gates, Bill* or *Bill Gates*). Authority files (discussed in Chapter 3) are frequently used to store lists of preferred terms, and also to provide scope notes defining the meaning of particular terms; any term can then be copied from the authority file when it is needed.

Systems based on structured data sometimes use uncontrolled or 'natural' language, but searching is normally more effective when controlled language is used. If the preferred term *Gates, William* has been used consistently, anyone searching for *Gates, William* should be confident of finding all the records associated with that individual.

Use of an agreed terminology can also help searchers when a single word or phrase has more than one meaning. Thus if *Reading [Berkshire, UK]* is consistently distinguished from *Reading [Pennsylvania, USA]* and from *reading [for study or pastime]*, the searcher should find all the records that are relevant but no others.

When compared with natural-language indexing, the use of controlled language may add further to the burden of assigning metadata to records, as each entry needs to be checked against an approved list. Before computerization, approved terms usually had to be transcribed onto index cards from a paper dictionary of terms, a task that was laborious and prone to error. Automated systems enhance the speed and accuracy of indexing: when records are captured, the appropriate names, subjects or other terms can be verified from an electronic authority file and inserted automatically into a record profile or database. This process can still be time-consuming, but much less so than purely manual systems. It is worthwhile, especially when accurate retrieval is critical or when heavy demand is expected, because the use of controlled language will enhance precision or recall through its control of synonyms and its guarantee of terminological consistency over time. Search results will be more useful, because effective searching does not depend on both searchers and creators fortuitously choosing the same words.

Creators of documentary records are not normally expected to use controlled language in the body of the record. When writing letters or reports, creators can use any words that they wish; controlled terms are used only when metadata are assigned. However, if records are wholly or partly in the form of structured data, creators may be required to use controlled language within the record, and software controls may be applied to prevent them from using unauthorized terms.

Pre-coordination and post-coordination

Language control systems may be pre-coordinate or post-coordinate. In pre-coordinate systems, individual controlled terms are combined at or before the time when the record is indexed; for example, *history of education* might appear in the authority file as a single indexing term. Post-coordinate systems are based on the assumption that terms can be combined at the search stage. In a post-coordinate system, *history* and *education* would be treated as separate indexing terms, so that searchers can retrieve either of them independently or use a Boolean search to combine them when required. Post-coordination is usually employed in computerized environments where Boolean search techniques can be supported.

Pre-coordinate systems raise questions about the order in which terms should be combined within the authority file. A concept such as *repair of brick walls* may be represented in a number of ways:

walls, brick, repair
brick walls, repair of
repairs: walls, brick

and so on. Choosing the most useful order for a pre-coordinate authority file entry is unlikely to be straightforward, and appropriate rules will be required. Rules may also be needed about punctuation between terms and the use or absence of prepositions. Post-coordinate systems avoid these difficulties and offer the additional benefit that searchers are not limited to the combinations that the indexer has predicted.

Record titles and index terms

The title of a record gives it a concise name that is meaningful to users. Titles also provide one of the principal means of retrieving records. They can be composed using either natural or controlled language. A controlled-language title may comprise a single term or a set of pre-coordinate terms. Figures 7.1 to 7.3 give examples of the options for constructing titles at file or folder level. Similar options are available for titles at other levels of aggregation.

Natural-language titles:	Mary Green
	Mr John James Smith
Controlled-language titles:	Green, Mary
	Smith, John James

Fig. 7.1 *Examples of file or folder titles in a series of client records*

Natural-language titles:	Trends and developments in gambling
	Recent developments in the use of credit cards
Controlled-language titles (single term):	Gambling
	Credit cards

Fig. 7.2 *Examples of file or folder titles in a series of consumer surveys*

Natural-language titles:	Trends and developments in gambling in Belgium
	Credit card use in India
	Canadian vacationing trends
Controlled-language titles	
(pre-coordinated combination of terms):	Gambling: Belgium
	Credit cards: India
	Vacationing: Canada

Fig. 7.3 *Examples of more complex titles*

In its fullest form, the title of a record should normally incorporate title elements derived from higher levels in the classification scheme. A file title, for example, might be composed of three elements: one derived from a function title, a second derived from a series title and a third specific to the file itself. On this basis, the complete title of the series in Figure 7.2 might be *Marketing – Consumer surveys*, and the complete title of one of its files would be *Marketing – Consumer surveys – Gambling*. In everyday use this might be referred to as the *gambling* file, and on a paper file cover it might also be labelled only with the word *Gambling*; but this word alone does not provide adequate information about the context of the file, and it is better practice for the complete (or 'concatenated') title to be made explicit on the label. In automated systems, titles need be entered only at the level to which they relate: well designed software applications will be able to maintain each title separately, while concatenating them for display purposes when required.

Within a hierarchy of levels, it is sometimes appropriate for titles to use natural language at one level and controlled language at another. Thus a concatenated title may contain a mixture of the two. For example, if natural language is used at file level, a concatenated title might read *Marketing – Consumer surveys – Trends and developments in gambling in Belgium*. If controlled language is used throughout, this would become *Marketing – Consumer surveys – Gambling: Belgium*.

The use of controlled language is driven by retrieval requirements and does not take account of the need for titles that are fully descriptive. At file level, titles such as *Gambling: Belgium* are less informative than more discursive titles such as *Trends and developments in gambling in Belgium*. The advantage of natural language is that it can often more accurately reflect the nature and scope of the records. However, in paper systems natural-language titles cannot be searched effectively; in computerized systems searches are possible but suffer the same limitations as the full-text searches discussed earlier in this chapter. When natural-language titles are used there is usually a requirement for additional indexing using controlled terms.

Titles that employ controlled language should reduce or eliminate the need for separate index terms: most users can expect to retrieve the record by relying on the title alone. However, there are obvious limitations when pre-coordinated terms are used: a title such as *Gambling: Belgium* can support direct retrieval of the word *Gambling*, but in a manual system the word *Belgium* can only be found when the initial term *Gambling* has already been located.

In computerized systems there may be little point in using pre-coordinated titles. It is often better to use natural-language titles and derive post-coordinate index terms from each title (as in Figure 7.4). In this example, searching the index for *Gambling* will find T1 and T2; searching for *France* will find T2 and T3; searching for *Belgium* will find T1 and T3. A Boolean search for *Gambling* and *Belgium* will find only T1.

This approach easily supports the indexing of lengthier titles, and eliminates the elaborate cross-references (*Credit cards: Belgium* see *Credit cards: France and Belgium*) that are often required in paper and pre-coordinate systems. As Figure 7.5 shows, it also supports the use of index terms at different levels of accumulation.

Database systems for records management normally provide dedicated fields for index terms using controlled language. Since several index terms may be needed for

Fig. 7.4   *Single-level database entries using post-coordinate index terms*

	Level: Series
	Unique identifier: LM
	Title: Grants of permits for repairs
	Index terms: Permits
	Repairs

	Level: Item
	Unique identifier: LM1
	Title: Making good the brick wall at Newtown warehouse
	Index terms: Walls
	Brick
	Newtown
	Warehouses

	Level: Item
	Unique identifier: LM2
	Title: Restoring stone walling at Newtown and Oldbury
	Index terms: Walls
	Stone
	Newtown
	Oldbury

Fig. 7.5   *Multilevel database entries using post-coordinate index terms*

each title, a well designed system should impose no limit on the number of times that the index field can occur. Depending on the configuration of the system, lower-level records may also inherit index terms from a higher-level record (see Figure 7.6). In this way, 'indexing . . . mak[es] it possible to give each record as many labels as might be needed for its retrieval' (Kennedy and Schauder, 1998, 119).

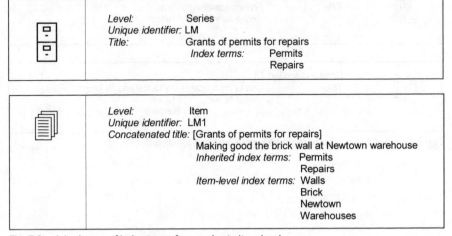

Level:	Series
Unique identifier:	LM
Title:	Grants of permits for repairs
	Index terms: Permits
	Repairs

Level:	Item
Unique identifier:	LM1
Concatenated title:	[Grants of permits for repairs]
	Making good the brick wall at Newtown warehouse
	Inherited index terms: Permits
	Repairs
	Item-level index terms: Walls
	Brick
	Newtown
	Warehouses

Fig. 7.6 *Inheritance of index terms from series to item level*

Controlled terminology can also be used for other elements of metadata, including the names of record creators or recipients, languages and dates. As with subject terms, if any of these elements is represented by a field in a database, repeated occurrences of the field may be required: a record may have several creators or recipients or contain text in several languages.

Record titles should be concise, but where necessary can be supplemented by an abstract of the scope and content of the record. Database systems may have optional 'free-text' fields where lengthier information about the content, structure or context of records can be entered using natural language. If more detailed indexing is required, controlled-language index terms can be derived from abstracts of this kind as well as from record titles. Additional resources will be required at the indexing stage but improved retrieval may result.

At item level, controlled-language terms can also be used to index the text of the record itself, but this is very labour-intensive. It is more usual to assign index terms only to entities and concepts mentioned in the record title or other elements of natural-language metadata.

In the future, intelligent electronic systems may be able to read natural-language text to identify appropriate terms, automatically convert them to controlled language and copy them to an index. Some text-retrieval systems already have a limited capability for automatic capture of approved index terms, but this functionality is not yet widely included in records management packages. Normally, the creator or indexer must review the appropriate natural-language elements to identify the entities and concepts that need to be indexed, and must then translate them into the approved indexing terminology. A well designed authority file should assist by referring the indexer from non-preferred to preferred terms.

Rules and standards

If the content of metadata is to be controlled, decisions are needed about the rules to be applied. Should *United Kingdom,* for example, be the preferred terminology, or *Great Britain and Northern Ireland*? Or should a coded abbreviation such as *UK* or *GB* be employed? If dates are to be entered in a standard form, should this be *YYYYMMDD, MMDDYYYY* or *DDMMYYYY*? Should months be entered in full (*December*), as abbreviations (*Dec*) or as numbers (*12*)?

Where appropriate, metadata for records management should conform to usage that has been formally approved and standardized for all of the organization's information resources. Users seeking *evidence* can be expected to focus their searches on records alone, but those needing *information* often require other sources besides records, and consistent use of metadata will help to provide common access routes. If the records management system can be linked to databases elsewhere in the organization that contain more extensive data about personnel, customers or suppliers, consistency of terminology can be ensured and duplication of data reduced or eliminated.

Published standards are available for some of the metadata elements that are likely to be required. These include:

- ISO 8601:2000 *Data elements and interchange formats – information interchange – representation of dates and times*
- ISO 639-1:2002 and ISO 639-2:1998 *Codes for the representation of names of languages*
- ISO 3166-1:1997, ISO 3166-2:1998 and ISO 3166-3:1999 *Codes for the representation of names of countries and their subdivisions.*

In addition, a growing number of standards (such as the *Universal standard products and services classification*, http://eccma.org/unspsc/) can be used for the representation of commercial products, facilities and services.

Published standards may also be used to support consistency in the form of names of persons, corporate bodies and places. Standards such as *AACR2*, the *Anglo-American cataloguing rules* (1988) for libraries, or the UK National Council on Archives *Rules for the construction of personal, place and corporate names* (1997), do not provide lists of approved terms but give considered advice on areas of potential difficulty such as names in non-European languages or double-barrelled names. Indexers can use these rules when creating metadata for newly captured records: the name can be taken from the title or the body of the record, and the rules applied to ensure that it is indexed to a consistent form. These rules may also be used in the creation of name authority files.

Constructing and using a thesaurus

In systems that use controlled language, approved terms for subjects and place names are often managed in a specialized type of authority file known as a *thesaurus*. Besides handling synonyms, the thesaurus is intended to recognize and take advantage of other semantic associations between words. For example, a pig is a type of animal, and so a thesaurus will recognize *pigs* as a 'narrower term' of *animals*. A 'broader term' such as *animals* will have a number of narrower terms: not just *pigs*, but also *cows*, *sheep* and so on.

To the indexer, the advantage of using a thesaurus is that a record of pig-farming need only be indexed under *pigs* and *farming*; if the relationship between *pigs* and *animals* is already recognized in the thesaurus, the word *animals* need not be entered as a separate index term. In addition, the thesaurus should ensure that a searcher looking for *animals* can be directed to the records indexed under all the relevant narrower terms (*pigs*, *cows*, *sheep*) as well as those indexed under the broader term *animals*.

The construction of a thesaurus has many pitfalls for the inexperienced. The relationships within the thesaurus must remain true irrespective of the context in which each term is used. Thus *dogs* is correctly described as a narrower term of *animals*, but not as a narrower term of *domesticated animals* or *pets* because some dogs are wild. Broader and narrower relationships should be restricted to terms that are related in one of the following ways:

1 Genus–species: e.g. *animals–dogs*. This example passes a simple test (Aitchison, Gilchrist and Bawden, 2000, 57): some animals are dogs; all dogs are animals.
2 Whole–part: parts of the body (e.g. *hands–fingers*), disciplines (e.g. *surgery–orthopaedics*), place names (e.g. *Scotland–Edinburgh*) and organizational units (e.g. *Roman Catholic Church–Papal Curia*).
3 Type–instance: e.g. *mountains–Kilimanjaro*.

A narrower term may have more than one broader term. For example, *Kilimanjaro* may be a narrower term of *Tanzania* and also of *mountains*; and *Tanzania* may be a narrower term both of *Africa* and of *countries*.

Categories of terms recognized in thesaurus construction include:

- entities (physical objects and other entities)
- actions (things done)
- agents (performers of actions)
- properties (attributes).

A broader term and its narrower terms must belong to the same category: *shoemaking*, *shoemakers* and *shoes* do not have broader–narrower term relationships because *shoemaking* is an action, *shoemakers* are agents and *shoes* are entities. These three are called 'related terms'. When designing a thesaurus it is important to beware of constructing 'false hierarchies'. Inexperienced indexers may be prone to identifying *shoes* as a narrower term of *shoemaking*, or perhaps of *shoe shops* or *sales*, but it is none of these; it is correctly a narrower term of *footwear* (Will, 1992).

The construction of a thesaurus to meet the needs of a particular organization is a task for specialist staff. Internationally recognized best practice is set out in ISO 2788:1986, *Documentation – guidelines for the establishment and development of monolingual thesauri*. Will (1992) provides a brief guide to thesaurus construction; Aitchison, Gilchrist and Bawden (2000) offer more detailed advice.

Computer software to support the development and use of thesauri is often built into records management applications. Thesaurus software is also available as a standalone application. It maintains the relationships between terms chosen by users; when integrated with a records management application it also allows terms to be selected for direct entry into record metadata.

Despite the availability of software tools to support the work, the time and cost of constructing and maintaining thesauri are often major obstacles to their use in records management. An alternative is to use a published thesaurus (such as the *UNESCO thesaurus*, www.ulcc.ac.uk/unesco/, the *Getty thesaurus of geographic names*, www.getty.edu/research/tools/vocabulary/tgn/, the *Art and architecture thesaurus*, www.getty.edu/research/tools/vocabulary/aat/, or one of the many other thesauri concerned with specific subject areas). However, their content may not always meet local needs, or a degree of adaptation may be required.

Functional 'thesauri' and the use of language control to describe functions, processes and activities

Controlled language can also be used to good effect in naming functions, processes and activities. Records managers in the Australian public sector, recognizing that many functions are common to numerous government agencies, have devised and published controlled vocabularies to describe these functions and their components, in order to promote consistency between agencies in the terms used to classify and retrieve records. Since these vocabularies focus on common functions, rather than those that are unique to particular agencies, they are likely to be of value to records managers in other sectors and other countries.

Two such vocabularies are available at the time of writing, both described by their publishers as 'thesauri'. *Keyword AAA: thesaurus of general terms*, produced by the State Records Authority of New South Wales (1998), is the more detailed of the two. The *Australian governments' interactive functions thesaurus (AGIFT)*, produced by the National Archives of Australia (2000), is a more generalized tool designed primarily for use with government materials made available through a web-based locator service.

Keyword AAA provides a comprehensive set of preferred terms (called 'descriptors') for common functions, and further sets of descriptors for the 'activities' identified as components of each function. The functional descriptors can be used to provide controlled-language titles for functions, while an 'activity' descriptor can be concatenated with the relevant functional descriptor to provide a title at process level: for example, *Health and safety – Inspections* or *Fleet management – Acquisitions*.

It also provides a third tier of 'subject descriptors', which are associated with particular activity descriptors but can be used with any activity descriptor that is deemed appropriate. At the third level, a descriptor can be taken from an approved list of 'subject descriptors' or can be the name of an organization, individual or project (Robinson, 1997, 293).

Keyword AAA is intended for use in conjunction with specially created authority files of terms relating to an organization's core or unique functions. One such derivative, entitled *Keyword for councils* (State Records Authority of New South Wales, 2000), has been created for Australian local government bodies. In the context of a functional classification scheme, *Keyword AAA* provides a base on which an organization-wide set of controlled-language terms can be built. However, it has some limitations: it is focused on the needs of organizations in the public sector; it provides for up to three levels of classification, but additional levels are not supported; and it assumes that the third level will normally be a subject grouping rather than an aggregation of records representing a lower level of activity. Records management systems that do not conform to this pattern may not be able to use it without adaptation.

Despite its name, *Keyword AAA: thesaurus of general terms* is not a thesaurus in the accepted sense. It uses some of the terminology of a conventional thesaurus, including phrases such as 'broader term' and 'narrower term', but gives them a different meaning: its 'broader terms' denote a higher level in a classification of functions, activities and subject descriptors, but may not always have a genus–species, whole–part or type–instance relationship to the 'narrower terms' below them. Records managers can use *Keyword AAA* to good effect in assigning record titles, but should be aware that it does not provide the kind of terminological relationships usually employed in indexing.

The retrieval interface

In computerized retrieval systems it is important that issues of human–computer interaction are taken into account. Browse and search interfaces that are welcoming and self-explanatory are essential if users of records are to have direct access to the system, but ease of operation is important even when a system is to be operated only by records management staff. In practice, there may be a trade-off between the range of functionality offered by the system and the need for an interface that avoids unnecessary complexity.

Enquiry screens for full-text searches are simple to present to the user, who merely has to fill in a search box and wait to see what results are achieved. Enquiry screens for searches of structured metadata usually raise more complex issues of presentation. A range of metadata elements should be searchable, including those relating to functional classification, forms of material and dates, as well as indexes of names, places or subjects. Since users often seek records of processes or activities that extended over a period of time, date range searches should be supported as well as searches for records from a single day, month or year. Users will need advice, preferably on-screen, about how to choose or combine the elements appropriate for their particular search.

Where controlled language is employed, searchers should also be enabled to use the preferred terms. It is helpful if searchers can consult indexes or thesauri when formulating their searches. Some applications offer automated term switching: if a non-preferred term is requested by a searcher, the preferred term is substituted automatically. Other options may include the facility to search on one term and find all occurrences of its related terms, or to search on a broader term and find relevant narrower terms as well.

Natural-language and controlled-language systems can both offer truncation and wildcard searches, and other search aids such as Boolean, adjacency and proximity searching. Systems that support the searching of metadata are more complex than those that rely only on full-text searching, since there is a choice of combining fields or indexes as well as combining search terms. For example, term A can be sought in fields X, Y and Z, or term A can be sought in field X, term B in field Y and term C in field Z. Boolean operators (**and, or, not**) can also be applied in appropriate combinations. Staff who are familiar with search techniques will understand the range of options but interfaces suitable for novices may be hard to achieve.

Many users will restrict their enquiry to the records of a single organizational function or a specific record series, but others may wish to look across several series or across all the records of the organization. An automated system should allow users to define the boundaries of their search, subject to the access rights assigned to them.

Presenting the full range of choice to users is often a challenge to the designers of system interfaces, and applications differ in their approach to presentation as well as in their underlying capabilities. Some offer multiple options or an expert search language to skilled users, while presenting a simplified interface to novices; this can be a helpful approach.

To meet the needs of users who may be uncertain of their exact requirements, the system should provide features to support browsing as well as searching. Such users may need to make a fairly broad search and then browse or navigate through the search results to identify records of potential interest. Online browsing is not always easy, but search results should be presented in a way that supports this.

Search results must also be presented in a way that makes clear the context of the records that have been retrieved. It is not enough for an automated system merely to present a set of results that match the search criteria: users must be able to interpret the records they have found, by access to contextual metadata or by being enabled to view records at higher or lower levels of aggregation.

Confidentiality and rights of access

Access regimes

Rights of access to records vary according to local needs and conditions. Some organizations have strict rules on confidentiality and restrict access to closely defined categories of user; even information about what records exist may be treated as confidential. Others have a policy of openness, with almost all records open to inspection by anyone, including members of the public.

Intermediate regimes are also common; for example, an organization may place no restriction on access to information about what records are available but may limit access to the records themselves, especially when access is sought by external enquirers. Records management staff need to know what records exist across the whole organization, although they may not have access to the contents of every record.

Freedom of information, privacy and data protection

Access rules are often imposed by legislation or other external constraints; for example, laws on freedom of information (FOI) may provide for public rights of access to the records of government agencies, but these rights may be tempered by other laws on privacy or data protection, which restrict the disclosure of information about named individuals.

Legislation on FOI has been enacted in a number of countries, with the intention of promoting accountability and transparency by giving citizens a right of access to information about the workings of government. The scope of FOI legislation varies from one jurisdiction to another. Some FOI laws may purport to give public access only to 'information' but most refer specifically to 'records' or 'official documents'; these terms may be variously defined in the legislation, or may not be defined at all. In practice, wherever FOI legislation is in force, members of the public have a right of access to a wide range of government records, although exceptionally sensitive or confidential records are usually exempt from the disclosure provisions.

FOI legislation normally indicates the procedures to be followed by members of the public who wish to make an access request, the time limits for responding to requests, the charges (if any) that may be levied, the circumstances in which access to original records may be granted and those in which requests may be met by supplying an abstract or a copy. There may also be a requirement for government agencies to publish a description of each series of records that they hold, so that citizens may know what types of record are being kept. FOI legislation normally applies to agencies of the central government; in some jurisdictions it also applies to local government bodies or other agencies that perform public functions. Commercial organizations are not usually subject to FOI laws, although there may be other legislation that provides for public access to some of their records.

Records that contain personal information about individuals are normally protected from disclosure under FOI legislation. Many countries have separate privacy laws, which are framed to prevent government agencies from disclosing such information to third parties. In some jurisdictions the same laws may also apply to non-governmental bodies, or there may be sector-specific laws regulating individual privacy rights in, for example, the banking sector.

European countries have comprehensive data protection regimes, which cover both the private and the public sector. Under the UK Data Protection Act 1998, personal data relating to identifiable living persons must be managed in accordance with a set of data protection principles: the data must be accurate, must be used only for fair and lawful purposes, must be relevant and adequate for those purposes, and must be protected against unauthorized access. Data subjects (the individuals about whom data are maintained) have a right to inspect their personal data and to have inaccurate data corrected. As with FOI legislation, data protection laws impose time limits for responding to access requests and regulate the level of charges that may be made. To protect individual privacy, the circumstances under which data may be disclosed to third parties are strictly limited. Access to data within the organization is also regulated: measures must be in place to prevent members of staff from gaining access to personal data about customers or colleagues, where such data are not relevant to their work. While the wording of data protection laws refers mainly to 'data' rather than 'records', the protection extends to personal information found in records as well as informational databases.

Access policies and procedures

Where there are no legal or regulatory requirements, organizations are free to apply their own rules on access to their records. In small organizations a single rule may be applied to all records, but in more complex organizations different processes or activities are likely to be subject to different levels of confidentiality. Each record series may have its own access rule, or rules may be applied at item or file level if part of a series is exceptionally sensitive. There may also be separate rules for different categories of staff, and for handling access requests from outside the organization.

Since the confidentiality of records diminishes over time, external access requests are often subject to a rule that records are available without restriction after the lapse of a stated number of years. A '30-year rule' is common, though other periods of time may also be specified, and for some records the period of 'closure' may be as long as 100 years. In many countries, closure rules for the records of public sector bodies are enshrined in legislation, although these rules may now have more limited application in the light of FOI laws that provide for access to many government records at an early stage in their life. Organizations in the private sector often choose to apply similar rules, although enforced at management discretion rather than imposed by statute. Provision may be made for external enquirers to apply for special permission to view records that are normally considered confidential: for example, some organizations grant access to academic researchers if they give a signed undertaking not to breach confidentiality guidelines in any published work.

An organization-wide access policy should be set at senior management level. It should state the general rules that apply to internal and external use of the organization's records, and any terms and conditions that are imposed on users across the organization as a whole. The role of the records manager is not to determine the policy but to provide appropriate advice to policymakers, ensure that the policy is clear and widely understood and take responsibility for its implementation. Within the policy, individual decisions about confidentiality, especially at item or file level, are normally made by business unit managers.

To enforce the policy, systems are needed to ensure that unauthorized access is not granted and that those who have access rights are not denied. There should be defined procedures for documenting the rights of different users and the access rules that apply to particular records, and for ensuring that this information is updated as staff responsibilities change or perceptions of confidentiality alter. The records management unit may take direct responsibility for these tasks or may be responsible for monitoring and checking the work done by others.

For any given record there are broadly three options: it may be open to all; open to defined users only; or freely open to one group of users while others have to make a formal application or meet certain conditions to gain access. In manual systems the terms of access may be marked on file covers, storage units, lists or index cards; to ensure that they are not overlooked, it is often necessary to repeat them in more than one place or highlight them using prominent labels in bold colours. Access may be controlled by restricting the availability of keys or codes used to unlock storage areas, cabinets or shelving units. Paper files may also be kept in sealed packages to reduce the likelihood of unauthorized opening. For these measures to be successful, staff employed in retrieving records must be trained in their operation. Regular monitoring may also be required.

Automated systems for paper records and electronic records systems can provide more sophisticated controls. A well-designed system should be able to manage the access rights of each user or group of users, by matching user rights against metadata describing the terms of access for particular records. When a user consults the database, it runs a test to see if the sought records are available to the user concerned. Users without full access rights may be debarred from seeing the description of a record, or may be allowed to see summary details but prevented from requesting the record itself. In an online environment, where users can retrieve electronic records directly from a central server, controls must be enforced automatically so that users are denied access to records for which they have no authorization. Access control is usually achieved through software functionality in combination with passwords or other identifiers used to log on to the system.

Problems occasionally arise when different items in a file or folder have different levels of confidentiality. If the records are on paper the sensitive items may have to be stored separately, so that users with limited access rights can still consult the rest of the file. Electronic records systems can handle this more easily, allowing separate online access rights to be assigned to each item. Some systems may also allow particular parts of an item to be concealed from unauthorized users, for example by obscuring sensitive words, phrases or paragraphs. Alternatively, systems can be configured so that the presence of one or more confidential items bars access to the whole of an electronic folder.

Electronic systems can be designed to ensure that when records are viewed full details are captured in an audit log. In highly sensitive environments, such logs can provide proof that records were seen only by authorized users. By logging the use of records automatically, electronic systems also offer an efficient method of gathering usage statistics for retention planning and management reports.

Managing external access to records

Even in organizations where internal users have direct access to records and no human intermediaries are employed to service their requests, there is still a need for staff to manage external enquiries.

In countries where citizens have rights of access under FOI or other legislation, access requests must be handled by someone with appropriate knowledge of the legal obligations as well as the organization's information and records systems. In addition, the organization will be contacted from time to time by external enquirers wishing to use its records for research purposes. Enquiries of this kind may relate to current or historical records. If the organization has retained its older records it will need to handle all these enquiries; if older records have been transferred to a separate archival institution historical enquiries can be passed on to the institution concerned, but enquiries about current records must still be handled in-house. Replies to external enquiries may be the responsibility of the records management unit; alternatively some or all may be handled by separate data protection, freedom of information or archives staff.

Some organizations, including most public sector bodies in many countries, are legally obliged to make some or all of their records available to the public. Even where there is no legal obligation, an organization may wish to provide access in the interests of goodwill, public relations or accountability. In either case, research enquiries may be handled by providing facilities for enquirers to make personal visits, or by undertaking research on their behalf. Either or both of these services may be provided free of charge, or a fee may be levied to cover the organization's costs or generate income.

External enquirers often seek to obtain copies of records, and it is normally appropriate to charge a fee for any photocopies or other reproductions supplied. The provision of copies is regulated by copyright laws, which apply to organizational records as well as published works. Broadly speaking, these laws state that reproduction of material in copyright requires the permission of the copyright owner. Copyright in records created within an organization is normally vested in the organization itself, but the organization does not own copyright in incoming correspondence and other records received from outside, and care should be taken not to breach the law by improper copying of records of this kind. Legal advice should be sought where necessary.

Archival services

Organizations that maintain their own archives usually need to provide a wider range of services, especially if external users are allowed or encouraged to use the archives for cultural purposes. If users are expected to consult archival records in person, accommodation for them must be provided; depending on the scale of the service, this may range from a single desk to one or more searchrooms where large numbers can be accommodated simultaneously. Staff are needed to provide assistance to users and to ensure that records are not misused. Visitors may be asked to take notice of, or sign assent to, a statement of the terms and conditions of access to the organization's records. Where original records on paper are consulted by external users, it is good practice to ensure that constant supervision is maintained, as a safeguard against mishandling, theft or damage. The risk of loss can also be reduced by providing access to copies of paper records on microform or as digital images.

Full descriptions of records and aids to retrieval are essential for archival services. Traditional practice has required the production of a descriptive list or catalogue of records on or after their transfer to archival custody. *ISAD(G)*, the *General international standard archival description* published by the International Council on Archives (2000), is a standard for retrospective cataloguing of older records that have been designated as archives. Its use in records management is limited, since it is not designed to support classification and description of records at the point of their creation. However, records that have been classified and assigned other metadata following the recommendations in Chapters 3 and 4 should need little further descriptive processing if a description complying with *ISAD(G)* is required for archival purposes. Practical applications of *ISAD(G)*, and other standards and practices for arranging and describing archival records, are discussed in Procter and Cook (2000).

Organizations wishing to encourage external use of their archives may publish a guide to their holdings, or give access to metadata about their archives through a website. In an integrated service that supports the management of records for internal use as well as providing for the needs of external users, external access to metadata may be restricted to those parts of the organization's records that are open to the public. Information about archival materials can also be contributed to regional or national networks, where users can find details of research sources from a variety of organizations. In many countries, compliance with *ISAD(G)* is deemed essential for metadata contributed to archival networks.

Archival records can be used in a variety of other ways to the benefit of the organization. Archives, particularly those that are visually attractive, are a prime resource for marketing and public relations activities. Reproductions of archival records may be used in advertising or in producing promotional materials for gift or sale. Depending on the focus of the organization, such materials may be targeted at customers, educational users or the wider community. Exhibitions and corporate histories can also increase awareness and understanding of the organization and its development over time, both for staff and for external markets. Audiovisual media may be used to similar effect, especially in educational programmes. Images of the organization's archives may be published on a corporate website, thus providing a service to distant researchers and a promotional tool for the organization as a whole.

There are many good texts that offer further guidance on the management of archives and archival services. A selective list is included in the Bibliography at the end of this book.

References

Aitchison, J., Gilchrist, A. and Bawden, D. (2000) *Thesaurus construction and use: a practical manual*, 4th edn, Aslib IMI.

Anglo-American cataloguing rules, 2nd edn 1988 revision, American Library Association, Canadian Library Association and Library Association Publishing.

International Council on Archives (2000) *ISAD(G): general international standard archival description*, 2nd edn, International Council on Archives. Also available at www.ica.org/ biblio/com/cds/isad_g_2e.pdf.

Kennedy, J. and Schauder, C. (1998) *Records management: a guide to corporate record keeping*, 2nd edn, Addison Wesley Longman Australia.

National Archives of Australia (2000) *Australian governments' interactive functions thesaurus*, National Archives of Australia.

National Council on Archives (1997) *Rules for the construction of personal, place and corporate names*, [UK] National Council on Archives. Also available at www.hmc.gov.uk/ nca/title.htm.

Procter, M. and Cook, M. (2000) *Manual of archival description*, 3rd edn, Gower.

Robinson, C. (1997) Records control and disposal using functional analysis, *Archives and Manuscripts*, **25** (2), 288–303. Also available at www.records.nsw.gov.au/publicsector/rk/ classification/record~1.htm.

State Records Authority of New South Wales (1998) *Keyword AAA: thesaurus of general terms*, 2nd edn, State Records Authority of New South Wales.

State Records Authority of New South Wales (2000) *Keyword for councils*, State Records Authority of New South Wales.

Will, L. (1992) *Thesaurus principles and practice*. Available at www.willpowerinfo.co.uk/ thesprin.htm.

ISO 639-1:2002 and ISO 639-2:1998 *Codes for the representation of names of languages*, International Standards Organization.

ISO 2788:1986 *Documentation – guidelines for the establishment and development of monolingual thesauri*, International Standards Organization.

ISO 3166-1:1997, ISO 3166-2:1998 and ISO 3166-3:1999 *Codes for the representation of names of countries and their subdivisions*, International Standards Organization.

ISO 8601:2000 *Data elements and interchange formats – information interchange – representation of dates and times*, International Standards Organization.

8

Implementing records management: practical and managerial issues

This chapter examines the practical and managerial issues surrounding the establishment and operation of a successful records management programme. It provides advice on the development and maintenance of effective records systems for organizations that already have the human and financial resources to support a records management programme, and guidance on establishing the necessary infrastructure for those at an earlier stage of implementation. It uses the framework recommended in the international standard on records management (ISO 15489-1:2001) and the accompanying technical report (ISO/TR 15489-2:2001).

Getting started

Establishing a records management policy

All organizations should have a formally agreed policy for the management of their records. The goal of the policy 'should be the creation and management of authentic, reliable and useable records, capable of supporting business functions and activities for as long as they are required. . . . The policy should be adopted and endorsed at the highest decision-making level and promulgated throughout the organization' (ISO 15489-1:2001, clause 6.2).

An example of a records management policy is given in Figure 8.2 (page 255). When records management is first under consideration, however, it will not be possible to prepare a fully detailed policy statement. The initial focus must be on obtaining a high-level policy decision that the organization will proceed to set up a programme of records management. When the need for a programme has been formally recognized, decisions are required to establish its broad parameters: in particular, whether it will embrace newly created as well as older records and whether it will cover the whole of the organization or only a part. Once these decisions have been made, the policy can be refined as work proceeds on developing the programme.

Reaching agreement on these initial policy decisions may not be easy. Some individuals at senior level may think that records 'manage themselves', or that decisions about records can safely be left to the initiative of local workgroups or individual staff members; others may not recognize a need for well-managed records or may consider it a low priority. Sometimes a crisis occurs – an organization suffers financial loss because records are unavailable for a legal dispute or for recovery from a disaster – and the case for records management becomes self-evident. In other circumstances some marketing may be required to convince every key senior manager of the need to manage records systematically.

Traditionally, records management programmes were promoted as a means of space saving and cost reduction, and this argument is still valid in paper environments where efficient management of records can offer substantial savings on storage costs. In the world of electronic and hybrid systems storage space has a lower profile, and records management is more effectively promoted in terms of the need to manage evidence and information to improve business performance and support accountability and legal and regulatory compliance.

Ideally, senior management will agree that the programme is to encompass all records in all media throughout the organization. Even if some parts of the organization already have local systems in place, these should be reviewed and incorporated into an organization-wide programme.

Sometimes key players need to be convinced of the need for a programme that is truly comprehensive. Some individuals may believe that records management is only concerned with paper records. A common misapprehension is that back-up systems operated by computing units will provide for the 'archiving' of electronic records, and it may be necessary to explain that back-up mechanisms designed to allow recovery from hardware or software failures are not sufficient to support the ongoing management, accessibility and use of records. Sometimes it is proposed that records management should be concerned only with records that are no longer required for the current business of the organization. While older paper records have often been the focus of records management programmes in the past, organizations now need to recognize that requirements for trustworthy evidence of their activities can only be met in full when all media are covered, and when records management issues are addressed at the point where records creation systems are designed and used.

In practice, however, resource limitations or political factors sometimes mean that a comprehensive programme appears to be an unrealistic aim. In such cases, the initial policy decision may be to establish a programme of more limited scope. It is common for organizations new to the concept of records management to start on a small scale, and for systems to spread across the organization as the benefits become clear and top management support increases. In some cases a small pilot programme may be formally agreed, with future decisions dependent on the success of the pilot. However modest the initial programme, a systematic approach to planning, design and implementation will be required.

Defining initial responsibilities

When a records management programme is introduced, responsibility rests at several levels. Senior management support is vital to the success of the project. It is essential to involve the chief executive or management board from the start, so that they support the programme, endorse the policy and provide resources.

At an early stage, key stakeholders can be brought together in a records management policy group or committee. Members of the group are likely to include business unit managers and senior computing, information management, financial, legal and corporate governance specialists. Such a group will provide a high level of management expertise to direct the project and assist in decision making and implementation.

An appropriate individual must be designated to take the lead role in planning and implementing the programme. The organization may choose to:

- appoint a consultant
- assign responsibility to an existing member of staff
- employ an experienced records manager on a long- or short-term contract.

Consultants can bring an impartial and experienced view and are often available at fairly short notice. They will undertake a project quickly and produce recommendations that are likely to be taken seriously by senior managers. However, it is important to select consultants with proven expertise in records management (rather than in, for example, library and information management, which requires a different balance of skills) and who can show a real understanding of the organization's needs. Consultants who import their standard blueprint should be avoided in favour of those who can tailor a solution to organizational requirements. Consultants may be used only for preliminary advice and planning or may also assist with implementation; in either case the organization will need to find staff to develop and maintain the programme after the consultant has left.

Assigning responsibility to an existing staff member has the advantage that the employee already knows the organization well. However, existing employees may lack the necessary skills (and thus need retraining). If records management is simply added to their other duties, staff with sufficient seniority to establish a records management programme may lack the time or interest to devote to its design and implementation. If more junior staff such as registry or filing supervisors are assigned to the task, they will lack the credibility or authority to implement significant changes. However, if the organization has staff such as archivists who have been trained in records management, their responsibilities could be extended accordingly.

Probably the ideal solution is to employ a suitably qualified and experienced records manager. The initial recruitment of a records manager sometimes follows a consultant's recommendations and a short-term appointment may be made until the organization becomes fully committed to a long-term investment.

The individual appointed to establish the records management programme will become a key member of the policy group and will need to call on the expertise of other group members. In an organization of any size, more than one individual will be required and a multidisciplinary team of project workers will be set up, perhaps including appropriate members of the policy group as well as others with relevant skills and interests. The records manager may lead the team or a separate project manager may be employed to oversee the project while leaving the professional decisions to those with records management qualifications or experience. Whichever model is followed, account must be taken of the project management issues discussed in Chapter 2.

Developing records management programmes and systems

The ISO 15489 methodology

A design and implementation methodology for sustainable records management is recommended in ISO 15489-1:2001, clause 8.4. The methodology is based on the Australian records management standard AS 4390.3-1996, clause 6.2.2. It has eight components:

- preliminary investigation
- analysis of business activity
- identification of requirements for records
- assessment of existing systems
- identification of strategies for satisfying records requirements

- design of a records system
- implementation of a records system
- post-implementation review.

The methodology is valid for the establishment of the records management programme as a whole and for the development of particular systems within it. When a new records management programme is established some systems and subsystems will necessarily be introduced before others, but if records management is to be adopted in a uniform manner across the whole organization it will be essential to keep the 'big picture' in mind throughout the development process. ISO 15489-1 emphasizes that the methodology need not be linear: the tasks can be undertaken iteratively or gradually.

Detailed guidelines originally based on the AS 4390.3 version of this methodology are available in the *Designing and implementing recordkeeping systems (DIRKS)* manual published by the National Archives of Australia (2001). These guidelines set out a rigorous approach and were designed primarily for Australian public sector organizations, but offer useful and practical advice applicable to all sectors. The British Standards Institution has published shorter guidelines based on the ISO version of the methodology: PD 0025-2:2002, *Effective records management: practical implementation of BS ISO 15489-1*.

Preliminary investigation and analysis of business activity

When establishing a records management programme, the starting point is to gain an understanding of the role, purpose and environment of the organization and to analyse its structures, functions, processes and activities (ISO 15489-1:2001, clause 8.4). This involves examining why the organization exists, what products or services it offers, how it operates in the present, how it plans to operate in the future and what changes to its operations and methods have been made in the past. It also involves an investigation of external factors affecting the way the organization operates, including its economic, political, legal, regulatory and social environment.

Techniques that can be used in these investigations have been discussed in Chapter 2, which also describes how a detailed analysis can be made of the functions and processes that the organization undertakes.

Identification of requirements for records

The preliminary investigation and the analysis of functions and processes provide essential background information about factors that influence or determine requirements for the creation and maintenance of records. Such requirements will vary from one function or process to another. Some will be stated explicitly in legislation or regulations but others are likely to be implicit in the business, accountability or cultural needs of the organization or the wider community. If the organization has a formal compliance programme, measures may already be in place to ensure that relevant laws, regulations and standards are observed; but account must also be taken of the other needs of internal and external stakeholders, including the organization's staff and customers.

As the records management programme develops, judgments must also be made on the extent to which the organization will seek to meet each particular requirement. As well as identifying stakeholders' needs for records of particular processes, it will be necessary to assess the costs that the organization will incur in meeting those needs and the possible consequences if the needs are not met. Sometimes it may be decided that the cost of creating or capturing records of a process cannot be justified, since the risk attaching to their absence is low; or that records of a process will be captured but the costs of long-term retention or maximum security provision are unwarranted. In other cases the need for records may be judged to be critical: if the risk attaching to their absence or defectiveness is high, requirements for records will be met in full. Such decisions must be ratified at senior level within the organization.

Assessment of existing systems

Records managers rarely work in virgin territory. Occasionally they may have the opportunity to design systems for newly established functional areas, or even for a new organization, but more often their work is concerned with the records of functions and processes that have been in operation for some time. In this situation they must take account of the existing records as well as plan for the management of those created in the future.

The key tool for gaining control of these legacy records is the records survey. As noted in Chapter 2, a survey enables records managers to assess the records themselves and the systems used to manage them in the past. It provides the opportunity to learn how the organization's functions, structures and environment have affected the creation and maintenance of its existing records. It also provides the opportunity to discover how far the existing systems match up to the requirements that have been identified and where they fall short.

In organizations where no structured records management programme has been in place, surveys often reveal a variety of problems. Typically a survey may find that:

- paper records systems are congested, and in some cases have been used to store information products and other materials that are not records
- paper records are poorly organized and difficult to retrieve, and their arrangement does not fully reflect the processes and activities that led to their creation
- parts of some record series appear to be missing from the paper systems, but some of the missing records are believed to be held in electronic form on personal computers
- computer storage is not organized to match the paper system, but each worker follows their own system: most store records alongside work in progress, and many use random and seemingly meaningless file titles, so that correlating electronic and paper documentation is impossible
- records stored on personal computers are inaccessible when the worker is absent
- further records that are needed appear to have been lost or destroyed, but no one knows exactly what exists or where
- when employees leave or change jobs, computing staff clear the contents of their hard disk or personal account: everything is deleted regardless of any continuing value it may have for the organization
- older paper records, together with some unlabelled computer tapes or floppy disks, are in unmarked cabinets and boxes in a basement.

Surveys do not always find the existing situation as dire as this. Sometimes a survey discovers that fairly adequate systems are in place even if they have not been designed to professional standards. There may be an existing infrastructure of records staff, accommodation and equipment, which can be used as a basis for future development.

Where an embryo records management service already exists, it is often helpful to evaluate it by means of a SWOT analysis (see Figure 8.1). The acronym SWOT refers to the *strengths* and *weaknesses* of the service and the *opportunities* and *threats* that it faces. SWOT analysis can be applied to develop and extend the conclusions drawn from investigation of the external environment. It seeks to identify the opportunities and threats in the external environment and the strengths and weaknesses of existing resources and activities, which might be used to take advantage of opportunities or avert threats. The analysis enables informed decisions to be taken

Internal factors	External factors
Strengths • long-serving and committed records staff • good relations between records staff and users • capacious and well-equipped storage areas for paper records • established systems for controlling access and maintaining confidentiality.	**Opportunities** • new privacy and freedom of information legislation highlights the importance of effective records management systems • new senior executive has a more open attitude to records management • outsourcing of support services means that the need for documentation of contracts and service level agreements has a high profile.
Weaknesses • lack of staff skills, especially in managing electronic records • lack of integration between electronic and paper records • no co-ordination between systems in different parts of the organization • inadequate funding.	**Threats** • management of electronic record creating systems is driven by information systems provision; software packages and hardware combinations are chosen by computing specialists with little or no regard for records management implications • outsourcing of support services means that there is little in-house access to information technology expertise for advice on electronic records issues.

Fig. 8.1 *Example of a SWOT analysis for a records service*

about the ability of the existing records service to contribute to the development of a new programme.

Identification of strategies for satisfying records requirements

Strategies to satisfy the requirements that have been identified may include adopting policies, standards, guidelines, procedures and practices; such strategies can be applied separately or in combination (ISO 15489-1:2001, clause 8.4). When establishing a new programme, it is also necessary to agree the balance between centralization and decentralization, as discussed in Chapter 6. The strategies chosen must suit the environment, culture and technical capabilities of the organization, and will guide the design and implementation of the programme and its components.

Organizational culture is an important factor in selecting appropriate strategies. For example, in recent years most organizations have actively encouraged employees to focus on outcomes and productivity; while commendable in many ways, this has sometimes created a culture where capture and maintenance of records is perceived as unimportant. Similarly where staff turnover is high, or where staff are employed on short-term contracts, many employees are likely to have little concern for the organization's longer-term needs for records of their activities. If operational staff appear to lack motivation to capture or maintain records systematically, policies and guidelines must be supplemented by other strategies. Particularly in highly decentralized systems, promotional or training strategies are likely to have a major role.

Strategies in a paper environment will include the use of agreed procedures (such as procedures for capturing and classifying records correctly and for transferring them to alternative storage). Additional strategies must then be selected to ensure that the procedures are followed. In some organizations, it may be appropriate to rely on assigning responsibility for these tasks to records management staff or other designated postholders. Where day-to-day responsibility is to rest with operational staff, there may be a need for senior management directives, supervisory checks or regular monitoring to enforce compliance.

In electronic environments similar choices must be made, but there is an additional option of using system functionality to ensure that records management requirements are met. For example, computer systems could be configured to purge personal directories or e-mail accounts of any items that have not been accessed for a stated number of weeks, thus obliging the user to capture records to a formal records management system if they are not to be lost. As noted in Chapter 4, with many routine processes it is also possible to rely on purely technological strategies that allow records capture and other requirements to be met automatically.

As decisions are made on records requirements and strategies, the initial policy statement is likely to need amplification or revision. An overarching records management policy should be developed, setting out the aim, scope and objectives of the records management programme (see Figure 8.2); where necessary it should be supported by more specific policies on creation, capture, retention, access or other aspects of the programme.

Once the policy statement has been drafted, perhaps by a records policy group or committee, it needs to be approved by senior managers and endorsed by the chief executive or management board. When this has been achieved, the organization's directors have formally accepted responsibility for good records management and have given their authority for the inauguration of the programme.

Responsibilities for records management must also be defined more precisely at this stage. Primary responsibility should be assigned to a records manager, who may be supported by other staff. Especially in role culture organizations, consideration must be given to the location of the records management service within the organizational structure. It may be an independent unit or a part of a larger department such as information services, facilities management, legal services or central administration.

Decisions are also needed on the extent of the records manager's responsibilities. For example:

Component	Example of wording
• Outline of the legislative or regulatory framework, or reference to other standards or best practice	'Our records management programme will seek to comply with ISO 15489-1 *Records management* and ISO 9000 *Quality management systems*. As a public body, we are also bound under the Freedom of Information Act 2000 to maintain and make available records to which citizens have a right of access.'
• Aim and scope of the programme	'The aim of the programme is the effective management of our records as a source of evidence and information. It encompasses records in all media and in all parts of the organization.'
• Key objectives for the programme	'The programme's objectives are to ensure that: • adequate records of our business activities are created • appropriate access to those records is provided for all authorized users • records required for business, accountability or cultural purposes are retained and remain usable for as long as they are needed • records of long-term value are identified and preserved as archives • other records are confidentially destroyed when no longer required.'
• Statement of responsibilities for records management	'The Central Records Service is responsible for ensuring the implementation of the programme. It provides records management services to all departments, including those at satellite sites. All staff are responsible for the proper management of the records they create and use and should follow the procedures and guidance of the Central Records Service. Central Records staff are responsible for offering support and training and for monitoring of standards. Liaison staff in each department can give local advice and assistance. The Information Services Division is responsible for the technical aspects of managing electronic records and the Central Records Service will work closely with Information Services to provide a comprehensive service.'
• Definitions of technical terms	'In this policy, *records* means any documents or data which form recorded evidence of a business activity.'
• References to specific policies and other more detailed documentation	'Policy guidelines on records capture, media conversion and migration ... and records procedure manuals, classification schemes and retention schedules ... are available on the intranet.'

Fig. 8.2 *Components of a records management policy statement*

1 If storage of current paper records is to become or remain decentralized, how much authority will the records manager have with regard to records held in business units?

2 If the records manager is to assume custody of such records later in their life, what rights and obligations will be transferred along with the records, and how much responsibility for their control and management will remain with business units?

3 Are the organization's archival records to be managed separately or will they form part of the records manager's remit?

Decisions on these matters should be incorporated into the policy document, together with statements on the records management responsibilities of operational staff and information technology specialists.

Since records management must be adopted across functional and departmental boundaries, and needs formal links with other business functions such as information technology and compliance management, the policy group overseeing the initial project can usefully be given a permanent status. Such a group should be a formally established body, which can contribute to the further development of the records management policy, advise on procedural issues and act as a forum for communication between records experts and senior operational managers. It might be chaired by a management board member or by the records manager or another senior member of staff.

Designing systems and identifying resources

When appropriate strategies have been agreed, records management systems can be designed in detail. Designs should be based on the requirements and strategies that have been identified and should follow the principles and techniques discussed in earlier chapters of this book. They must take account of the size and resources of the organization, and the extent to which its operations are concentrated on one site or geographically dispersed. At an operational level, systems must also be designed so that they comply with regulatory or best practice requirements for health and safety in the workplace.

It was noted in Chapter 1 that a single organization-wide records management system may be feasible in a small organization, but in larger organizations separate systems will probably be needed in different functional areas. While common models should be used where appropriate, it is also important that each system is designed to match the needs of the relevant business processes and activities. When technological solutions are to be employed for records capture, relevant functionality should be built into operational systems as far as possible. If operational staff are to be asked to follow specific procedures, instructions can usefully be incorporated into guidelines that have wider scope; for example, records management rules about the capture of e-mail messages can be included in corporate guidelines on e-mail use, or instructions for managing records of a particular business process included in procedural manuals relating to the process concerned.

Depending on organizational requirements, retrieval mechanisms for records may be designed to stand alone, or may need to be integrated with particular business process tools or corporate information systems. While their evidential qualities differentiate records from other information sources, many users wish to use records simply to gain access to their information content. If structured information from records is widely used beyond the process where the records are created, it may be appropriate to design records management systems so that they can support the copying of the relevant data to a dedicated information environment such as a statistical or decision-support application. Alternatively, if wide-ranging use is made of information obtained by direct consultation of the records themselves, records management systems may be designed to share an interface with library systems, corporate databases or information products published on an intranet. Particularly in larger organizations, records or metadata maintained electronically may be accessed through a corporate information portal. For optimum integration, both technical and semantic interoperability will be required; as well as appropriate technological standards it will be necessary to use index terms that share a common vocabulary.

In geographically dispersed organizations it may be necessary to make provision for staff at one location to gain access to records created or held at another. Internet technology can facilitate remote access to electronic records as well as the provision of common gateways for records and other information resources. However, the advantages of shared access to corporate information must be balanced against the overriding need to design systems that protect the evidential value of records by preserving their functional context and integrity.

Resources are a prerequisite for a new records management service. Staff with specialist skills, accommodation and equipment will be required, and these requirements must be identified and costed when programmes and systems are designed.

In larger organizations, several types of *records management staff* will be needed. One or more professional members of staff will be responsible for the direction of the records management service and for systems development (see Figure 8.3). The senior records professional may also be responsible for other services such as data protection or freedom of information compliance, mailroom services or internal communications.

It can sometimes be difficult to identify a 'professional records manager'. Many people working in records management have added records management skills to a professional background in information management, librarianship or business administration. Others have a postgraduate qualification in records or archives management. Many countries have a framework for the training and

---

Job description : Records Manager

Job purpose: to develop and manage a records management programme that meets the business, accountability and cultural needs of the organization.

Reporting to the Deputy Chief Executive, the postholder is responsible for:

1. managing the Central Records Service and its operations
2. undertaking needs analysis, strategic planning and policy development for records management
3. developing and maintaining appropriate records management systems, liaising with client departments as necessary and ensuring that all legal and regulatory obligations are met
4. managing the implementation of a system for electronic records management, in conjunction with the Information Services Division, and ensuring its full integration with existing paper records systems
5. devising and delivering records management training for staff throughout the organization
6. devising and maintaining quality control and compliance procedures for records management
7. supervising other records management staff and assisting them to develop appropriate skills and capabilities
8. planning and managing the budget for the Central Records Service.

Person specification

Qualifications and experience:

1. postgraduate qualification in records management
2. at least five years' experience in a records management service.

Aptitudes:

1. financial and staff management skills, or aptitude to acquire them
2. familiarity with office automation systems and specialist software applications for records management
3. ability to communicate effectively in writing and orally with staff at all levels.

Fig. 8.3   *Example of a job description for a professional records manager*

development of records managers. A survey in 1997 (Yusof and Chell, 1998, 33–51) identified more than 80 academic institutions in 26 countries worldwide that offered undergraduate or postgraduate training in records management, either as standalone courses or in conjunction with educational programmes in archives, information science or other subjects. Distance learning courses are increasingly available. Links to the websites of many training providers can be found on the UNESCO Archives Portal at www.unesco.org/webworld/portal_archives/pages/ Education_and_Training/Institutions/.

Membership of a professional association is often an indicator of commitment to a professional career in records management. Some of the major professional associations are listed in Appendix C. Formal routes for continuing professional development are offered in some countries. The certification programme of the Institute of Certified Records Managers, based in the USA, requires its members to undertake 100 hours of approved educational activity every five years. In the UK and Ireland, the Society of Archivists' Professional Register requires candidates to have three years' post-qualification experience and to show evidence of professional development in this period.

Especially where records are maintained on paper, professional staff in larger organizations will be supported by records assistants responsible for carrying out day-to-day procedures (see Figure 8.4). Intermediate tiers of supervisory staff may also be employed. In some organizations clerical, portering, cleaning or maintenance staff are dedicated to the records management unit; elsewhere these services may be provided centrally.

Job description : Records Assistant

Job purpose: to assist in the running of the University's records centre.

Reporting to the Records Centre Manager, the postholder is responsible for:

1. processing user requests, including retrieving and reshelving paper records
2. preparing records for transfer from current storage to the records centre, and checking deliveries and transfer lists
3. preparing records for scanning or conversion to microfilm
4. checking the quality of scanned or filmed images
5. processing records designated for destruction or transfer to the University Archives
6. completing documentation associated with the tasks set out above, and entering relevant data into the Central Records Service database
7. assisting professional records management staff in other tasks as appropriate.

Person specification

Qualifications and experience:

1. a school leaver or graduate
2. at least one year's general office experience or experience in a records management service.

Aptitudes:

1. fair keyboard skills (40 wpm)
2. familiarity with office automation systems, including word-processing, e-mail and databases
3. ability to interact with users courteously and effectively.

Fig. 8.4   *Example of a job description for a records assistant*

Records assistants and paraprofessionals may be school leavers or graduates with information technology, keyboard or administrative skills. Sometimes paraprofessional posts are used to give experience to aspiring professionals. In some countries there are technical courses offering task and skill centred training for paraprofessional staff working in records management, although where such courses exist they do not always lead to formal qualifications.

In practice the head of the records management unit will not have line management responsibility for all staff involved in records activities. Most records creation is necessarily the responsibility of operational staff across the organization. In decentralized systems, some records staff may work locally within business units: such staff may form part of the central records management team or report to a manager within the business unit concerned. Ideally they should be professionally responsible to the head of records management even if they report to another manager for operational purposes.

Where business units have no dedicated records staff, some organizations establish a liaison network, whose members might meet periodically but mainly work remotely. Each business unit nominates a liaison officer to take responsibility for records management locally. This type of network can supplement a senior policy group in bringing ownership of records management into business units and providing a focus of expertise to contribute to development of the programme. The records manager can use the network to disseminate procedures and monitor implementation.

In addition to suitable staff and office facilities for them, a records management unit is likely to require the use of *accommodation or equipment* for a number of specialist purposes. These may include mail sorting and delivery facilities, one or more records storage areas, microfilm or digitization facilities and access to services such as transport and confidential waste destruction. Issues relating to the planning of accommodation have been discussed in Chapter 6. Advice should also be sought from architects, structural engineers, builders or equipment suppliers.

Technological solutions are almost certain to form part of any systems design. These may include the addition of enhanced records management functionality to existing software applications, the acquisition of a new application to support records management, or both. When acquiring a new application the first steps are to define the functionality that is needed and draw up a specification of requirements. In some organizations there may be an option to have a system specially built to match the specification, but more commonly an existing commercial product will be purchased. For paper records, organizations have sometimes chosen to use a number of separate small databases to manage different aspects of a records management programme, but where resources allow it is preferable to use a single integrated application. In a hybrid environment the application should be able to support the management of records in any medium. It should provide a range of retrieval and reporting tools that can be used to find information about the records, instigate disposal or other actions when required and produce reports and statistical analyses so that the records management unit can account for its activities and plan for the future.

The published standards listed in Figure 4.5 (page 123) may be used to help identify necessary enhancements to existing applications to support the management of electronic records, and can also be used or adapted when specifying the functionality required from a new ERM application. Some national bodies, such as the US Department of Defense and the UK Public Record Office, have issued lists of records management software applications that they have tested and approved.

While some commercial packages for records management are bought ready to run, others allow or require varying degrees of adaptation or further development of the supplier's core product. Whichever route is followed, the software must be compatible with existing or available hardware platforms and operating systems, portable to future platforms and scalable for expected rates of growth. Where necessary it must also provide technical interoperability with other relevant applications.

Procedures for software purchases vary between organizations, but usually it is appropriate to contact a number of suppliers and make a preliminary evaluation of available products against the specification of requirements. The reputation and financial stability of suppliers should also be investigated, before making a shortlist of suppliers who are formally invited to tender. All tenderers should be sent a copy of the specification and a statement of compatibility, scalability and interoperability requirements, and asked to provide a detailed written response stating precisely how their product matches what is required. They should be advised that, when a selection has been made, their response will be incorporated into any eventual contract together with the organization's requirements for maintenance and support services and the supply of future upgrades.

Records systems design necessarily includes the planning of *documentation*. Traditionally this required the design and production of numerous control forms: internal forms such as charge-out sheets, location registers and survey forms for use by records management staff, and also forms such as transfer lists and records request forms for interaction with users. Today most of the data provided on such forms are collected and maintained electronically, and if a records management software package is acquired it will provide most or all of the necessary infrastructure. Nevertheless there will still be a need for decisions about documentation and data collection, whether in customizing the interface provided by a software package or in preparing documentation for distribution on paper or through an intranet.

There are three broad categories of records management documentation:

1 *Programme documentation* includes policy statements, organizational records management standards and guidelines, and business plans for the records management service.
2 *Systems documentation* captures information about the logical infrastructure of the system (including logical models of functions and activities, classification schemes and retention schedules), its physical infrastructure (including storage plans and location metadata) and operational procedures for records management staff and users (including procedural guidelines, which may be brought together in a procedure manual). Systems documentation may need to be made available in different versions for records staff and for users; records management software packages often support this by providing different views of relevant metadata.
3 *Promotional materials* include publicity brochures, leaflets and web pages giving general information about records management services.

Whatever the systems design, its implementation will require adequate *financial resources*. There will also be recurrent costs for staff, accommodation, supplies, equipment and services purchased. To meet these costs, records management will need a budget. Depending on the organizational structure this may be an independent cost centre under the control of the senior records manager, which enables priorities to be set and expenditure controlled locally, or part of the budget of a larger business unit of which records management forms part.

Sometimes records managers are expected to negotiate agreements with business units for delivery of records management services and to derive the records management budget from internal contracts of this kind. If successful, this approach can provide records management with close user links and a high profile within the organization. If records management is funded centrally, its funding is simpler to manage but may be vulnerable to cuts in budgets for non-income earning functions. Sometimes records management is funded from a mixture of sources: an allocation for central services ensures a spread of good practice across the organization, and can be supplemented by charging for value added services delivered in individual business areas.

Planning and managing implementation

When the prerequisites are in place, decisions must be made about priorities for implementation. New systems may have to be introduced in stages, allowing time for piloting and testing each component before full implementation. Existing systems may have to be partly or wholly restructured; while it is sometimes possible to implement a new system independently of any need to resolve problems inherited from past practice, more usually existing arrangements must be integrated into the new design.

Priorities will vary according to local circumstances, but in general it is unwise to attempt the implementation of new systems for electronic records until paper systems are in good order. Business managers sometimes assume that the introduction of information technology is all that is needed to solve problems of managing paper records, but if the paper records are in disarray automation may simply transfer the problem to a different medium.

Often the first step is to decongest the existing systems by establishing appraisal criteria and eliminating records that are redundant. Records that are identified for retention but are not expected to be used for the current business of the organization can be separated and removed to off-floor or offline storage.

If information products such as trade catalogues, magazines or instruction manuals for office equipment have been interfiled with paper records they should be moved to separate information files. Stocks of office supplies and blank forms should also be segregated from the records management system. Members of staff who keep personal papers or memorabilia in their offices should be encouraged to establish a personal file so that these do not become confused with organizational records.

Functional classification schemes are the intellectual basis on which effective records systems are built. Once materials that are not records have been separated out, record series corresponding to business processes can be identified, classification schemes implemented and systems for the capture, retention, maintenance and retrieval of records built around them.

When a new classification scheme is introduced or an old scheme revised, existing records may be reclassified or the new scheme applied only to records created subsequently. Reclassifying existing records is labour-intensive and can be prone to error. It is often more appropriate to identify a date when the new scheme will come into use, and to leave records created before that date with their classification under the old scheme. Existing paper files should be closed on the agreed date, while electronic folders can be made read-only so that no new items are added to them. It will then be necessary to run the two schemes in tandem, often for several years. Both will be required for retrieval, although only one will be used to classify newly created records.

If this is likely to be difficult, or if management of the existing records is critically hindered by the inadequacy of the previous scheme, reclassification must be undertaken. Each file, folder or item must be inspected so that a new classification can be assigned to it. In a busy organization this is often impractical during working hours when records are in use for business purposes, and it may be best for the task to be undertaken during holiday periods or at weekends. Once started, the work needs to be finished as quickly as the need for care and accuracy will allow, so that business operations that use the records are not impeded. Sometimes it is possible to reduce the scale of the task by limiting reclassification to the most critical records or those created after a fixed date in the recent past. Teamwork is likely to produce faster results than an exercise undertaken by one person working alone, but it is important to ensure that all team members work to the same standards. Another option is to reclassify on demand as old records are needed.

Similar options are available for other retrospective conversion tasks, such as converting paper-based metadata to digital form, scanning paper records to create digital images or importing electronic files from office suites into electronic records management software applications. When records are to be digitized or moved to a more robust software environment it is likely that additional metadata will need to be captured. If this requires records to be reviewed individually, this can be done while scanning or importing is in progress or as a separate exercise when scanning or importing is complete. While import processes may be largely automatic, upgrading of metadata usually requires staff or contractors with specialist skills. The timing and scope of retrospective conversion must take account of their availability.

Those parts of a system that relate to the off-floor or offline management of older records are often easiest to introduce. While the establishment of new current records systems can bring substantial benefits in the medium and longer terms, nevertheless in the short term it inevitably disrupts established working patterns; on the other hand, improved systems for paper records whose usage rate has declined are usually welcomed, because staff see an immediate benefit in the decongestion of their working areas.

The introduction of new systems for managing records will have an impact on all members of staff who create or use them in their daily work. Training staff in the new systems is essential, but the issue extends beyond training into wider areas of change management. Records managers have a delicate task to perform in working with staff who are often very possessive about 'their' records and may be apprehensive or unsympathetic when records management systems are devised and standards imposed.

While the introduction of any corporate system of records management brings a loss of personal control over records, additional culture change issues often arise with electronic records management:

1 Some individuals may only feel comfortable with keeping records on paper, because of its obvious visibility and its independence from computer technology.
2 Some may accept the introduction of corporate systems for paper records, but resist it where electronic records are concerned because of an assumption that computer storage is essentially personal.
3 Many people find that an electronic records management system imposes more discipline than the paper systems to which they are accustomed, particularly if it changes the way that they use standard office software or obliges them to complete record profiles when records are captured.
4 Others become so committed to using electronic systems that they forget paper resources altogether.

The starting point is usually the need to promote an awareness of records as a corporate resource and an understanding that, whether on paper or in electronic form, they are not merely for personal use. Culture change often includes motivating staff to recognize the importance of good records management, as well as building confidence in the new systems. The organization's records management policy should be communicated to all staff, together with a directive for its implementation. By itself, however, this will not be sufficient. 'Records managers will have to meet with staff throughout the organization to express their enthusiasm' for records management and develop 'a corporate culture in which employees take the documentation of their activities seriously' (Bearman, 1994, 112; 1995, 392). Staff must feel ownership of the new systems and so it is essential that they participate as fully as possible in the change process. A communications strategy should be adopted, with workshops, demonstrations, meetings and interviews held as necessary. Particularly in larger organizations, change agents (individuals who can influence others and promote involvement in workshops and training sessions) can be identified and used to assist the records manager in achieving a smooth transition.

Post-implementation review

Design and implementation are the beginning of an ongoing records management programme. After implementation, the programme and each of its components must be reviewed and evaluated. The purpose of such reviews is to monitor progress and measure success, so that senior management can be informed of results and revisions to the programme can be made as necessary. Review and evaluation will also be ongoing processes. Policies and procedures should be examined regularly to ensure that they still meet the organization's requirements. Targets may be set and performance measured against them. Records management services may also aim at compliance with independent quality standards such as the ISO 9000 series *Quality management systems*.

Performance measurement seeks to define the relationship between the resources going into a records management service and its achievements, using quantitative and qualitative measures. If a records management software application is used, much quantitative information (for example, on the frequency of records use) can be obtained from report output. Other indicators of performance (such as the time taken to retrieve paper files from storage) may have to be measured manually. Qualitative evaluation (assessing how effectively the records requirements of the organization and the needs of individual users are being met) requires techniques such as interviews, questionnaires and observation of systems in operation. Quality audits can be undertaken internally or by external bodies.

Maintaining the impetus

Planning for the future and responding to change

The records management programme should have a place in the strategic plans for the organization as a whole, and the records management unit charged with carrying out the programme should produce a business plan of its own. Where appropriate, a long-term business plan setting out objectives over several years can be supplemented by short-term plans indicating immediate operational priorities. Business plans should be regularly reviewed and updated and should also be sufficiently flexible to allow a rapid and effective response to changing requirements for records management.

The analytical techniques examined in Chapter 2 can be reused when necessary in the ongoing management of the programme. Particularly in times of organizational or legislative change, or at points of significant technological evolution, it is helpful to deploy some of these techniques to undertake a new analysis of the strategic position of the records management service and to shape ideas on its future direction. For example, reuse of the PEST analysis technique described in Chapter 2 can be valuable to maintain current awareness of the wider environment. The SWOT analysis described earlier in this chapter can be repeated periodically to analyse the resources available within the organization and help to ensure that strengths are maximized and weaknesses minimized, so that opportunities can be taken and threats avoided.

Records managers must be ready to react to changes both to organizational structures and to the functions, processes and activities that the organization performs. Structural changes occur frequently in contemporary organizations, and records managers need to log information about each change, in order to document the resultant shifts in responsibility for functional areas of work and thus for the creation, capture or maintenance of records. The functions of the organization, though relatively stable, may also change over time, and changes to individual processes will be made at more or less frequent intervals. Records managers may need to introduce new systems when new functions are established and will certainly need to modify existing systems from time to time in response to changes in the way that functions are carried out. Such changes will require revision of the logical model of functions and processes, and of the classification schemes and retention schedules derived from it, to ensure that they are kept up to date as new types of record creating activity are introduced or old ones discontinued.

Existing systems may also need revision to meet other changes in requirements for records. Within the organization, these may be triggered by new internal regulations or control measures, changes in organizational culture or evolving business needs. Other events that may call for a response are office moves, reductions in the size of the workforce, or the introduction or revision of service agreements, market testing or outsourcing requirements. Records managers must be constantly alert to such developments and should respond appropriately.

In the wider environment, technological changes can also be expected to have a major impact on a records management programme. Records managers need to maintain an awareness of the arrival of new formats for the creation and preservation of records, and of the implications of the obsolescence of older formats. While the rapid rate of change in information technology can sometimes appear daunting, it can also bring benefits in terms of improved functionality for users and records management staff.

Other external factors include changes to laws or statutory regulations, which may require the creation of new types of record or the alteration of existing retention periods or access rights. In addition, external pressures such as the passage of new legislation can sometimes provide leverage and opportunity to raise the profile of records management or to improve practices in difficult areas.

Records management programmes must remain focused on the needs of their users, not on records retention for its own sake. Monitoring new developments, responding to change and taking advantage of opportunities all form part of the ongoing management of an effective programme. When there is a need for significant modification of the programme components, some or all of the design and implementation methodology recommended in ISO 15489-1:2001 should be applied. Appropriate elements from the methodology should be selected to ensure that the changes are managed systematically.

Promoting competence, understanding and awareness

Ongoing training for users and records staff should be provided, to ensure that records management objectives are understood and best practices communicated throughout the organization. New staff in particular will need to be informed about records management policies and trained in the relevant procedures. Many organizations include a briefing by the records manager in induction courses for new employees.

Awareness of records management issues can also be promoted using newsletters (in paper or electronic form), posters, mouse mats, records centre open days and other marketing techniques. If the programme is to be successful the benefits of effective records management must be demonstrated and emphasized to managers and staff at all levels in the organization.

Recording records management

Records management activities must be subject to the same records management discipline as other organizational activities. Records of policy development and operational procedures in records management must be captured and managed systematically. Operational records traditionally comprised paper forms completed by users, records management staff or contractors, but now often take the form of transactional data captured in a database or records management software application. Retention decisions and access controls should be applied to these records as rigorously as to records created elsewhere in the organization.

Records of quality control processes in records management must also be created, captured and managed over time. Evidence of systematic monitoring and auditing of practices and procedures should be maintained for as long as it is needed.

References

Bearman, D. (1994) *Electronic evidence: strategies for managing records in contemporary organizations*, Archives and Museum Informatics.

Bearman, D. (1995) Archival strategies, *American Archivist*, **58** (4), 380–413. Also available at www.archimuse.com/publishing/archival_strategies/.

National Archives of Australia (2001) *DIRKS: a strategic approach to managing business information*. Available at www.naa.gov.au/recordkeeping/dirks/dirksman/dirks.html.

Yusof, Z. M. and Chell, R. W. (1998) Records management education and training worldwide: a general overview of the current situation, *Records Management Journal*, **8** (1), 25–54.

AS 4390-1996 *Records management*, Standards Australia.

ISO 9000 series: ISO 9000:2000 *Quality management systems – fundamentals and vocabulary*, ISO 9001:2000 *Quality management systems – requirements* and ISO 9004:2000 *Quality management systems – guidelines for performance improvements*, International Standards Organization.

ISO 15489-1:2001 *Information and documentation – records management – part 1: general*, International Standards Organization.

ISO/TR 15489-2:2001 *Information and documentation – records management – part 2: guidelines*, International Standards Organization.

PD 0025-2:2002 *Effective records management: practical implementation of BS ISO 15489-1*, British Standards Institution.

Conclusion

In common with many other professions, records management is experiencing rapid changes and in recent years has moved beyond its traditional boundaries. No longer focused wholly on space and cost saving, or restricted to the channelling of historical records into archival institutions, it has acquired a much greater visibility and a more proactive role. The priority given to accountability and corporate governance initiatives in many countries has given records managers a new sense of direction and has increased the range of stakeholders whose needs are served by effective and successful records management programmes. At the same time, the development of national and international standards for records management has provided a framework for best practice. The growth in the availability of professional literature, to which this book contributes, also shows the increasing maturity of the discipline.

Records management practices were originally developed to manage the large quantities of paper files generated by governments and commercial organizations, and for many years these remained the primary concern of records managers. Today paper is only one of a number of media used to create, maintain or provide access to records. The increasing prevalence of 'born digital' records, many of which will never have a paper manifestation, has required the traditional approaches to be rethought and reinterpreted. It has shifted the emphasis from the warehousing of older records to the development of systems for records creation and capture, and has encouraged records managers to work more closely with professionals in other disciplines and to develop new analytical skills. It has also called into question the long-standing distinction between records and archives management: in particular, the growing acceptance of the records continuum concept has highlighted the common principles that records managers and archivists share, as well as providing a richer view of the ongoing management of records and their use by organizations and the wider community. Many records managers have also welcomed the rediscovery of the evidential nature of records and the importance of protecting their authenticity and integrity in a world increasingly dominated by fast-changing information technology.

These trends are likely to continue in the coming decades, while new challenges and opportunities may arise from the globalization of business, the growth of e-government and e-commerce, the expansion of mobile computing and distributed storage technologies, or the use of artificial intelligence in classification and retrieval.

This book gives an overview of professional principles and records management practices at the beginning of the 21st century. Its authors hope that it will deepen its readers' understanding of the discipline and help records managers to develop their knowledge and skills.

Appendix A
Bibliography and sources of further information

Records management websites

The following websites are particularly useful for the breadth of their coverage of records management issues. Most of them provide information about both paper and electronic records. Some of their content focuses on the needs of public sector organizations in particular countries, but most is of considerably wider relevance.

International Records Management Trust
  www.irmt.org/.
National Archives and Records Administration, USA
  www.archives.gov/.
National Archives of Australia
  www.naa.gov.au/.
National Archives of Canada
  www.archives.ca/.
New York State Archives and Records Administration, USA
  www.archives.nysed.gov/.
Public Record Office, UK
  www.pro.gov.uk/.
  In 2003 the name of the UK Public Record Office is expected to change to the National Archives, and its web address may also change.
State Records Authority of New South Wales, Australia
  www.records.nsw.gov.au/.

Further information about developments in electronic records management can be found on the following websites.

Digital Longevity (Digitale Duurzaamheid)
   www.digitaleduurzaamheid.nl/.
DLM-Forum on Electronic Records
   www.dlmforum.eu.org/.
e-TERM (European Training in Electronic Records Management)
   www.ucl.ac.uk/e-term/.
Interpares Project
   www.interpares.org/.
Persistent Archives and Electronic Records Management
   www.sdsc.edu/NARA/.
Records Continuum Research Group
   http://rcrg.dstc.edu.au/.
VERS (Victorian Electronic Records Strategy)
   www.prov.vic.gov.au/vers/.

General works in print

Recent works that provide coverage of electronic as well as paper records

Kennedy, J. and Schauder, C. (1998) *Records management: a guide to corporate record keeping*, 2nd edn, Addison Wesley Longman Australia. Widely used Australian text, revised in 1998 to conform with the Australian records management standard AS 4390.

Parker, E. (1999) *Managing your organization's records*, Library Association Publishing. Practical manual in an informal style.

Short introductions to records management

Hare, C. and McLeod, J. (1997) *Developing a records management programme*, Aslib. Succinct account of the components of a records management programme.

McLeod, J. and Hare, C. (2001) Records management. In Scammell, A. (ed.) *Handbook of information management*, 8th edn, Aslib IMI. Overview of records management principles, approaches and trends.

Saffady, W. (1999) *The value of records management: a manager's briefing*, ARMA International. Brief explanation of records management, emphasizing the value that it can deliver to an organization.

Works focusing mainly or wholly on the management of electronic records

Bearman, D. (1994) *Electronic evidence: strategies for managing records in contemporary organizations*, Archives and Museum Informatics. Seminal work including reprints of articles by a leading theorist.

Dearstyne, B. (ed.) (2002) *Effective approaches for managing electronic records and archives*, Scarecrow Press. Collection of essays, mainly by US authors.

Duranti, L. (1998) *Diplomatics: new uses for an old science*, Scarecrow Press. Reprint of articles originally published between 1989 and 1991 in *Archivaria*, **28–33**.

Ellis, J. (ed.) (2000) *Selected essays in electronic recordkeeping in Australia*, Australian Society of Archivists. Reliable and practical overview of electronic records solutions.

European Commission (1997) *Guidelines on best practice for using electronic information*, INSAR Supplement III, Office for Official Publications of the European Communities. Also available at www.europa.eu.int/ISPO/dlm/documents/guidelines.html. Multidisciplinary guidelines applicable to electronic information products as well as records.

Public Record Office (1999) *Management, appraisal and preservation of electronic records*, 2 vols, [UK] Public Record Office. Also available at www.pro.gov.uk/recordsmanagement/eros/guidelines/. Intended for UK public sector but offers guidance that is applicable more widely.

Saffady, W. (1998) *Managing electronic records*, 2nd edn, ARMA International. Good coverage of digital file formats and storage media, but not a comprehensive account of electronic records management.

Shepherd, E. (1996) *The management of electronic records*, Library and Information Briefings 69, South Bank University. A summary of the characteristics of electronic records and the issues arising in their management.

Older works focusing mainly or wholly on paper records

Most of these books present a traditional view of records management, emphasizing the informational rather than the evidential role of records and concentrating on the management of records no longer required for current business.

Benedon, W. (1969) *Records management*, Prentice Hall.

Diamond, S. Z. (1995) *Records management: a practical approach*, 3rd edn, AMACOM.

Emmerson, P. (ed.) (1989) *How to manage your records: a guide to effective practice*, ICSA.

Kallaus, N. F. and Johnson, M. M. (1992) *Records management*, 5th edn, South-Western Publishing Co.

Leahy, E. J. and Cameron, C. A. (1965) *Modern records management*, McGraw-Hill.

Linton, J. E. (1990) *Organising the office memory: the theory and practice of records management*, Sydney University of Technology.

Penn, I. A., Pennix, G. and Coulson, J. (1994) *Records management handbook*, 2nd edn, Gower.

Ricks, B. R., Swafford, A. J. and Gow, K. F. (1992) *Information and image management: a records system approach*, 3rd edn, South-Western Publishing Co.

Robek, M. F., Brown, G. F. and Stephens, D. O. (1995) *Information and records management: document-based information systems*, 4th edn, Glencoe/McGraw-Hill.

Schellenberg, T. R. (1956) *Modern archives: principles and techniques*, F. W. Cheshire. Reprinted by University of Chicago Press 1957 et seq. and by Society of American Archivists 1996.

Schwartz, C. and Hernon, P. (1993) *Records management and the library*, Ablex.

Smith, P. A. et al. (1995) *Introduction to records management*, Macmillan Education Australia.

Wallace, P. E., Lee, J. A. and Schubert, D. R. (1992) *Records management: integrated information systems*, 3rd edn, Prentice Hall.

Journals

The main English-language records management journals

Informaa Quarterly (Australia).

Information Management Journal (formerly *Records Management Quarterly*) (USA).

Records & Information Management Report (USA).

Records Management Bulletin (UK).

Records Management Journal (UK).

Archives journals that publish articles on records management

American Archivist (USA).

Archival Science: International Journal on Recorded Information (Netherlands).

Archivaria (Canada).
Archives and Manuscripts (Australia).
Archives and Museum Informatics (USA).
Journal of the Society of Archivists (UK).

Journals focusing on document and content management and related technologies

e-doc, www.edocmagazine.com/ (USA).
Information Management & Technology (UK).
Transform Magazine, www.transformmag.com/ (USA).

Selected further reading on specific topics

Accountability

McKemmish, S. (1998) *The smoking gun: recordkeeping and accountability*. Available at http://rcrg.dstc.edu.au/publications/recordscontinuum/smoking.html.

McKemmish, S. and Upward, F. (eds.) (1993) *Archival documents: providing accountability through recordkeeping*, Ancora Press.

Appraisal and retention

Association of Records Managers and Administrators (1986) *Developing and operating a records retention program*, ARMA International.

Bailey, S. (1999) The metadatabase: the future of the retention schedule as a records management tool, *Records Management Journal*, **9** (1), 33–45.

Brown, C. (1999) Keeping or destroying records: some current issues in retention, *Business Archives*, **77**, 31–44.

Cook, T. (1992) Mind over matter: towards a new theory of archival appraisal. In Craig, B. L. (ed.) *The archival imagination: essays in honour of Hugh A. Taylor*, Association of Canadian Archivists.

Eastwood, T. (1992) Towards a social theory of appraisal. In Craig, B. L. (ed.) *The archival imagination: essays in honour of Hugh A. Taylor*, Association of Canadian Archivists.

International Records Management Trust (1999) *Building records appraisal systems*, Managing Public Sector Records Study Programme 3, International Records Management Trust.

Kennedy, J. and Schauder, C. (1998) *Records management: a guide to corporate record keeping*, 2nd edn, Addison Wesley Longman Australia, Chapter 4 'Records appraisal and disposal: strategies and tools'.

Montana, J. C. (1997) Statutes of limitation and records retention, *Records Management Quarterly*, **31** (1), 33–6, 74.

National Archives of Australia (no date) *Why records are kept: directions in appraisal.* Available at www.naa.gov.au/recordkeeping/disposal/why_keep/intro.html.

Stephens, D. O. (1988) Making records retention decisions: practical and theoretical considerations, *Records Management Quarterly*, **22** (1), 3–7.

Terenna, B. J. (2001) Risky business: proactive strategies help reduce records-related risks, *InfoPro*, **3** (1), 25–32.

Archives management

Bradsher, J. G. (ed.) (1988) *Managing archives and archival institutions*, University of Chicago Press.

Cook, M. (1993) *Information management and archival data*, Library Association Publishing.

Cook, M. (1999) *The management of information from archives*, 2nd edn, Gower.

Cox, R. J. (1992) *Managing institutional archives: foundational principles and practices*, Greenwood.

Dearstyne, B. (ed.) (2001) *Leadership and administration of successful archival programs*, Greenwood.

Ellis, J. (ed.) (1993) *Keeping archives*, 2nd edn, D. W. Thorpe.

Hunter, G. S. (1997) *Developing and maintaining practical archives: a how-to-do-it manual*, Neal-Schuman.

International Records Management Trust (1999) *Managing archives*, Managing Public Sector Records Study Programme 5, International Records Management Trust.

Jenkinson, H. (1937) *A manual of archive administration*, 2nd edn, Lund Humphries. Reprinted 1965.

O'Toole, J. M. (1990) *Understanding archives and manuscripts*, Society of American Archivists.

Ritzenthaler, M. L. (1993) *Preserving archives and manuscripts*, Society of American Archivists.

Turton, A. (ed.) (1991) *Managing business archives*, Butterworth-Heinemann.

Authenticity

Duranti, L. (1995) Reliability and authenticity: the concepts and their implications, *Archivaria*, **39**, 5–10.

MacNeil, H. (2000) *Conceptualizing an authentic electronic record*. Available at www.interpares.org/documents/hm_saa_2000.pdf.

Business continuity planning

Association of Records Managers and Administrators (1993) *Vital records*, ARMA International.

Barnes, J. C. (2001) *A guide to business continuity planning*, John Wiley and Sons.

Jones, V. A. and Keyes, K. E. (2001) *Emergency management for records and information programs*, 2nd edn, ARMA International.

National Fire Protection Association (1995) *Guide for fire protection for archives and records centers*, NFPA 232A, [US] National Fire Protection Association.

Penn, I. A., Pennix, G. and Coulson, J. (1994) *Records management handbook*, 2nd edn, Gower, Chapter 10 'Vital records' and Chapter 11 'Disaster planning and recovery'.

Ricks, B. R., Swafford, A. J. and Gow, K. F. (1992) *Information and image management: a records system approach*, 3rd edn, South-Western Publishing Co., Chapter 9 'Vital records' and Chapter 18 'Records disaster prevention and recovery'.

Walsh, B. (1997) *Salvage at a glance*. Available at http://palimpsest.stanford.edu/waac/wn/wn19/wn19-2/wn19-207.html.

Wellheiser, J. and Scott, J. (2002) *An ounce of prevention: integrated disaster planning for archives, libraries and record centers*, 2nd edn, Scarecrow Press.

Classification and metadata

Bearman, D. (1996) Item level control and electronic recordkeeping, *Archives and Museum Informatics*, **10** (3), 195–245. Also available at www.archimuse.com/papers/nhprc/item-lvl.html.

Bearman, D. and Sochats, K. (1996) Metadata requirements for evidence. In Lysakowski, R. and Schmidt, S. (eds) *Automating 21st century science*, Team-Science Publishing. Also available at www.archimuse.com/papers/nhprc/BACartic.html.

Keay, S. (1999) Developing a business classification scheme for the Ministry of Premier and Cabinet, Western Australia: a living perspective, *Informaa Quarterly*, **15** (3), 7–11.

McKemmish, S., Acland, G. and Reed, B. (1999) Towards a framework for standardising recordkeeping metadata: the Australian recordkeeping metadata schema, *Records Management Journal*, **9** (3), 177–202. Also available at http://rcrg.dstc.edu.au/publications/framewrk.html.

McKemmish, S., Cunningham, A. and Parer, D. (1998) Metadata mania. In *Place, interface and cyberspace: archives at the edge. Proceedings of the Conference of the Australian Society of Archivists, Fremantle 6–8 August 1998*, Australian Society of Archivists. Also available at http://rcrg.dstc.edu.au/publications/recordkeepingmetadata/sm01.html.

Parker, E. (1999) *Managing your organization's records*, Library Association Publishing, Chapter 2 'Well . . . it's only filing, isn't it? Designing filing systems that really work'.

Robinson, C. (1999) *Functional analysis and keyword classification*. Available at www.records.nsw.gov.au/publicsector/rk/edmonton/functional_analysis1.htm.

Schellenberg, T. R. (1956) *Modern archives: principles and techniques*, F. W. Cheshire, Chapter 7 'Classification principles'.

Continuum and lifecycle concepts

Atherton, J. (1985–6) From life cycle to continuum: some thoughts on the records management – archives relationship, *Archivaria*, **21**, 43–51. Reprinted in Nesmith, T. (ed.) (1993) *Canadian archival studies and the rediscovery of provenance*, Scarecrow Press.

Marshall, P. (2000) Life cycle versus continuum: what is the difference?, *Informaa Quarterly*, **16** (2), 20–5.

McLeod, J. (1996) The record's lifecycle: myth, mantra or misnomer?, *Records Management Journal*, **6** (1), 5–11.

McKemmish, S. (1997) Yesterday, today and tomorrow: a continuum of responsibility. In *Proceedings of the Records Management Association of Australia 14th National Convention, 15–17 September 1997*, Records Management Association of Australia. Also available at http://rcrg.dstc.edu.au/publications/recordscontinuum/smckp2.html.

Upward, F. (2000) Modelling the continuum as paradigm shift in recordkeeping and archiving processes and beyond: a personal reflection, *Records Management Journal*, **10** (3), 115–39.

Cost analysis

Dmytrenko, A. (1997) Cost benefit analysis, *Records Management Quarterly*, **31** (1), 16–20.

Saffady, W. (1998) *Cost analysis concepts and methods for records management projects*, ARMA International.

Creation and capture

Kennedy, J. and Schauder, C. (1998) *Records management: a guide to corporate record keeping*, 2nd edn, Addison Wesley Longman Australia, Chapter 5 'Creating and capturing full and accurate records'.

Southwood, G. (1993) Records creation: the key to successful records management, *Records Management Bulletin*, **56**, 8–12.

State Records Authority of New South Wales (2001) *Create and capture*. Available at www.records.nsw.gov.au/publicsector/rk/creation/entry.htm.

Cultural and corporate memory

Cox, R. J. (2000) *Closing an era: historical perspectives on modern archives and records management*, Greenwood, Chapter 6 'Archives, records and memory'.

Foote, K. E. (1990) To remember and forget: archives, memory and culture, *American Archivist*, **53** (3), 378–92.

Megill, K. (1997) *Corporate memory: information management in the electronic age*, Bowker-Saur.

Current paper records systems

International Records Management Trust (1999) *Organising and controlling current records*, Managing Public Sector Records Study Programme 2, International Records Management Trust.

Kennedy, J. and Schauder, C. (1998) *Records management: a guide to corporate record keeping*, 2nd edn, Addison Wesley Longman Australia, Chapter 8 'Managing active paper records'.

Robek, M. F., Brown, G. F. and Stephens, D. O. (1995) *Information and records management: document-based information systems*, 4th edn, Glencoe/McGraw-Hill, Chapter 6 'Filing system maintenance'.

State Records Authority of New South Wales (1993) *File format: a guide to the physical design and construction of files*, Guideline 1, State Records Authority of New South Wales. Also available at www.records.nsw.gov.au/publicsector/rk/fileformat/fileformattoc.htm.

State Records Authority of New South Wales (1994) *File creation: a guide to file systems and the file creation process*, Guideline 2, State Records Authority of New South Wales. Also available at www.records.nsw.gov.au/publicsector/rk/filecreation/filecreationtoc.htm.

Stephens, D. O. (1995) The registry: the world's most predominant recordkeeping system, *Records Management Quarterly*, **29** (1), 64–6.

Design, implementation and restructuring of records management programmes and systems

International Records Management Trust (1999) *Restructuring current records systems: a procedures manual*, Managing Public Sector Records Study Programme 20, International Records Management Trust.

National Archives of Australia (2001) *DIRKS: a strategic approach to managing business information*. Available at www.naa.gov.au/recordkeeping/dirks/ dirksman/dirks.html.

State Records Authority of New South Wales (1999) *Principles in practice: guidelines on establishing and maintaining a records management program*, Guideline 9, State Records Authority of New South Wales. Also available at www.records.nsw. gov.au/publicsector/rk/guidelines/rm_program/rmprogram_guidelines.htm.

Destruction methods and procedures

Parker, E. (1999) *Managing your organization's records*, Library Association Publishing, Chapter 8 'It's just a load of rubbish: destroying records when you no longer need them'.

State Records Authority of New South Wales (2000) *Destruction of records: a practical guide*, Guideline 3, State Records Authority of New South Wales. Also available at www.records.nsw.gov.au/publicsector/disposal/guideline3-dest/guideline3.htm.

Digital preservation

Digitale Bewaring Testbed (2001) *Migration: context and current status*. Available at www.digitaleduurzaamheid.nl/bibliotheek/Migration.pdf.

Dollar, C. (1999) *Authentic electronic records: strategies for long-term access*, Cohasset Associates.

Feeney, M. (ed.) (1999) *Digital culture: maximising the nation's investment*, [UK] National Preservation Office. Also available at www.ukoln.ac.uk/services/ elib/papers/other/jisc-npo-dig/intro.html.

Heazlewood, J. (2000) Management of electronic records over time. In Ellis, J. (ed.) *Selected essays in electronic recordkeeping in Australia*, Australian Society of Archivists.

Hendley, T. (1998) *Comparison of methods & costs of digital preservation*, Research and Innovation Report 106, British Library. Also available at www.ukoln.ac.uk/ services/elib/papers/tavistock/hendley/hendley.html.

New York State Archives and Records Administration (1998) *Guidelines for ensuring the long-term accessibility and usability of records stored as digital images*, Government Records Technical Information Series 22, New York State Archives and Records Administration. Also available at www.archives.nysed.gov/pubs/ local-pub/grtip22.pdf.

State Records Authority of New South Wales (2002) *Future proof: ensuring the accessibility of equipment/technology dependent records*. Available at www.records.gov.au/ publicsector/rk/guidelines/techdependent/entry-page.htm.

Digital storage media

Dollar, C. (1999) Selecting storage media for long-term access to digital records, *Information Management Journal*, **33** (3), 36–43.

Kahn, R. A. (2000) *Evidentiary benefits and business implications of write-once-read-many ('WORM') optical disk storage for records management*. Available at www.aiim.org/ documents/wp/HP_WORM.pdf.

National Archives of Australia (1999) *Protecting and handling magnetic media*, Archives Advice 5, National Archives of Australia. Also available at www.naa.gov.au/publicat/advices/HTML/advice5.htm.

National Archives of Australia (1999) *Protecting and handling optical discs*, Archives Advice 6, National Archives of Australia. Also available at www.naa.gov.au/ publicat/advices/HTML/advice6.htm.

Saffady, W. (1998) *Managing electronic records*, 2nd edn, ARMA International, Chapter 2 'Electronic storage media and formats' and Chapter 7 'Managing files and media'.

Document management

Craine, K. (2000) *Designing a document strategy*, MC2 Books.

Kampffmeyer, U. (2000) Electronic document management market: technologies and solutions. In *Proceedings of the DLM-Forum on Electronic Records, Brussels, 18–19 October 1999*, Office for Official Publications of the European Communities. Also available at www.europa.eu.int/ISPO/dlm/fulltext/full_kampf_en.htm.

Veal, D. C. (2001) Techniques of document management: a review of text retrieval and related technologies, *Journal of Documentation*, **57** (2), 192–217.

Wiggins, B. (2000) *Effective document management: unlocking corporate knowledge*, Gower.

Wilkinson, R. et al. (1998) *Document computing: technologies for managing electronic document collections*, Kluwer.

Documentation of records systems

Diamond, S. Z. (1995) *Records management: a practical approach*, 3rd edn, AMACOM, Chapter 13 'Documenting the records management program'.

Doyle, M. and Frénière, A. (1991) *The preparation of records management hand-books for government agencies: a RAMP study*, UNESCO. Also available at www.unesco.org/webworld/ramp/html/r9118e/r9118e00.htm.

Robek, M. F., Brown, G. F. and Stephens, D. O. (1995) *Information and records management: document-based information systems*, 4th edn, Glencoe/McGraw-Hill, Chapter 16 'Records management manuals'.

E-government, e-commerce and records of web-based activities

E-government Sub-group for Electronic Records Management (2001) *E-government policy framework for electronic records management*, [UK] Public Record Office. Also available at www.e-envoy.gov.uk/publications/frameworks/erm2/.

Frye, E. (2001) Legal issues in documenting e-commerce transactions, *Information Management Journal*, **35** (4), 10–14.

Harries, S. (2000) Capturing and managing electronic records from websites and intranets in the Government environment. In *Proceedings of the DLM-Forum on Electronic Records, Brussels, 18–19 October 1999*, Office for Official Publications of the European Communities. Also available at www.europa.eu.int/ISPO/dlm/fulltext/full_harr_en.htm.

Iacovino, L. (1998) Regulating net transactions: the legal implications for record-keeping in Australia. In *Place, interface and cyberspace: archives at the edge. Proceedings of the Conference of the Australian Society of Archivists, Fremantle 6–8 August*

1998, Australian Society of Archivists. Also available at http://rcrg.dstc.edu.au/ publications/recordscontinuum/li01.html.

IMForum Internet and Intranet Working Group (1999) *Managing internet and intranet information for long term access and accountability: implementation guide*, National Archives of Canada. Also available at www.imforumgi.gc.ca/consult/ inter_intra/implement2_e.pdf.

McClure, C. R. and Sprehe, J. T. (1998) *Guidelines for electronic records management on state and federal agency websites*. Available at http://istweb.syr.edu/~mcclure/ guidelines.html.

National Archives of Australia (2001) *Archiving web resources: a policy for keeping records of web-based activity in the Commonwealth Government*. Available at www.naa.gov.au/recordkeeping/er/web_records/intro.html.

O'Neill, J. (2000) *E-government*, New York State Archives and Records Administration. Also available at www.archives.nysed.gov/pubs/recmgmt/egovernment/ index.htm.

E-mail

Association of Records Managers and Administrators (2000) *Guideline for managing e-mail*, ARMA International.

Baron, J. R. (2000) E-mail litigation wars: the US National Archivist strikes back. In Sarno, L. (ed.) *Authentic records in the electronic age*, Interpares Project.

DiGilio, J. J. (2001) Electronic mail: from computer to courtroom, *Information Management Journal*, **35** (2), 32–44.

Enneking, N. E. (1998) Managing e-mail: working toward an effective solution, *Records Management Quarterly*, **32** (3), 24–43.

Kahn, R. A. (2000) *Managing e-mail is essential in today's business environment: carrots and sticks abound to ensure companies manage e-mail*. Available at www.aiim.org/documents/wp/HP_EmailManagement.pdf.

Wallace, D. (1998) *Recordkeeping and electronic mail policy: the state of thought and the state of the practice*. Available at www.mybestdocs.com/dwallace.html.

Encryption and electronic signatures

Atreya, M. et al. (2002) *Digital signatures*, McGraw-Hill/Osborne.

Greenwood, D. (1997) *Electronic signatures and records: legal, policy and technical considerations*. Available at www.state.ma.us/itd/legal/e-sig.htm.

Minihan, J. (2001) Electronic signature technologies: a tutorial, *Information Management Journal*, **35** (4), 4–8.

National Archives of Canada (2001) *Guidelines for records created under a public key infrastructure using encryption and digital signatures*. Available at www.archives. ca/06/0618_e.html.

Financial records

Barata, K., Cain, P. and Routledge, D. (2001) *Principles and practices in managing financial records: a reference model and assessment tool*, International Records Management Trust. Also available at www.irmt.org/download/DOCUME~1/ DEVELO~1/RESEAR~1/mfsr.pdf.

International Records Management Trust (1999) *Managing financial records*, Managing Public Sector Records Study Programme 15, International Records Management Trust.

Forms design, forms management and recognition technology

Gingrande, A. (1998) *Forms automation: from ICR to e-forms to the Internet*, AIIM.

Phillips, J. T. (2000) Does ICR keep paper forms viable?, *Information Management Journal*, **34** (2), 58–61.

Robek, M. F., Brown, G. F. and Stephens, D. O. (1995) *Information and records management: document-based information systems*, 4th edn, Glencoe/McGraw-Hill, Chapter 13 'Forms management'.

Woods, J. (1995) *Recognition technology for data entry*, Cimtech.

History of records management

Cox, R. J. (2000) *Closing an era: historical perspectives on modern archives and records management*, Greenwood.

Duranti, L. (1989) The odyssey of records managers, *Records Management Quarterly*, **23** (3), 3–11 and **23** (4), 3–11. Reprinted in Nesmith, T. (ed.) (1993) *Canadian archival studies and the rediscovery of provenance*, Scarecrow Press.

Evans, F. B. (1990) Records and administrative processes: retrospect and prospects. In Durance, C. (ed.) *Management of recorded information: converging disciplines*, K. G. Saur.

Shepherd, E. (1994) Records management in Britain: a review of some developments in professional principles and practice, *Business Archives*, **67**, 13–25.

Information retrieval and language control

Aitchison, J., Gilchrist, A. and Bawden, D. (2000) *Thesaurus construction and use: a practical manual*, 4th edn, Aslib IMI.

Hoy, M. (1998) *Understanding government terminology: natural language searching and government thesauri*. Available at www.naa.gov.au/recordkeeping/gov_online/ agift/gov_term/intro.html.

Rowley, J. (1994) The controlled versus natural indexing languages debate revisited: a perspective on information retrieval practice and research, *Journal of Information Science*, **20** (2), 108–19.

Smith, D. A. (1997) Use of a thesaurus in two-stage information retrieval of electronic records. In *Proceedings of the DLM-Forum on Electronic Records, Brussels, 18–20 December 1996*, Office for Official Publications of the European Communities. Also available at www.europa.eu.int/ISPO/dlm/dlm96/proceed-en4.pdf.

Treasury Board [of Canada] Information Technology Standards Programme, Thesaurus Standards Working Group (1996) *Thesaurus as a tool for the management of government information*. Available at www.archives.ca/06/docs/ thesaur.wpd.

Will, L. (1992) *Thesaurus principles and practice*. Available at www.willpowerinfo.co.uk/ thesprin.htm.

Legislation, legal admissibility and evidential weight of records in court

Alabama Department of Archives and History (1996) *Legal admissibility of public records*. Available at www.archives.state.al.us/ol_pubs/leg_adm.html.

Hulbert, B. J. (1997) *As a trial attorney, how would I attack the way you manage your electronic records?* Available at www.cohasset.com/main/library/legal_issues/ hulbert/presentation.htm.

Hunter, I. (2000) Auditing an electronic records system at the Wellcome Trust to reinforce the records' value as legal evidence, *Business Archives*, **79**, 43–54.

Iacovino, L. (1998) The nature of the nexus between recordkeeping and the law, *Archives and Manuscripts*, **26** (2), 216–46. Also available at http://rcrg.dstc.edu.au/ publications/la03.html.

Montana, J. C. (1995) It can make you or break you: the importance of records management in litigation, *Records Management Quarterly*, **29** (1), 3–8.

Stephens, D. O. (1995) Recordkeeping provisions of international laws, *Records Management Quarterly*, **29** (3), 60–5.

Management skills

Diamond, S. Z. (1995) *Records management: a practical approach*, 3rd edn, AMACOM, Chapter 3 'Developing and staffing the program' and Chapter 4 'Using project management tools to plan and control the program'.

Goodman, S. K. (1998) Business politics for the records manager and archivist, *Records Management Quarterly*, **32** (1), 19–34.

International Records Management Trust (1999) *Managing resources for records and archives services*, Managing Public Sector Records Study Programme 9, International Records Management Trust.

International Records Management Trust (1999) *Strategic planning for records and archives services*, Managing Public Sector Records Study Programme 10, International Records Management Trust.

Ricks, B. R., Swafford, A. J. and Gow, K. F. (1992) *Information and image management: a records system approach*, 3rd edn, South-Western Publishing Co., Chapter 2 'The records manager and the records management staff'.

Marketing and advocacy

De Saez, E. E. (1995) Marketing for the records manager, *Records Management Journal*, **5** (1), 23–33.

Diamond, S. Z. (1995) *Records management: a practical approach*, 3rd edn, AMACOM, Chapter 2 'Getting support for the records management program'.

Jones, R. D. (1989) Don't 'sell' records management – give it away, *Records Management Quarterly*, **23** (1), 3–10. Reprinted (1998), *Records Management Quarterly*, **32** (4), 36–44.

Sanders, R. L. (1998) The records manager steps out of the comfort zone: the problem with selling records management, *Records Management Quarterly*, **32** (2), 56–63.

Tower Software (2000) *The Tower guide: advocating electronic records management*. Available at www.dialog-uk.co.uk/http/acrobat_files/Record%20Management%20Support.pdf.

Media conversion

Adler, M. S. (2000) Avoiding the perils of imaging system implementations, *Information Management Journal*, **34** (4), 4–22.

Avedon, D. (1996) *Introduction to electronic imaging*, 3rd edn, AIIM.

Avedon, D. (1998) *Film-based imaging: new views and applications*, AIIM.

Kowlowitz, A. (1999) *Guidelines for determining if a stand-alone imaging system is the best choice for you*, New York State Archives and Records Administration. Also available at ftp://ftp.sara.nysed.gov/pub/rec-pub/local-rec-pub/lgtis20.pdf.

Saffady, W. (2000) *Micrographics: technology for the twenty-first century*, ARMA International.

Saffady, W. (2001) *Electronic document imaging: technology, applications, implementation*, ARMA International.

Organizational structures and cultures; organizational change

Barry, R. (1993) Getting it right: managing organizations in a runaway electronic age. In Menne-Haritz, A. (ed.) *Information handling in offices and archives*, K. G. Saur.

Barry, R. (1997) *Keeping records for changing organizations: who's minding the store?* Available at www.mybestdocs.com/rb-nag1.html.

Capon, C. (2000) *Understanding organisational context*, Financial Times/Prentice Hall.

Charman, D. (ed.) (1995) *Records management and organisational change*, Society of Archivists.

Dawson, S. (1996) *Analysing organisations*, 3rd edn, Palgrave.

Handy, C. B. (1993) *Understanding organizations*, 4th edn, Penguin.

Robbins, S. P. (2001) *Organizational behaviour*, 9th edn, Prentice Hall.

Sellen, A. J. and Harper, R. (2001) *The myth of the paperless office*, MIT Press.

Skyrme, D. J. (1994) When information culture encounters organisational culture, *Records Management Bulletin*, **64**, 3–5.

Stephens, D. O. (2000) *Information management issues in mergers and acquisitions*, ARMA International.

Performance measurement and quality standards

Brumm, E. K. (1995) *Managing records for ISO 9000 compliance*, ASQC Quality Press.

Goodman, S. K. (1994) Measuring the value added by records and information management programs, *Records Management Quarterly*, **28** (2), 3–13.

Lemieux, V. (1996) The use of Total Quality Management in a records management environment, *Records Management Quarterly*, **30** (3), 28–38, 74.

Place, I. and Hyslop, D. J. (1982) *Records management: controlling business information*, Reston Publishing, Chapter 4 'Evaluating the information and records management system'.

Van Houten, G. (2000) ISO 9001:2000: a standard for all industries, *Information Management Journal*, **34** (2), 28–37.

Personnel records

Cain, P. and Thurston, A. (1998) *Personnel records: a strategic resource for public sector management in developing countries*, Commonwealth Secretariat.

International Records Management Trust (1999) *Managing personnel records*, Managing Public Sector Records Study Programme 18, International Records Management Trust.

Preservation and handling of traditional records media

International Records Management Trust (1999) *Preserving records*, Managing Public Sector Records Study Programme 6, International Records Management Trust.

National Archives of Australia (1999) *Protecting and handling paper files*, Archives Advice 1, National Archives of Australia. Also available at www.naa.gov.au/ recordkeeping/rkpubs/advices/advice1.html.

Privacy, confidentiality and freedom of information

Booz, C. R. (2001) Electronic records and the right to privacy, *Information Management Journal*, **35** (3), 18–24.

Bull, H. P. (1998) Access to information: legal aspects. In *CITRA 1997: proceedings of the 32nd International Conference of the Round Table on Archives*, International Council on Archives.

Cady, G. H. and McGregor, P. (2001) *Protect your digital privacy: survival skills for the information age*, Que.

Hornfeldt, T. (2000) Freedom of information and data privacy. In Sarno, L. (ed.) *Authentic records in the electronic age*, Interpares Project.

Incomes Data Services (1999) Data protection: disclose and be damned!, *Records Management Bulletin*, **92**, 9–16.

McDonald, A. and Terrill, G. (eds) (1998) *Open government: freedom of information and privacy*, Macmillan.

Pope, J. (2000) *Transparency International source book 2000. Confronting corruption: the elements of a national integrity system*, Transparency International, Chapter 24 'The right to information – information, public awareness and public records'. Also available at www.transparency.org/sourcebook/24.html.

Records centres

Association of Records Managers and Administrators (1986) *Records center operations*, ARMA International.

Diamond, S. Z. (1995) *Records management: a practical approach*, 3rd edn, AMACOM, Chapters 7 and 8 'The records center'.

Faber, M. J. (1997) Selecting an offsite commercial records center, *Records Management Quarterly*, **31** (1), 28–32. Also available at www.paxton.com/recdstrg/select2.htm.

International Records Management Trust (1999) *Managing records in records centres*, Managing Public Sector Records Study Programme 4, International Records Management Trust.

Robek, M. F., Brown, G. F. and Stephens, D. O. (1995) *Information and records management: document-based information systems*, 4th edn, Glencoe/McGraw-Hill, Chapter 17 'Records center planning and design' and Chapter 18 'Records center management'.

Sectoral records: central and local government

Dearstyne, B. W. (1988) *The management of local government records: a guide for local officials*, AASLH Press.

Dearstyne, B. W. (1999) *Managing government records and information*, ARMA International.

Mims, J. L. (1996) *Records management: a practical guide for cities and counties*, International City/County Management Association.

Sectoral records: healthcare

Dick, R. S., Steen, E. B. and Detmer, D. E. (eds) (1997) *The computer-based patient record: an essential technology for health care*, 2nd edn, National Academy Press. Also available at www.nap.edu/books/0309055326/html/.

Huffman, E. K. (1994) *Health information management*, 10th edn, Physicians' Record Co.

Maxwell-Stewart, H., Sheppard, J. and Yeo, G. (1996) *Hospital patient case records: a guide to their retention and disposal*, Health Archives Group.

Sectoral records: private sector organizations

Morrissette, N. H. (1993) *Setting up a bank records management program*, Greenwood.

Saffady, W. (2002) *Records and information management: a benchmarking study of large US industrial companies*, ARMA International.

Security

Boyce, J. G. and Jennings, D. W. (2002) *Information assurance: managing organizational IT security risks*, Butterworth-Heinemann.

Morgan, O. J. and Welch, M. (1995) Protecting confidential computer records against careless loss, *Records Management Quarterly*, **29** (3), 16–20, 65.

Ricks, B. R., Swafford, A. J. and Gow, K. F. (1992) *Information and image management: a records system approach*, 3rd edn, South-Western Publishing Co., Chapter 17 'Records security'.

Stephens, D. O. (1997) Document security and international records management, *Records Management Quarterly*, **31** (4), 69–74.

Software specification and acquisition

Department of Defense (2002) *Design criteria standard for electronic records management software applications*, DoD5015.2-STD, [US] Department of Defense. Also available at http://jitc.fhu.disa.mil/recmgt/standards.htm.

European Commission (2002) *Model requirements for the management of electronic records*, INSAR Supplement VI, Office for Official Publications of the European Communities. Also available at www.cornwell.co.uk/moreq.html.

International Records Management Trust (1999) *Automating records services*, Managing Public Sector Records Study Programme 13, International Records Management Trust.

Kennedy, J. and Schauder, C. (1998) *Records management: a guide to corporate record keeping*, 2nd edn, Addison Wesley Longman Australia, Chapter 9 'Selecting and implementing automated records management systems'.

Mark, T. J. and Owens, J. M. (1996) Comparing apples to oranges: methods for evaluating and selecting records management software, *Records Management Quarterly*, **30** (1), 30–6.

Public Record Office (1999) *Functional requirements for electronic records management systems*, [UK] Public Record Office. Also available at www.pro.gov.uk/recordsmanagement/eros/invest/. Revision in progress, 2002.

Standards for records management

Connelly, J. C. (2001) The new international records management standard: its content and how it can be used, *Information Management Journal*, **35** (3), 26–36.

Cumming, K. (2002) Two peas in a pod: comparison of ISO 15489 and AS 4390, *Informaa Quarterly*, **18** (1), 9–13.

Hoyle, M. (1999) *Standards and recordkeeping in the New Zealand public sector*. Available at www.archives.govt.nz/statutory_regulatory/standards/record_keeping/contents.html.

Storage accommodation and equipment

Hardcastle, S. (1989) Providing storage facilities. In Emmerson, P. (ed.) *How to manage your records: a guide to effective practice*, ICSA.

Public Record Office (1999) *Storage of semi-current records*, Standards for the Management of Government Records RMS 3.1, [UK] Public Record Office. Also available at www.pro.gov.uk/recordsmanagement/standards/semicurrent.pdf.

Robek, M. F., Brown, G. F. and Stephens, D. O. (1995) *Information and records management: document-based information systems*, 4th edn, Glencoe/McGraw-Hill, Chapter 7 'Facilities and equipment for filing'.

State Records Authority of New South Wales (2000) *Standard on the physical storage of state records*, State Records Authority of New South Wales. Also available at www.records.nsw.gov.au/publicsector/rk/storage/toc.htm.

Surveys and fact-finding

Gannon, A. (1992) Know your merchandise: the records management inventory, *Records Management Quarterly*, **26** (2), 12–19.

Gunther, H. M. and Lang, B. (1983–4) Planning for an operational audit of active files, *Records Management Quarterly*, **17** (3), 30–41; continued as 'Conducting an operational audit of active files', **17** (4), 5–11; continued as 'Analysis and interpretation of data from an operational audit of active files', **18** (1), 5–13.

Parker, E. (1999) *Managing your organization's records*, Library Association Publishing, Chapter 11 'What have you got to work with? Finding out about your organization and its records'.

Penn, I. A., Pennix, G. and Coulson, J. (1994) *Records management handbook*, 2nd edn, Gower, Chapters 6–7 'Management analysis' and Chapter 8 'Records inventory'.

Systems theory and practice

Bantin, P. C. and Bernbom, G. (1996) The Indiana University electronic records project: analyzing functions, identifying transactions, and evaluating record-keeping systems; a report on methodology, *Archives and Museum Informatics*, **10** (3), 246–66. Also available at www.indiana.edu/~libarch/ER/NHPRC-1/article1.html.

International Records Management Trust (1999) *Analysing business systems*, Managing Public Sector Records Study Programme 11, International Records Management Trust.

Layzell, P. J. and Loucopoulos, P. (1989) *Systems analysis and development*, 3rd edn, Chartwell-Bratt.

Maddison, R. and Darnton, G. (1996) *Information systems in organizations: improving business processes*, Chapman and Hall.

Patching, D. (1990) *Practical soft systems analysis*, Pitman.

Smith, A. M. (2000) Business processes and logical process modeling: an overview, *Data Administration Newsletter* (April). Available at www.tdan.com/i012ht03.htm.

Users of records

Chown, J. (1997) Establishing a profile of the users of a records management system, *Records Management Journal*, **7** (2), 115–29.

Watson, M. (1994) Records management: a user's perspective, *Records Management Journal*, **4** (2), 85–94.

Appendix B
Select list of national and international standards

Details given in this list are believed to be correct at the time of going to press, but new and revised standards are issued regularly. The list includes only recognized national or international standards, and related publications of standards organizations. It does not include standards promoted solely by commercial or professional bodies.

Records management standards and related publications

AS 4390-1996 *Records management*, Standards Australia. This standard was withdrawn following the publication of ISO 15489, but it remains a valuable source of guidance.

ISO 15489-1:2001 *Information and documentation – records management – part 1: general*, International Standards Organization.

ISO/TR 15489-2:2001 *Information and documentation – records management – part 2: guidelines*, International Standards Organization.

PD 0025-1:2002 *Effective records management: a management guide to the value of BS ISO 15489-1*, British Standards Institution.

PD 0025-2:2002 *Effective records management: practical implementation of BS ISO 15489-1*, British Standards Institution.

Alphabetical filing rules

ANSI/ARMA 1-1997 *Alphabetic filing rules*, ARMA International.

ISO 12199:2000 *Alphabetical ordering of multilingual terminological and lexicographical data represented in the Latin alphabet*, International Standards Organization.

Digital storage media

ANSI/AIIM TR 25-1995 *The use of optical disks for public records*, AIIM.

BS 4783:1988 *Storage, transportation and maintenance of media for use in data processing and information storage*, British Standards Institution.

ISO 18923:2000 *Imaging materials – polyester-base magnetic tape – storage practices*, International Standards Organization.

ISO 18925:2002 *Imaging materials – optical disc media – storage practices*, International Standards Organization.

Forms and documents: creation and markup

ANSI/AIIM TR 32-1994 *Paper forms design optimization for electronic image management*, AIIM.

ISO 8879:1986 *Information processing – text and office systems – standard generalized markup language (SGML)*, International Standards Organization.

ISO/IEC 15445:2000 *Information technology – document description and processing languages – hypertext markup language (ISO-HTML)*, International Standards Organization.

PD0017:2001 *Guide to the preparation of business documents*, British Standards Institution.

Information retrieval and language control

ISO 639-1:2002 and ISO 639-2:1998 *Codes for the representation of names of languages*, International Standards Organization.

ISO 2788:1986 *Documentation – guidelines for the establishment and development of monolingual thesauri*, International Standards Organization.

ISO 3166-1:1997, ISO 3166-2:1998 and ISO 3166-3:1999 *Codes for the representation of names of countries and their subdivisions*, International Standards Organization.

ISO 8601:2000 *Data elements and interchange formats – information interchange – representation of dates and times*, International Standards Organization.

Legal admissibility and evidential weight

BS 6498:2002 *Guide to preparation of microfilm and other microforms that may be required as evidence*, British Standards Institution.

ISO/TR 10200:1991 *Legal admissibility of microforms*, International Standards Organization.

PD 0008:1999 *Code of practice for legal admissibility and evidential weight of information stored electronically*, British Standards Institution.

PD 5000:2002 *Legal admissibility: an international code of practice for electronic documents and e-business transactions for evidence, audit, long term duty of care*, British Standards Institution.

Media conversion

ANSI/AIIM MS 44-1993 *Recommended practice for quality control of image scanners*, AIIM.

ANSI/AIIM MS 48-1999 *Recommended practice for microfilming public records on silver-halide film*, AIIM.

ANSI/AIIM TR 15-1997 *Planning considerations addressing preparation of documents for image capture*, AIIM.

ANSI/AIIM TR 35-1995 *Human and organizational issues for successful electronic image management system implementation*, AIIM.

BS 6660:1985 *Guide to setting up and maintaining micrographics units*, British Standards Institution.

ISO 6199:1991 *Micrographics – microfilming of documents on 16mm and 35mm silver-gelatin type microfilm – operating procedures*, International Standards Organization.

PD 0016:2001 *Guide to scanning business documents*, British Standards Institution.

Microform storage and preservation

AS 3674-1989 *Storage of microfilm*, Standards Australia.

ISO/TR 12031:2000 *Micrographics – inspection of silver-gelatin microforms for evidence of deterioration*, International Standards Organization.

ISO 18902:2001 *Imaging materials – processed photographic films, plates and papers – filing enclosures and storage containers*, International Standards Organization.

ISO 18911:2000 *Imaging materials – processed safety photographic films – storage practices*, International Standards Organization.

ISO 18919:1999 *Imaging materials – thermally processed silver microfilm – specifications for stability*, International Standards Organization.

Paper: permanence and durability

ISO 9706:1994 *Information and documentation – paper for documents – requirements for permanence*, International Standards Organization.

ISO 11108:1996 *Information and documentation – archival paper – requirements for permanence and durability*, International Standards Organization.

ISO 11798:1999 *Information and documentation – permanence and durability of writing, printing and copying on paper – requirements and test methods*, International Standards Organization.

Performance measurement and quality management

ISO 9000 series: ISO 9000:2000 *Quality management systems – fundamentals and vocabulary*, ISO 9001:2000 *Quality management systems – requirements* and ISO 9004:2000 *Quality management systems – guidelines for performance improvements*, International Standards Organization.

PD0025-3 *Effective records management: measuring performance in records management programmes*, British Standards Institution (to be published 2002).

Security

BS 4737:1986 *Intruder alarm systems*, British Standards Institution.

ISO/IEC TR 13335-1:1996 *Information technology – guidelines for the management of IT security*, International Standards Organization.

ISO/IEC 17799:2000 *Information technology – code of practice for information security management*, International Standards Organization.

Storage accommodation and equipment

BS 5454:2000 *Recommendations for the storage and exhibition of archival documents*, British Standards Institution.

BS 7083:1996 *Accommodation and operating environment for information technology equipment*, British Standards Institution.

HB 96-1997 *Guidelines for mobile shelving for archives, libraries and museums*, Standards Australia and Standards New Zealand.

NISO TR 01-1995 *Environmental guidelines for the storage of paper records*, [US] National Information Standards Organization. Also available at www.niso.org/standards/resources/tr01.pdf.

Appendix C
Professional organizations for records managers in English-speaking countries

Most developed countries have a professional body that operates a publications programme and arranges conferences, meetings and other professional development opportunities for records managers. Most professional organizations for archivists and some organizations for information managers also take an active interest in matters relating to records management. Details of the main professional bodies based in English-speaking countries or operating internationally are given below, together with the titles of their published journals.

ARMA International
13725 W 109th Street, Suite 101, Lenexa, KS 66215, USA
E-mail: hq@arma.org
www.arma.org/
Information Management Journal

Aslib
Temple Chambers, 3–7 Temple Avenue, London EC4Y 0HP, UK
E-mail: aslib@aslib.com
www.aslib.co.uk/
Records Management Journal

Association of Canadian Archivists
PO Box 2596, Station D, Ottawa, Ontario K1P 5W6, Canada
E-mail: aca@magma.ca
http://archivists.ca/
Archivaria

Association of Commonwealth Archivists and Records Managers
c/o IRMT, 12 John Street, London WC1N 2EB, UK
E-mail: info@irmt.org
www.acarm.org/
ACARM Newsletter

Australian Society of Archivists
>PO Box 83, O'Connor, ACT 2602, Australia
>E-mail: asa@asap.unimelb.edu.au
>www.archivists.org.au/
>*Archives and Manuscripts*

Business Archives Council
>101 Whitechapel High Street, London E1 7RE, UK
>www.archives.gla.ac.uk/bac/
>*Business Archives*

Institute of Certified Records Managers
>318 Oak Street, Syracuse, NY 13203, USA
>E-mail: admin@icrm.org
>www.icrm.org/

The International Council on Archives
>60 rue des Francs-Bourgeois, 75003 Paris, France
>E-mail: ica@ica.org
>www.ica.org/
>*Comma, International Journal on Archives*

International Records Management Council
>Church Bank, Main Street, Holcot, Northampton NN6 9SP, UK
>E-mail: charman.irm@btinternet.com
>*International Records Management Journal*

National Association of Government Archives and Records Administrators
>48 Howard Street, Albany, NY 12207, USA
>E-mail: nagara@caphill.com
>www.nagara.org/
>*NAGARA Clearinghouse*

Records Management Association of Australia
>GPO Box 1059, Brisbane, Queensland 4001, Australia
>E-mail: admin@rmaa.com.au
>www.rmaa.com.au/
>*Informaa Quarterly*

Records Management Institute
>PO Box 2856, Ottawa, Ontario K1P 5W8, Canada
>E-mail: bknox@archives.ca
>www.rmicanada.com/

Records Management Society of Great Britain
  Woodside, Coleheath Bottom, Speen, Princes Risborough, Buckinghamshire
  HP27 0SZ, UK
  E-mail: rms@rms-gb.org.uk
  www.rms-gb.org.uk/
  Records Management Bulletin
Society of American Archivists
  527 S Wells Street, 5th Floor, Chicago, IL 60607, USA
  E-mail: info@archivists.org
  www.archivists.org/
  American Archivist
Society of Archivists, Records Management Group
  40 Northampton Road, London EC1R 0HB, UK
  E-mail: societyofarchivists@archives.org.uk
  www.archives.org.uk/
  Journal of the Society of Archivists

Index

access
  copies and images made to support
    110–11, 191–2, 244
  external 220, 239–41, 242–4
  policies for 239, 240–1
  restrictions, conditions and controls
    on 38, 140, 173, 204–5, 207–9,
    216, 218, 220, 239, 240–2, 243–4
  rights of 38, 117, 139, 167, 204, 218,
    220, 239–42
  to archival records 243–5
  users' requirements for 113, 175,
    216–21, 237–8
  see also retrieval
accessibility
  compromised when records are
    poorly managed 112–13
  in centralized and decentralized
    records systems 173–4, 175
  of electronic records 20, 92, 112,
    120–1, 195–7, 205, 207, 219–20,
    222, 242, 257
  of offline discs and tapes 183, 220,
    221
accountability xi–xii, 45, 102–3, 147,
    151, 155, 157, 158–9, 160, 172,
    239

activities 2–3, 15–16, 19–20, 24, 49–50,
    52–7, 58, 65, 73–4, 76–7, 85,
    102–3, 114, 156, 158, 167, 236–7
  definition of 2
  see also creative activities and
    processes; routine activities and
    processes
adjacency searching 224, 238
'administrative value', Schellenberg's
    view of 148
alphabetical filing order 189
analytical techniques 30–71, 266–7
appraisal
  criteria and frameworks for 147–62,
    166–9
  documentation of 162–5, 171
  for records capture 108–9, 146
  for records retention 146, 147–62,
    166–9
  Grigg system 149–51
  macro 151–3
  of functions and processes 152–3,
    154–5, 169
  Schellenberg's taxonomy of 'values'
    148–9, 150–1
archives
  conditions of access to 243–4